Spelling:

Connecting the Pieces

Ruth McQuirter Scott
Sharon Siamon

gagelearning

© **2004 Gage Learning Corporation**
1120 Birchmount Road
Toronto ON M1K 5G4
www.gagelearning.com

National Library of Canada Cataloguing in Publication

Scott, Ruth, 1949-
    Spelling : connecting the pieces / Ruth McQuirter Scott, Sharon Siamon.

Includes bibliographical references and index.
ISBN 0-7715-1868-4

    1. English language--Orthography and spelling--Study and teaching (Elementary) I. Siamon, Sharon II. Title.

LB1574.S278 2003   372.63'2   C2003-905595-7

We would like to thank the following educators for their helpful advice:
Gwen Babcock, Andrea Bishop, Colette Foran, Faye Gertz, Charmaine Graves, Marilynn Hayhow, Maureen Innes, Sue Jackson, Diana Knight, Kimberly A. McKay, Brenda McCarron Newcombe, and Peter Veltri.

Any Web sites visited through www.gagelearning.com have been checked for appropriate content. However, these Web sites and any other suggested links should be periodically checked before the addresses are given to students. Web addresses change constantly. Teachers should locate the URL through a search engine, and check the site for appropriate content.

We acknowledge the financial support of the Government of Canada through the Book Publishing Industry Development Program for our publishing activities.

Senior Project Editor: Patrice Peterkin
Production: Bev Crann
Permissions: Linda Tanaka
Design: Word & Image
Cover Photos: Bonnie Kamin/PhotoEdit; ROB & SAS/CORBIS; Richard Hutchings/PhotoEdit

  5 TPI 08

ISBN-13: 978-0-7715-**1868-3**
ISBN-10: 0-7715-**1868-4**

Written, printed, and bound in Canada

TABLE OF CONTENTS

Introduction

● ●

Before we began writing this book, we spoke to teachers who had years of experience and had taught many different grade levels. We asked them this question: "What would you like to see in a professional book on the teaching of spelling?" Over and over again, we heard variations of this response: "How do I put it all together? I know that spelling should be a part of my word-study program and tied to writing. But I have so many needs in my classroom and so many curriculum expectations to cover, that I need advice on bringing all the parts together." And so, *Spelling: Connecting the Pieces* was born.

As a writing team, we share a particular fascination with words and spelling. We join Richard Lederer in being "self-confessed and unrepentant verbivores." Lederer coined the term *verbivore* to describe people who devour words. He says, "My whole life I have feasted on words—ogled their appetizing shapes, colours, and textures; swished them around in my mouth…"

Over the past two decades, we have collaborated on over 30 books, and never tire of looking for new ways to share our interest in spelling with teachers and their students. We believe that classrooms should be laboratories where children can explore words and acquire the skills they need to make language a powerful tool for personal expression.

We are delighted when we receive feedback from children who are confident spellers. We know, however, that many children still view spelling as an albatross that damages their self-esteem and prevents them from writing with ease. Even though computer spell checks help mask poor spelling, this is only a temporary solution at best. Our society is still too quick to link poor spelling with a lack of intelligence, and the child who lags behind in spelling is indeed at a disadvantage.

The English spelling system is not easy to master, with its lack of one-sound-one-letter consistency, its preponderance of homophones, and its tendency to borrow words freely from other languages. For most children, learning to spell requires skilled instruction on the part of their teachers.

With the many demands on teachers in today's multi-needs, multi-language classrooms, this is a tall order. The school day has not expanded, but the needs of children and the expectations placed on teachers have.

We believe strongly that the time you and your students spend on spelling must be focused and productive. This does not mean spending a great deal of time on spelling or throwing out everything you have been doing and starting over again. It does mean having a knowledge base about English spelling and acquiring the instructional skills to link spelling with all aspects of the curriculum.

This book provides a framework for understanding spelling, both from the perspective of children who are learning to spell and teachers who are vital links in the process. As the title of the book suggests, spelling does not exist in isolation from other areas of language. It is vitally connected to reading, speaking, listening, viewing, representing, and writing. Spelling needs to be addressed in all areas of the curriculum, so the puzzle becomes even more complex. Our goal in writing this book is to help you, the classroom teacher, put the pieces of the spelling puzzle together in a way that meets the unique needs of your classroom setting.

HOW IS THE BOOK ORGANIZED?

We have structured the book in three sections. Part 1 provides the background information needed by teachers to understand how children learn to spell, the implications of current research for the classroom, and how to use this knowledge to assess student needs. The section concludes with a brief description of the English spelling system, and the features that make English spelling rich in patterns while at the same time challenging in its inconsistencies.

Part 2 examines the links between spelling and other aspects of your literacy program: listening and speaking, viewing and representing, reading and writing. We argue that growth in each of these areas can lead to growth in spelling, but also that as children become more proficient spellers, they often use this knowledge of language to become more effective speakers, readers, and writers. These language skills must then be applied throughout the school day, both in what is traditionally considered language time and every other subject area.

Part 3 explores the range of spelling needs within the typical classroom and provides a wealth of practical suggestions for accommodating each student, whether the struggling speller, the second-language learner, or the skilled speller. Families are a crucial source of background information, as well as vital partners in providing support to your classroom program. We present a number of ways to share your spelling program with the parents/guardians of your students.

SPECIAL FEATURES

While there is a logical progression from Parts 1 to 3, you may find you prefer to explore the contents of the book in your own way. We have built into each chapter features that will help you to navigate through the book. The key points of each chapter are summarized, and a quick reference is provided to related chapters.

The appendixes contain resources in the form of lists of recommended books, reproducible pages, and word lists, as well as a glossary of terms. The extensive bibliography contains over 100 references to research studies and professional texts in the field of spelling.

Whether you read this book on your own as part of your personal professional development, or study it in the context of a professional learning community, the section in each chapter entitled "Reflective Thinking" will help you to relate the contents of the book to your own teaching environment.

Throughout the book, we acknowledge the importance of providing instruction that meets the needs of a variety of learning styles. We try to model this principle in the design features of the book. Not every reader likes to read a chapter from start to finish, so the summaries will help those who prefer to scan a chapter first. We appeal to the needs of visual learners through the use of charts, graphic organizers, and cartoons that relate to the text.

Teachers who convey a love of language and who understand the role spelling plays in language development give their students a priceless gift—the ability to make sense of their world through writing, and to share those thoughts with accuracy and confidence. We hope that this book will play a part in making that happen in your classroom.

PART

1

The Child and the Spelling System

CHAPTER

1

Learning to Spell

"Spelling is easy as long as you guess the right letters."

The child in this cartoon is already confident that she is a good speller! As teachers, we know that learning to spell involves much more than guessing the right letters. Spelling maturity requires the knowledge of increasingly sophisticated language patterns on the levels of sound, structure, and meaning. It also demands the use of a variety of spelling strategies to deal with irregular spelling features. Becoming a skilled speller is a complex, life-long process. Gentry (1993) points out that "children do not learn to spell with equal ease or in the same way. While learning the language system for spelling may be easy and natural for some children, others—including many adults—may find it extremely difficult" (p. 3).

PROFILE OF A GOOD SPELLER

Researchers Hughes and Searle (1997) tracked the spelling development of a group of children from Kindergarten through Grade 6. They found it difficult to classify some children as good or poor spellers, but they were able to identify one group of nine children who stood out clearly as capable spellers. The members of this group shared a number of the following characteristics:

- **They moved quickly through the early phases of literacy** and continued to be excellent, avid readers.

- **They used their knowledge of the sound and visual features of words** and increasingly added meaning to their spelling logic.

- **They approached spelling as a system** that they could control.

- **They recognized their correct and misspelled words.** They were able to pinpoint problem areas in their misspellings and spontaneously generate a variety of viable alternatives. In most cases, they wrote out their alternative versions and compared them for correctness.

- **They treated editing as their personal responsibility** and developed effective editing strategies.

- **They showed interest in the meanings and the spellings of the words used in their environment.** The children often could pinpoint where they first saw a word.

- **They often collected words for use in their writing,** and reading was a vital source of their curiosity about the meaning and spelling of words.

- **They talked frequently about the relationship among reading, writing, and spelling,** and they viewed writing as a crucial way of helping them grow as spellers.

These children did not become proficient spellers overnight. In fact, they did not demonstrate the characteristics of good spellers until the end of Grade 6. Even then, they still had to grasp some of the higher-level understandings of the spelling system.

This point is important because it is too easy to support the view that "good spellers are born, not made." Although these children were advanced in overall language development, they still had to learn the complexities of the English spelling system over time. Their progress may have been more rapid than less skilled spellers, but they too followed the same road that most children take when learning to spell.

SPELLING RESEARCH: WHAT DOES IT SAY?

Developmental researchers (Beers and Henderson, 1977; Gentry, 1993; Henderson, 1990; Read, 1971) have made tremendous contributions to our understanding of how children learn to spell. This research describes the stages that children follow as they gradually master the English spelling system. Children progress at different rates and often show signs of being in different stages depending on the nature of the spelling task. Still, these broad categories are useful in charting a child's progress toward spelling maturity.

STAGES OF SPELLING DEVELOPMENT

Henderson (1990) proposed five stages of spelling development: Prephonetic, Phonetic, Patterns Within Words, Syllable Juncture, and Meaning-Derivation. In this framework, children progress from squiggles and marks on the page in their early years to the sophisticated use of spelling patterns and strategies that mark an accomplished speller.

1. Prephonetic Stage

The Prephonetic Stage occurs before children understand that letters are associated with sounds. This stage is characterized by squiggles, random marks, and letters or words that children have copied. It is likely that through their exposure to picture books, children have noticed that pictures are usually accompanied by print. Their use of scribbles and random letters are important clues that they have already made some valid inferences about written language.

In Figure 1.1, Zoë, age 4, prints random letters to accompany her picture. She has noticed the left to right progression of print.

Figure 1.1 Prephonetic Stage

2. Phonetic Stage

At the Phonetic Stage, true alphabetic writing begins. In Emileah's thank-you note (see Figure 1.2), she mixes sight words (*the*, *four*) with attempts to link letters and sounds. She uses a letter-name strategy to spell *you*. Emileah hears the word *you* and links it with the name of the alphabet letter that "says" that sound—in this case, the letter *U*.

Emileah takes the same approach to the end of *birthday*, spelling it *brethda*. She is able to use the digraph /*th*/ in *thank* and *birthday*. Her facility with short vowels is still in the early stages, and she leaves out all vowels in her spelling of present (*prznt*). She also omits the *n* before the final consonant in *thank* (*thak*), a typical characteristic of phonetic spelling. However, it is not difficult to read Emileah's note because she has learned that pairing sounds and letters allows her to convey her thoughts in print.

Figure 1.2 Phonetic Stage. Emileah, age 5, composes a thank-you note for a birthday present. It translates as follows: "Thank you for the birthday present. Love, Emileah."

3. Patterns Within Words Stage

If children stay at the Phonetic Stage of spelling, it may be possible to figure out what they are writing, but their work will contain many errors. This occurs because English often uses clusters of letters to spell a given sound, and there are frequently several ways to spell the same sound in print. Children enter the Patterns Within Words Stage when they move from spelling a word such as *boat* as *BOT* and try letter patterns instead. The resulting spelling may not be correct (*bowt*, *bote*), but it is important to acknowledge this major leap in thinking about spelling.

In Figure 1.3, Raduanul shows that he is still sorting out short vowel patterns (*want for went*), and he is inconsistent in his use of the digraph /*th*/. On the other hand, he is experimenting with letter clusters to spell the diphthongs /*ow*/ (*out—aot*; *house—hoes*) and /*oi*/ (*toys—tois*). He spells the long *o* in *home* correctly and makes phonetically accurate attempts at *came* (*c<u>ai</u>md*) and *made* (*ma<u>y</u>d*). The final syllable of *puzzle* is also spelled correctly, in contrast to a student at the Phonetic Stage who would likely spell the word as *pazl*. Although Raduanul is still making many spelling errors, his spelling reflects a more sophisticated understanding of the spelling system.

It is important to note that some of his attempts (*plyd*) are more characteristic of the Phonetic Stage, showing that children move back and forth between stages.

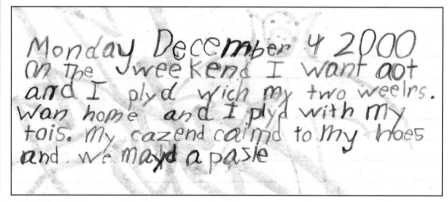

Figure 1.3 Patterns Within Words Stage. Raduanul's writing translates as follows: "On the weekend I went out and I played with my two-wheelers. I went home and I played with my toys. My cousin came to my house and we made a puzzle."

4. Syllable Juncture Stage

Children move on to the Syllable Juncture Stage when they have a basic spelling vocabulary and an understanding of many long and short vowel patterns. This stage focuses on the place within words where syllables meet. For example, when -ing is added to the base word *stop*, is the new word spelled *stopping* or *stoping*? Spellers who understand the doubling principle realize that the final consonant must be doubled in order to preserve the short vowel *o*. Similarly, they understand that the silent *e* in *hope* is no longer needed in *hoping* since the presence of a single *p* retains the long vowel sound.

In Figure 1.4, Danielle spells *hopping* correctly but neglects to double the consonant in *dropped* and *grabbed*.

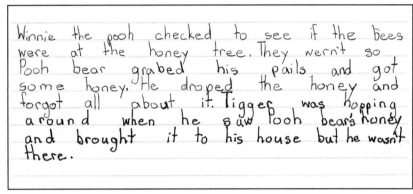

Figure 1.4 Syllable Juncture Stage

5. Meaning-Derivation Stage

The concept children acquire in the Meaning-Derivation Stage is that in written English meaning is more important than sound. Words that are related in meaning or have a common root are spelled alike even if they are pronounced differently. For example, the silent *g* in *sign* can be remembered if the student relates *sign* to *signal* and *signature*. All three words are related in meaning, and since meaning takes precedence over sound, the *g* in *sign* remains even though it is silent.

Children in the Meaning-Derivation Stage also show an ability to spell roots, prefixes, and suffixes of Greek and Latin origin. The suffix -tion, for example, is no longer spelled phonetically as /shun/.

"The spelling-meaning relationship illustrates the importance of vocabulary study as an essential part of the reading and spelling curriculum, particularly in Grades 4–8" (Cramer, 1998).

homophones

Homophones are words that have the same pronunciation but different meanings, origins, and sometimes, spellings (e.g., *pear/pair*).

Homophones are another indicator of spelling–meaning connections. Since homophones sound the same, a sounding-out strategy for spelling them will not be effective. Cramer and Cipielewski (1995) found that homophones were the most common error category in Grades 7 and 8, and the second most common in Grades 4 to 6. Students who spell homophones correctly have sorted out the meaning connections among homophones such as *there/their/they're* or *its/it's.*

In Figure 1.5, Lindsay shows a mastery of many polysyllabic words such as *intellectual* and *admirable.* She is comfortable adding suffixes in *commitment* and *dedication* and in spelling homophones such as *their.* Although she undoubtedly still faces spelling challenges with specific words, it appears that she has successfully negotiated the daunting twists and turns of learning to spell.

> The Masters Golf Tournament was created by a famous golf pro named Bobby Jones. Jones once said, "I can play this game only one way. I must play every shot for all that is in it." What an admirable message. I think about the athletes in our times, whose greed and selfishness are higher on their list than a true love of the game. Not only was Jones an incredible athlete, he was also a very intellectual person. This was made clear when he graduated from Harvard with a B.S. and later passed the bar exam after only one year in law school. When the Masters Tournament comes around each year, it is important for golf lovers worldwide to recognize the man who was behind it, his dedication to the game of golf, and the values that he lived by. His commitment to excellence was clear in every fibre of his being.

Figure 1.5 Meaning-Derivation Stage

The chart on page 9 provides a summary of the characteristics of the five stages of spelling development. Use the chart as you examine samples of students' writing.

Developmental Stages

Prephonetic	Phonetic	Patterns Within Words	Syllable Juncture	Meaning-Derivation
• scribbles in horizontal lines • writes from left to right eventually • can be "read" by student only right after it is written • letters are not linked with sounds • may include number symbols as part of the spelling of a word • often mixes upper-case and lower-case letters	• direct letter-to-sound matches (e.g., *U* for *you*) • many short vowels and ambiguous consonants omitted (e.g., *jup* for *jump*) • *m* and *n* often left out before final consonant (e.g., *stap* for *stamp*) • pattern of short vowel substitutions • long vowels spelled by the vowel letter-name alone (e.g., *KAK* for *cake*)	• silent "marking" vowel for long vowels (e.g., *RANE* for *rain*) • more correctly spelled words • regular appearance of correctly spelled short vowels • patterns of letters can represent a sound (e.g., *boat*, *boil*) • use of consonant blends and digraphs (e.g., *splash*, *pluck*, *that*)	• doubles consonants to mark the short vowel (e.g., *hopped*) • applies doubling principle properly to long vowels (e.g., *hope/hoping* vs. *hopeing/ hopping*) • conventional rules and generalizations about spelling beginning to be applied	• homophones are spelled correctly more consistently • sees relationship between words with common roots (e.g., *sign/signal*) • uses simple prefixes and suffixes

Figure 1.6 Summary of developmental stages of learning to spell

WHAT CAN WE CONCLUDE ABOUT DEVELOPMENTAL STAGES?

These developmental stages are broad categories that should not be used to pigeonhole children's spelling. Children often move back and forth between stages depending upon how familiar they are with a word, how complex the writing task is, and their level of stress. Still, by examining children's writing, especially their invented spellings, it is possible to learn much about their understanding of written English. Gentry (1993) writes, "Each time a child or adult invents a spelling, he or she produces a telling snapshot of how the mind conceives of spelling. Each invented spelling is a permanent record of an individual's journey to spelling competence" (p. 39).

There is a danger, however, in basing a spelling program strictly on the findings of developmental research. Developmental stage models are sometimes misinterpreted to mean that

- children naturally learn to spell
- all that is needed to ensure spelling success is a learning environment that encourages reading and writing

Such a view assumes that the English spelling system can be mastered by understanding spelling patterns from simple sound-level connections to more sophisticated rules for adding endings to words. While this is partially the case, English is also riddled with exceptions to rules. Chapter 4, "The English Spelling System," examines the spelling system of English in greater detail and explains why English presents so many spelling challenges.

SPELLING STRATEGIES

Research on spelling strategies has revealed that good spellers use a broad assortment of spelling strategies. Varnhagen (1997) warns against assuming that a child who is in the Phonetic Stage of development uses only sound-based strategies when spelling. Her study found that from a very early age, children use a variety of sources of knowledge and strategies in their spelling. More research needs to be conducted on the multiple strategies children use when spelling, how they select certain strategies, and how they acquire new ones.

Chapter 10, "Spelling Strategies and Word Study," describes a variety of spelling strategies and explains how teachers can incorporate this important aspect of spelling into their programs.

SPELLING IS CONNECTED TO READING, WRITING, AND ORAL LANGUAGE

The profile of good spellers presented on page 3 shows how closely spelling is related to other language skills and makes it clear that reading, oral language, and writing influence spelling.

SPELLING AND READING

Reading is the primary way in which children encounter the spellings of new words. In the process of decoding words using sound–symbol relationships, or by recognizing units such as prefixes and suffixes, the reader learns how "words work." In addition, the reader encounters high-frequency words that are often exceptions to patterns—for example, words such as *said* or *come*. These words often become part of the child's oral, written, and reading vocabularies. Even though words may be examined as single entities, it is important that children see them used in context and are aware of their meanings.

SPELLING AND ORAL LANGUAGE

A child's spoken vocabulary also has a major influence on spelling. In the early years, children who are familiar with rhyme through poetry, chants, and wordplay grasp word families that share common rime patterns, such as *blast*, *cast*, and *fast*. They also gain experience in hearing the sounds in words, leading to greater phonemic awareness. At later stages of development, children with extensive vocabularies can recognize the connections between words such as *compose* and *composition*, and use this knowledge in spelling. The schwa vowel in *composition* can be remembered by relating it to the base form *compose* where the *o* is clearly sounded.

SPELLING AND WRITING

As with reading and oral language, children practise and reinforce their spelling knowledge through the act of writing. Many writers just "know" a word is misspelled when they see it in print, and through editing and proofreading, they learn the correct spelling. The motivation to spell accurately is also tied to writing. When children realize that proper spelling is important for effective communication, they can see a real purpose in learning conventions such as spelling. In the final analysis, we teach spelling so that children develop the ability to communicate their thoughts clearly to others.

SPELLING ENHANCES OTHER LANGUAGE SKILLS

Researchers have recognized, however, that the relationship between spelling and other language areas is a two-way process. While spelling is clearly reinforced through reading, writing, and speaking, learning to spell also enhances these other language areas.

Cramer (2001) says, "Spelling serves as a gateway to reading; reading serves as a gateway to spelling. In either instance, there is mutual advantage" (p. 315). The knowledge a child acquires about written English through word solving in spelling is directly applicable to reading.

This is particularly true with respect to sound patterns in the early grades and to the meaning relationships in multisyllablic words in later years. Chapter 7, "Reading and Spelling," explores the relationship between these two skill areas in greater detail.

Good spellers also have an advantage comprehending oral language. As children learn about base words, prefixes, and suffixes, they are better able to understand the meaning of new words encountered in their environment. For example, the child who knows that the prefix *multi-* means "many" will likely understand the meaning of the term *multimedia*. The relationship between oral language and spelling is discussed in more detail in Chapter 5, "Listening and Speaking."

Proficiency in spelling also enhances the writing process. Children who feel competent as spellers are likely to use a more sophisticated level of vocabulary in their writing. Conversely, poor spellers often substitute simple or less precise words simply because they have a small spelling vocabulary. When attention is diverted from composing to worries about spelling, the quality of writing suffers. Even when using a computer, the need to correct errors detected by a spell check takes precious time and attention from composing. Furthermore, many errors, such as homophones, are not detected by spell checks. The important connections between writing and spelling are the topic of Chapter 8, "Writing and Presenting."

LEARNING TO SPELL IS A COMPLEX, LIFE-LONG PROCESS

We have seen that learning to spell is a complex, life-long process. The typical classroom is composed of students with different language skills. Some students are excellent readers and spellers. Others are excellent readers but struggle with spelling. Still others speak fluently but struggle with print, both as readers and spellers. Students with learning disabilities, who two decades ago might have been segregated in special classrooms, are now integrated into the regular classroom setting with varying levels of support.

Teachers are expected to provide the best possible program for all students, regardless of learning profiles. This book is devoted to helping you create a learning environment for the students that will encourage spelling growth for all children—the skilled speller, the second-language learner, the child who struggles to learn to spell, and all the other students in between.

SUMMARY

This chapter has presented the following main ideas:

1. **Good spellers share many common characteristics. They often**
   - are skilled and avid readers
   - see spelling as a system they can control
   - have effective proofreading strategies
   - treat editing of spelling as their personal responsibility
   - show great interest in words in their environment
   - use reading as a major source of information about the meaning and spelling of words
   - understand the connections among reading, writing, and spelling

2. **Spelling development occurs in five stages:**
   - Prephonetic Stage: Children experiment with squiggles, random marks, and letters or words they have copied.
   - Phonetic Stage: Children begin to link letters with sounds. This is the beginning of true alphabetic writing.
   - Patterns Within Words Stage: Children recognize that patterns of letters can represent a sound. They begin to use the silent *e* marker for long vowels, consonant blends and digraphs (*th*, *ph*, and so on), and diphthongs (*oy*, *oi*, *ow*, and so on).
   - Syllable Juncture Stage: Children discover the patterns for adding endings to words—dropping the final *e*, doubling final consonants, changing *y* to *i*.
   - Meaning-Derivation Stage: Children recognize that words related in meaning often share common spelling features. They understand the meaning connections among base words, prefixes, and suffixes.

3. **Spelling development evolves over many years.** Children often show the characteristics of more than one stage in their spelling, and move back and forth between stages depending on the circumstances and the difficulty of the task.

4. **Becoming a good speller involves more than just learning the patterns of written English.** Good spellers also use a range of spelling strategies to recall the spelling of words that do not fit patterns. Although certain strategies are most likely to be used at a given stage (for example, a sounding-out approach in the Phonetic Stage), children use a variety of strategies at each stage of development.

5. **Spelling is connected to growth in reading, writing, and oral language.** Not only is spelling influenced by these language skills, but learning to spell also enhances a child's development in reading, writing, and oral language.

6. **Learning to spell is a complex, life-long process.** While most children progress in a similar stage-like manner, there is great variability in the ease and rate at which they move toward spelling maturity.

REFLECTIVE THINKING

1. Hughes and Searle found many common characteristics among good spellers (see page 3). Do good spellers in your classroom share these qualities?

2. What is the most significant distinction between Prephonetic spelling and the remaining four stages of spelling development? Why is this difference so critical?

3. Why might it be unwise to say that a student is a Phonetic Stage or Within Words Stage speller?

4. Is a student a mature speller if he or she knows all the basic patterns or rules of spelling? Why or why not?

The following chart provides links with other chapters in the book that show how spelling research relates to instruction:

To learn more about...	see these chapters
What Does the Research Mean for the Classroom?	Chapter 2, page 15
The English Spelling System	Chapter 4, page 50
Listening and Speaking	Chapter 5, page 66
Reading and Spelling	Chapter 7, page 85
Writing and Presenting	Chapter 8, page 99
Spelling Strategies and Word Study	Chapter 10, page 129
Supporting Struggling Spellers	Chapter 12, page 170
Challenging Skilled Spellers	Chapter 13, page 182

What Does the Research Mean for the Classroom?

• •

Understanding that learning to spell is a complex, life-long process is the first step in addressing the many needs of students in your class. But how do you fit spelling into the literacy program so that spelling receives the attention it deserves without sacrificing other, equally important areas of learning? The specific answers will vary according to your classroom situation. There are, however, some general principles that will help you make decisions that best fit the students' needs. In this chapter, we outline these principles and discuss various points of view surrounding the teaching of spelling.

SIMPLE ANSWERS ABOUT TEACHING SPELLING ARE LIKELY TO FAIL

In the past, spelling was treated as a low-level memorization task. Instruction typically involved rote-learning activities, such as writing out corrected spelling errors multiple times. We now know that learning to spell is a complex, life-long process that involves thinking on a number of levels. Memorization is but one aspect of being a mature speller. Therefore, spelling instruction that is simplified to the level of writing out errors or completing exercises in a text is unlikely to be effective for most students.

At the other end of the spectrum was the belief that children could learn to spell "naturally" through reading and writing. It was thought by some that no formal systematic instruction was necessary. Teachers could teach whatever concepts were needed through incidental mini-lessons or editing conferences with their students. Spelling was viewed as a cosmetic feature of writing.

Shlagel (1992) argues that this view has marginalized spelling instruction and made it superfluous. He maintains that, "The belief that spelling is merely a subset of writing results from a fundamental misunderstanding of the research on developmental orthography" (p. 419).

Spelling development is tied closely to learning to read. Children's knowledge of words expands as they learn the patterns of written language through invented spelling and formal exposure to spelling patterns. If we downplay spelling instruction and assume the complexities of English spelling will be learned incidentally, we cut children off from a crucial source of word knowledge.

Effective Word Study Is Systematic

Many word-study opportunities present themselves naturally to teachers every day—interesting words encountered in reading, new words introduced into the language, or spelling errors in students' writing. On its own, however, this spontaneous approach to studying words is likely to be inadequate. Unless the teacher has a thorough knowledge of linguistics and is aware of students' needs at various stages of development, exploration of necessary word patterns is likely to suffer.

Cramer (2001) maintains that "children need consistent spelling instruction starting in first or second grade and continuing through grade eight. Many students would benefit from continued instruction throughout high school" (p. 316). There should be continuity from one grade to the next, so that children can build on what they learned in previous years. Cramer adds:

> Spelling instruction should concentrate on developing a serviceable spelling vocabulary, crucial spelling principles, and spelling strategies. If a core spelling vocabulary is not established early, children will not have a sufficient base upon which to build new spelling knowledge. (p. 316)

"Most children require explicit, planned instruction—as well as plenty of exposure to suitable books—to crack the complex code of written language" (The Report of the Expert Panel on Early Reading in Ontario, 2003).

FOCUSED WORD STUDY IS THE FOUNDATION FOR EFFECTIVE SPELLING INSTRUCTION

One of the main characteristics of both good readers and good spellers is that they know how to examine words effectively (Scott, 1991). Most poor spellers do not approach spelling as a system to be grasped, but instead memorize words. Over twenty years ago, Edmund Henderson (1981) stressed the need for classroom practices that include focused word study: "Correct spelling is not learned by sheer memory nor is it learned mechanically from rules…. What is learned cannot be learned in any other way than through the examination of words" (p. 95).

More recently, Pinnell and Fountas (1998) echoed the concern that while "some children will discover on their own the necessary principle of how words work…most will not" (p. 31). They say that brief teacher demonstrations of word patterns are often not enough. Many children "need even more direct attention and repetition of important principles as well as much practice with them" (p. 21).

An emphasis on focused word study does not mean a return to a drill approach to spelling instruction. It means providing children with many opportunities to explore words throughout their day, both in structured situations such as a word-study block, and informally as words present themselves in reading, writing, and every subject area. It means actively involving children in word solving.

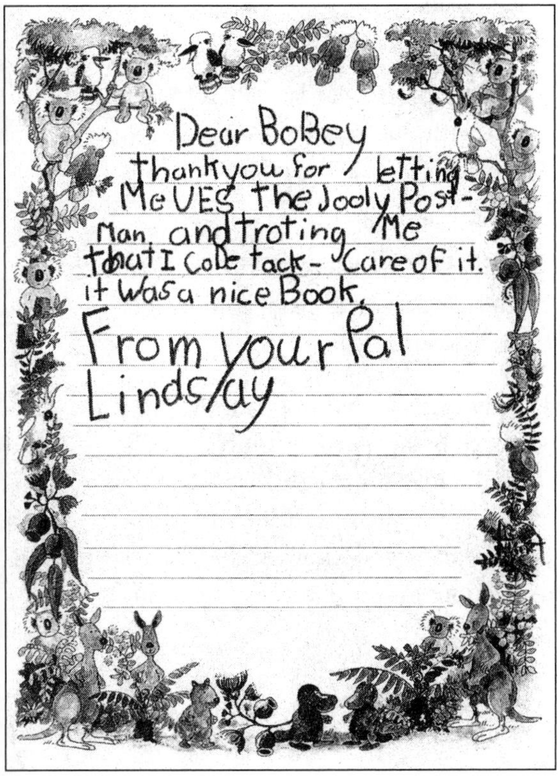

CHILDREN AS WORD DETECTIVES

Children of all ages should be encouraged to be word detectives, sniffing out interesting words they encounter in their daily lives.

Lindsay has been a word detective for much of her life. As a preschooler, she announced that s-a-y spelled zee. When her mother said, "No, s-a-y spells say," Lindsay replied, "Well, why at the end of Lindsay does it say zee?" Several years later, Lindsay heard an announcement of a lecture to be given in the community on the topic of "euthanasia." This was a new word for her, and after thinking about it for a moment, she asked, "Is that about child labour in India?" (youth in Asia!)

Being a word detective also extends to written language. When we encourage young children to use invented spelling in drafts of their writing, we are actively supporting word exploration. In Figure 2.1, six-year-old Lindsay writes a thank-you note to a friend for the loan of the book *The Jolly Postman*. Her writing shows that she can already spell a number of high-frequency words, and she is also experimenting with patterns within words (*code* for *could*; *tack* for *take*). She is even having some success with syllable juncture—*letting* is spelled with two *t*'s. Lindsay's invented spellings tell a great deal about her attempts to explore the English spelling system.

Figure 2.1

WORDS CAN BE STUDIED ON MANY LEVELS

Spelling Patterns

Children can explore spelling patterns such as the following:

- rhyming segments
- vowel sounds
- silent letters
- consonant clusters
- homophones
- compound words
- contractions
- plural forms
- root and base words
- possessives
- syllables
- stress patterns
- past-tense forms
- proper nouns
- prefixes and suffixes

Language Features

The English language also holds fascinating insights beyond basic spelling patterns. Try to incorporate some of these features of language into your literacy program:

- word origins
- new words created to describe technology
- idioms and expressions
- slang and jargon
- spelling strategies for tricky words
- borrowed words
- Canadianisms
- dialects
- acronyms (e.g., *UNESCO*) and abbreviations
- puns
- eponyms (words named after people, e.g., *sandwich*)
- portmanteau words (blended words, e.g., *brunch*)
- nicknames
- homographs (words spelled the same but with different pronunciations and meanings, e.g., *bow/bow*)
- alliteration
- euphemisms (e.g., *pre-owned car*)
- special categories (e.g., colours, music, autumn)

"Carnivores eat flesh and meat; piscivores eat fish; herbivores eat plants and vegetables; verbivores devour words. I am such a creature" (Lederer, 1994).

The manner in which word study is presented is as important as the concepts being studied. By actively exploring words, children gain a metacognitive understanding of the English language. Instead of just memorizing individual words, children see the multiple connections among words. They acquire the vocabulary and knowledge they need to manipulate words, so that words become tools for communication.

Word Sorts

Word sorts are an effective strategy for helping children examine word patterns. Present words individually on cards and have the students sort the cards in various ways. They can sort the words by sound, structure, or meaning patterns. In the early grades, for example, children might sort words by initial consonant sounds or vowel patterns. In the middle grades, they can sort words by more complex syllable-juncture patterns, such as ways of forming plurals. In later grades, sorting can focus on patterns of meaning. For example, cluster together words that share a common base word or words that have prefixes with common meanings. Figure 2.2 illustrates a word sort based on sound. If students are given the categories for sorting ahead of time, it is called a "closed sort." When they are allowed to sort the words in whatever way makes sense to them, it is called an "open sort."

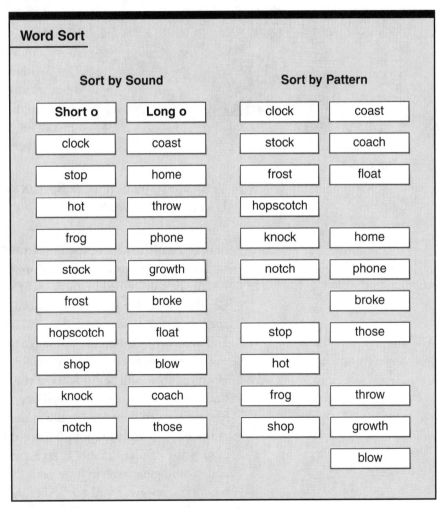

Figure 2.2 Word sort by sound: long and short vowels

Further descriptions of word sorting are found in Chapter 9, "Integrating Spelling Across the Curriculum." Other excellent resources include *Word Matters* (Pinnell and Fountas, 1998), *Words Their Way* (Bear, Invernizzi, Johnston, and Templeton, 2000), and *Guiding Readers and Writers* (Fountas and Pinnell, 2001).

Word Walls

Patricia Cunningham and Dorothy Hall introduced the concept of "Word Walls." As part of the "Working with Words Block" in their "Four Blocks Literacy Model," Word Walls provide an opportunity for students and teachers to study high-frequency words that students need to use in their writing. The teacher selects five words each week for study. Students examine the words by writing them, tracing the shape of the words, and by chanting and clapping the letters. The Word Wall is displayed prominently in the classroom, with words arranged alphabetically. The "Working with Words Block" also involves other word-study activities, such as building words from individual letters, word sorting, looking for patterns of rhyme, and noticing specific letter combinations in words.

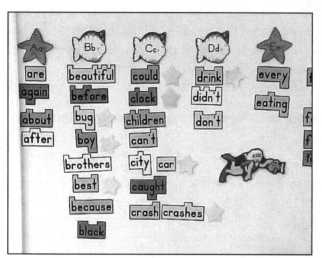

Figure 2.3

WORD STUDY SHOULD BE LINKED WITH DEVELOPMENTAL STAGES

The patterns introduced to students should also be in line with their developmental stages of spelling growth. The sequence recommended in Figure 2.4 on pages 22 and 23 follows the natural developmental progression described by stage theorists (Beers and Henderson, 1977; Gentry, 1993; Henderson, 1990; Read, 1971). Formal study of these spelling patterns supports what children learn through invented spelling and their own explorations of language in other areas.

These patterns are appropriate for most students at a given grade level. However, there will be students in your class who may not be ready for these concepts, or who may need to go beyond them. You are the best judge of whether a student can handle more or less complex spelling patterns.

Note that while the sound level of language is the focus of early grades, the emphasis shifts to structural patterns in the middle grades, and meaning patterns in later years. Sound patterns are not dropped, but tend to be reviewed and reinforced. Meaning patterns are addressed throughout, but they become more crucial in the later grades with the introduction of multisyllabic words containing prefixes and suffixes.

Many spelling patterns can be repeated from one year to the next, applying them to more complex words and consolidating an understanding of the pattern.

INSTRUCTION IN SPELLING STRATEGIES GOES HAND-IN-HAND WITH SPELLING PATTERNS

The patterns in English spelling work much of the time. Patterns allow the reader to "sort" words into memory files with labels such as "I before E" or "long vowel pattern" or "base word and prefix." Unfortunately, almost every pattern has its exceptions, and as Chapter 4, "The English Spelling System," clearly shows, English spelling is known for its liberal borrowing from other languages. As a result, mature spellers must go beyond the understanding of spelling rules and have an arsenal of spelling strategies to help them with the "tricky" parts of words.

Varnhagen (1997) found that even Grade 1 children use a number of spelling strategies, although a sounding-out strategy is the most common approach at this age. Poor spellers have a narrow range of spelling strategies (Hughes and Searle, 1997; Scott, 1991). It is important that you model a variety of spelling strategies with your students and encourage them to use these strategies when they are learning new words.

Chapter 10, "Spelling Strategies and Word Study," describes a wide range of spelling strategies.

Spelling Concepts

JK/SK and Grade 1 Prephonetic to Phonetic	Grade 2 Phonetic to Patterns Within Words	Grade 3 Patterns Within Words	Grade 4 Patterns Within Words to Syllable Juncture
• readiness activities • awareness of individual sounds and sequences of sounds • printing • holding pencil • letter sounds • short vowel patterns • onset/rime (e.g., *at*, *ug*, *est*) • one or two long vowel patterns (to contrast with short) • consonant digraphs • consonant blends • high frequency, irregular words	• review of short vowel patterns • common long vowel patterns • *r*-influenced patterns (e.g., *art*, *ore*) • review of digraphs (*th*, *ch*) • double consonant patterns (*hill*, *puff*) • compound words • homophones • inflected endings (*-s*, *-ed*, *-ing*) • concept of base word and endings • vowel sound /*ow*/ • high frequency, irregular words	• review of short and long vowel patterns • homophones • compound words • *r*-influenced vowels (*er*, *ir*, *ur*) • two-syllable words • syllable juncture (*button*, *batted*) • base words • compound words • *e*-drop and consonant doubling principles; *y* to *i* • common prefixes and suffixes • unstressed syllables (*er*, *le*) • contractions • possessives (singular) • plurals (regular) • high frequency, irregular words	• review of basic vowel patterns • *r*-influenced vowels • silent consonants • syllables and stress • schwa vowels • plurals (irregular) • possessives • contractions • homophones • compound words • simple prefixes and suffixes • review of *e*-drop, *y* to *i*, and consonant doubling principles • unstressed syllables • unusual spellings • borrowed words • new words in English • high frequency, irregular words

Spelling: Connecting the Pieces

Spelling Concepts

Grade 5 **Syllable Juncture to Meaning-Derivation Stages**	Grade 6 **Syllable Juncture to Meaning-Derivation Stages**	Grade 7 **Meaning-Derivation Stage**	Grade 8 **Meaning-Derivation Stage**
• similar to Grade 4 • review of basic spelling principles • pace more rapid • syllable juncture in both two- and three-syllable words (*happening*, *occurred*) • irregular plurals • homophones • compound words • possessives (singular and plural) • related words (*sign*/*signature*) • broader range of prefixes and suffixes • schwa vowels • high frequency, irregular words	• reinforce previous concepts using more sophisticated vocabulary • schwa vowels • final, unstressed syllables • common Latin prefixes and suffixes • irregular plurals • homophones • compound words • possessives (singular and plural) • contractions • syllable juncture in longer words (doubling, *e*-drop, *y* to *i*) • related words (*muscle*/*muscular*) • irregular past tense verbs (e.g., *brought*) • unusual spellings • high frequency, irregular words	• review of basic spelling principles • application to adult vocabulary • roots and meaning relations among derived forms (e.g., *divine*/*divinity*) • schwa vowels • use meaning principle to spell schwa vowels (*compose*/*composition*) • easily confused word pairs (*angle*, *angel*) • borrowed words • new words in English • homophones • high frequency, irregular words	• same as Grade 7, using increasingly sophisticated vocabulary • roots and meaning relations among derived forms (e.g., *column*/*columnist*) • schwa vowels • use meaning principle to spell schwa vowels (*define*/*definition*) • easily confused word pairs (*affect*, *effect*) • borrowed words • new words in English • homophones • high frequency, irregular words

Figure 2.4

Sources: Bear, D., and Templeton, S. (1998). *Explorations in developmental spelling*. Henderson, E. (1990). *Teaching spelling*. Scott, R. (1991). *The student editor's guide to words*. Toronto: Gage Learning. McQuirter Scott, R., and Siamon, S. (2004). *Canadian spelling*. Toronto: Gage Learning.

FORMAL WORD STUDY MAY INCLUDE BOTH A PUBLISHED SPELLING PROGRAM AND TEACHER-DESIGNED ACTIVITIES

The decision to use a published speller or to create your own spelling program should not be seen as a clear either/or matter. Some teachers do a highly competent job of planning a spelling program that is both flexible and thorough, based on students' needs. The demands of this approach, however, should not be underestimated. To be effective, teachers must be knowledgeable about the English spelling system and the benchmarks of normal spelling development. Word-study activities must be focused and cover the major spelling principles addressed in Figure 2.4. Attention to word study needs to be a feature of the literacy program throughout the year, and from one grade to the next within the school. These requirements are often difficult to meet in the midst of the packed curriculum mandated for most classrooms today.

Published Spelling Programs

Many teachers use a published speller as part of their overall spelling program. In addition to requirements set by specific school districts and provincial education departments, the following features should be considered when selecting a spelling resource:

- spelling concepts are addressed in a logical sequence based on developmental principles (see Figure 2.4)
- patterns are reinforced and consolidated from grade to grade, yet applied to an increasingly sophisticated vocabulary
- new concepts are introduced with the developmental stages of spelling growth in mind
- spelling strategies are incorporated into every unit
- word study goes beyond spelling patterns and also addresses word usage, grammar, vocabulary development, and wordplay
- word lists are appropriate to the grade level and reflect words students frequently use in their writing

For Better or For Worse®   **by Lynn Johnston**

- teachers have licence to delete words from the list
- provision is made for adding words from personal spelling lists and other contexts
- words are used in various contexts throughout the unit to show meaning, grammatical function, and spelling features, although the word list is initially presented in list form
- words are transferred to meaningful writing contexts using a variety of writing forms
- advice is provided in the teacher's edition for adjusting the program to a variety of learning styles, language backgrounds, and stages of spelling growth
- instructional language is clear and the layout is attractive

A published text, however, can never replace a rich writing and reading program or classroom-based word study. The two approaches should complement each other. While the published program may provide systematic coverage of key spelling concepts, these principles must be transferred and applied to reading and writing through purposeful links facilitated by the teacher. With the time pressures common in today's classroom, it is tempting to assign exercises from the speller as homework and simply dictate the words at the end of the week. However, unless the concepts are linked in weekly units to everyday writing and other word-study activities, the age-old problem of transferring word knowledge to writing is likely to continue. A Friday dictation should not be the measure of success of a student's spelling.

Chapter 9, "Integrating Spelling Across the Curriculum," offers suggestions for making effective links between formal word study and applications throughout the curriculum.

WORD LISTS SHOULD BE CAREFULLY SELECTED

Cramer (2001) suggests, "The goal of a spelling curriculum is to establish a core writing vocabulary and an understanding of basic spelling principles and strategies" (p. 327). Once students have acquired this core writing vocabulary, they will be able to spell thousands of other words that are either derived from words they know or can be spelled by analogy (e.g., the student thinks of *tight* to spell *flight*).

Choosing words for spelling is a complex task that should reflect a number of important considerations. Cramer outlines six components that should be present in the words students learn to spell over the course of a school year.

"A good spelling program starts with an appropriate set of words. Not only must the right words be taught, but they must be organized and presented in a sequence appropriate to the stages of spelling growth" (Cramer, 1998).

1. Developmentally Appropriate Words

Students should be exposed to words that are consistent with their stage of developmental growth. Whether the word list is generated by you or suggested by a published program, it is important to monitor the words for suitability for individual children. If, for example, a child is in the early Syllable Juncture Stage, it makes sense to teach words such as *slammed* or *hopping*. To expect the same child to apply the much more complex rules of doubling to multisyllabic words such as *occurred* or *commitment*, however, is unrealistic. Although at first glance, *slammed* and *occurred* seem quite similar, doubling in the latter requires an understanding of stress patterns and whether the affix begins with a vowel or consonant. Few students at this stage could be expected to juggle so many concepts simultaneously.

2. High-Frequency Words

There are many lists of words that are used frequently in children's writing and reading. Although certain words appear in almost all lists, there is significant variation from list to list. No single list should be considered definitive. Several sources for word lists are noted below:

- 2000 most frequently used words, on the Edict Virtual Language Centre Web site.

- Cunningham, P., Hall, D., and Sigmon, C. (1999). *The Teacher's Guide to the Four Blocks®*.

- Cunningham, P., and Hall, D. (1998). *Month-by-Month Phonics for Upper Grades*.

- Pinnell, G., and Fountas, I. (1998). *Word Matters: Teaching Phonics and Spelling in the Reading/Writing Classroom*.

3. Frequently Misspelled Words

You will be able to select words from your students' writing that are frequently misspelled. Many of these words will appear from year to year, and they should be taught more than once to help students consolidate the spellings. You can supplement these class lists by using research-based lists of frequently misspelled words. Figure 2.5 on page 27 contains an example of one such list.

100 Most Frequently Misspelled Words Grades 1–8

too	really	always	very	school
a lot	finally	I	into	getting
because	where	something	caught	started
there	again	would	one	was
their	then	want	Easter	which
that's	didn't	and	what	stopped
they	people	Halloween	there's	two
it's	until	house	little	Dad
when	with	once	doesn't	took
favourite	different	to	usually	friend's
went	outside	like	clothes	presents
Christmas	we're	whole	scared	are
were	through	another	everyone	morning
our	upon	believe	have	could
they're	probably	I'm	swimming	around
said	don't	thought	about	buy
know	sometimes	let's	first	maybe
your	off	before	happened	family
friend	everybody	beautiful	Mom	pretty
friends	heard	everything	especially	tried

Figure 2.5   Source: Cramer, R., and Cipielewski, J. (1995)

"If theme is the sole criterion for selecting words, however, then students are reduced to learning how to spell one word at a time, with no opportunity to discover and explore the spelling patterns that apply to many words" (Bear and Templeton, 1998).

4. Linguistically Patterned Words

The word lists for many published spelling series are organized around linguistic patterns. There is good reason for this since they reflect the major spelling principles underlying written English. These linguistic patterns can then be sequenced to match the developmental stages of spelling. Patterns can be reinforced from grade to grade by applying them to words suitable for the age level. In addition to the patterned words, most series also incorporate words reflecting the other five categories described in this section.

5. Content-Related Words

Grade-level curriculum in subjects such as science, social studies, mathematics, the arts, and physical/health education will provide a core list vocabulary that students should be able to spell. Consider carefully, however, which of these terms your students should be expected to spell independently. A Grade 2 science curriculum may include investigations on the metamorphosis of a butterfly, and students would undoubtedly need to understand the word *caterpillar* and use it in recording their observations. Rather than including this word on a spelling list, however, you may choose to post it on a theme chart so that students can refer to it when writing.

When adding content words to spelling lists, avoid having students just memorize the words. Look for patterns in the words that can be linked with other word-study principles. For example, if students are spelling *triceratops* in a dinosaur theme, focus on the prefix *tri-* and apply this prefix to other words they may know, such as *tricycle*, *tripod*, and *triangle*.

Two authors, however, Bear and Templeton (1998), warn against an overemphasis on lists of words drawn from themes and curriculum areas:

> In well-intentioned attempts to focus on meaningful word study, some teachers have used only content-related words for spelling study without consideration of developmental appropriateness…. If theme is the sole criterion for selecting words, however, then students are reduced to learning how to spell one word at a time, with no opportunity to discover and explore the spelling patterns that apply to many words. (p. 230)

6. Student-Selected Words

Personal word lists are an important component of word study. These lists are chosen by the students themselves, and usually reflect words they have misspelled in written work or encountered in reading. It is a good idea to steer students away from too many exotic words, as they may not be useful in establishing a core writing vocabulary. Cramer (2001) recommends three to five personal words a week if you are using a spelling textbook approach, and a balance between student-selected and teacher-selected words if you are using a teacher-designed approach to word study.

Compiling a word list for word study is a complicated task. If one of the categories above is overemphasized to the exclusion of others, you run the risk of having a spelling program that lacks balance or coverage.

THEORY MUST BE LINKED TO PRACTICE IN PURPOSEFUL WAYS

No matter how successful students are at word-study activities, they must also be able to apply this linguistic knowledge to real-life writing. Word study without writing is like learning to drive without a car. Just as young drivers are motivated by the hope of driving the family car, young writers need to see a purpose to word study beyond the mark they receive on spelling dictations. The classroom writing program is crucial in helping students to care about their spelling efforts. The works of Lucy McCormick Calkins (1994) or Nancie Atwell (1998) promote writing as a powerful medium through which children can make sense of their lives. If they are encouraged to write about what matters to them and given opportunities to share these insights with others, children are more likely to care about the quality of their final product.

"A shared spirit of inquiry may inspire everyone to make the study of words and spelling a lifelong pursuit" (Johnston, 2001).

Even highly motivated children, however, need help in transferring the knowledge gained through formal word study to their everyday writing. If we merely assign exercises for children to complete, and we do not link what is being learned about spelling to writing, the same errors will keep recurring in student writing. Using word-solving approaches consistently throughout the day allows students to

- tackle the spelling of tricky words
- decipher the meanings of new words
- apply proofreading skills in editing conferences

Providing authentic purposes for word study leads to a much greater chance of spelling improvement.

The act of composing also has the same kind of distractions that new drivers face on the road. A young driver has to cope with surrounding traffic, honking horns, and road hazards. The writer has to concentrate on the voice, content, audience, and purpose for writing. It is only later, when the piece is ready for editing, that spelling becomes a priority. Even then, it is more difficult to spot errors in spelling when words are embedded in a paragraph than when they stand alone on a Word Wall or in a text. Considering all these factors, is it any wonder that research shows that spelling is a more challenging task than reading?

SUMMARY

This chapter has presented the following main ideas:

1. **Spelling is a complex process.** Neither straight memorization nor immersion in reading and writing will, on its own, provide a satisfactory environment for spelling growth.

2. **Focused word study is the foundation for effective spelling instruction.** Formal activities should be planned so that students are guided as they learn to examine words.

3. **Word study should involve children actively in the examination of words.** Students should be encouraged to be word detectives as they encounter words in reading, writing, and oral language.

4. **Words can be studied on many levels.** Both spelling patterns and the various meaning levels of language will provide rich material for word study.

5. **Word sorts and Word Walls are teaching strategies that encourage the active involvement of children in word study.**

6. **Effective word study is systematic.** Children need consistent spelling instruction throughout their elementary school experiences. This instruction should concentrate on developing a serviceable spelling vocabulary, crucial spelling principles, and spelling strategies.

7. **Instruction should be linked with the developmental stages of spelling growth.** An outline of typical spelling concepts addressed at each grade level is summarized in Figure 2.4 on pages 22–23.

8. **Instruction in spelling strategies should be given along with spelling patterns.** Strategies are particularly important for spelling irregular words. Children use a variety of spelling strategies throughout the grades, although certain strategies tend to predominate at each stage of development.

9. **Formal word study may include both a published spelling program and teacher-designed activities.** There are advantages and drawbacks to either approach when used on its own. A combination of published resources and teacher-generated activities can maximize coverage of important spelling principles and facilitate the transfer to reading, writing, and oral vocabulary.

10. **Words chosen for study should come from a variety of sources:**
    - developmentally appropriate words
    - high-frequency words
    - frequently misspelled words
    - linguistically patterned words
    - content-related words
    - student-selected words

11. **Theory must be linked to practice in purposeful ways.** Word study without reading and writing is like learning to drive without a car. Both skills require a combination of knowledge and application in real-life contexts.

12. Spelling should be embedded in a balanced literacy program that offers support for learners through whole class, independent, guided small group, and shared reading and writing contexts.

REFLECTIVE THINKING

1. Reflect on how you learned to spell. Was memorization the key method, or were you encouraged to be a "word detective"? Do you feel this has had an impact on your spelling ability?

2. How might you use word sorts to accommodate students with varying levels of spelling knowledge in your classroom?

3. How do the spelling concepts in Figure 2.4 on pages 22–23 fit the expectations set out for your grade in local or provincial curriculum documents?

4. Many educators have strong views about the use of published spelling programs. What position do the authors take in this chapter? Do you agree with their views?

5. Do you currently use a variety of sources for word lists in spelling? Did the chapter provide you with further possibilities?

The following chart provides links with other chapters in the book:

To learn more about...	see these chapters
How children learn to spell	Chapter 1, page 2
Word solving	Chapter 4, page 50
Patterns in English spelling	Chapter 4, page 50
Linking spelling instruction across the curriculum	Chapter 9, page 115
Accommodating diverse needs	Chapter 11, page 155
	Chapter 12, page 170
	Chapter 13, page 182

CHAPTER

3

Spelling Assessment

• •

Our discussion of spelling assessment follows Chapters 1 and 2 because we believe teachers need to have an understanding of how children learn to spell before they make judgments about their students' spelling abilities. They need also to consider the implications of spelling research for their total literacy program, and fit spelling assessment into this framework.

Spelling assessment should be ongoing, combining both formal and informal methods of determining a student's profile as a speller. When teachers report a student's use of spelling in writing, their comments should be guided by information gathered from a variety of sources over the course of a term or school year.

Assessment and evaluation of a student's spelling performance is only useful if it leads to informed decisions about instruction and provides student feedback. In this chapter, we present ten basic principles that should underlie spelling assessment. Each principle is described in detail, and links are suggested to other chapters of the book.

Principles of Spelling Assessment
❶ Use student writing as the primary source of spelling assessment.
❷ Assess spelling within a developmental model of learning to spell.
❸ Gather information about the student's spelling throughout the school year.
❹ Examine the student's knowledge, use of strategies, and attitudes related to spelling.
❺ Include the student in the assessment process.
❻ Add other sources of information to your assessment profiles.
❼ Focus on what the student already knows about spelling.
❽ Link assessment with explicit instruction based on identified needs.
❾ Develop a classroom assessment plan that includes a systematic collection of data about your students' spelling development.
❿ Provide timely feedback and opportunities to practise new concepts and strategies.

USE STUDENT WRITING AS THE PRIMARY SOURCE OF SPELLING ASSESSMENT

The most revealing insights often come from examining a student's spelling attempts rather than the number of words spelled conventionally.

Children reveal a great deal about their spelling skills as they go about the everyday tasks of writing. By examining writing over time, teachers can chart a student's milestones along the road to spelling competence. In order to get an accurate picture of this journey, however, it is necessary to examine various forms of writing that represent both edited and draft pieces of work. Some students are reluctant to use words in their stories that they are unsure how to spell. If polished work is the only source of spelling assessment, the information gleaned from the student's writing may be limited. The most revealing insights often come from examining a student's spelling attempts rather than the number of words spelled conventionally.

Figure 3.1 suggests many writing activities that can provide rich information for spelling assessment.

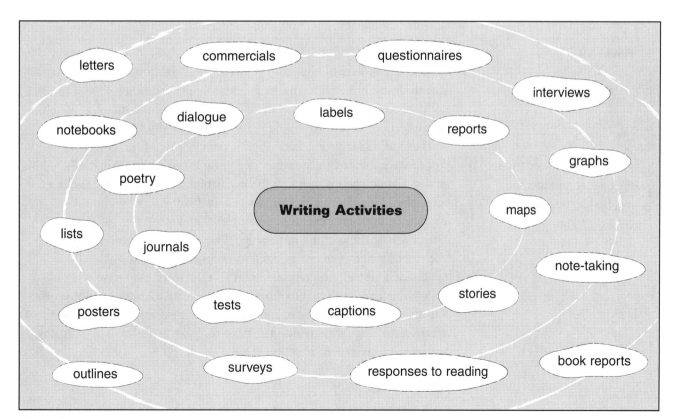

Figure 3.1

ASSESS SPELLING WITHIN A DEVELOPMENTAL MODEL OF LEARNING TO SPELL

Chapter 1 describes the stages most children pass through in becoming mature spellers. By viewing students' spelling through this framework, you will be able to make clearer judgments about how each student is progressing.

One parent treasures the following note "forged" by her six-year-old son, Michael. His Grade 1 teacher had sent home a letter describing Michael's inappropriate behaviour, and he decided to take matters into his own hands.

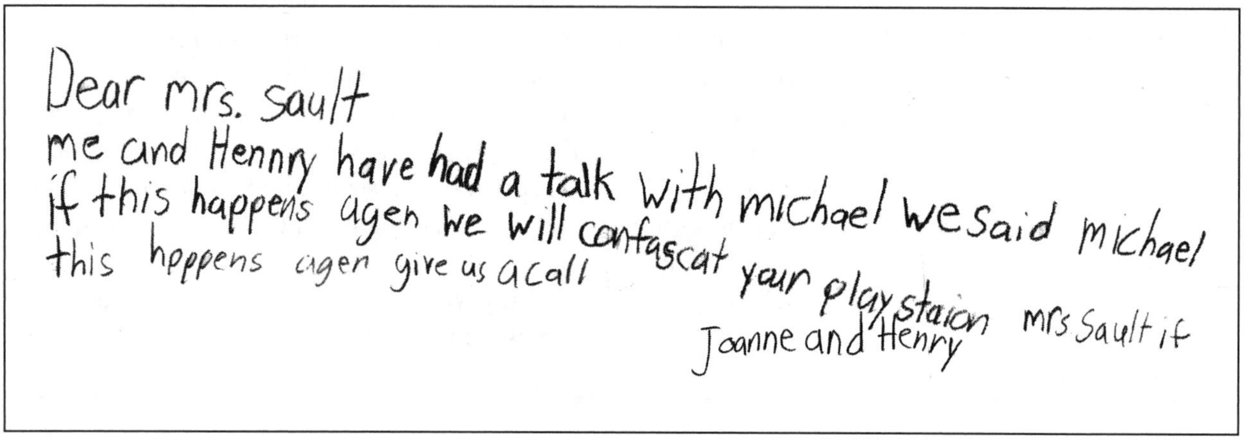

Dear mrs. sault
me and Hennry have had a talk with michael we said michael
if this happens agen we will confascat your play staion mrs sault if
this happens agen give us a call
Joanne and Henry

Figure 3.2

"Determining a stage of spelling for a student is not for creating a label but serves as a starting point for planning instruction" (Bear and Templeton, 1998).

While you may not approve of Michael's behaviour, if you analyse his note in developmental terms, he is certainly progressing well as a speller! He has a store of high-frequency words at his disposal, many of which have irregular features (*have, talk, said*). He uses double consonants (*happen*) and silent *e* markers (*give*) characteristic of the Patterns Within Words Stage. Although the word *confiscate* is misspelled, Michael's version (*confascat*) includes all three syllables. He presumably spells *again* as he says it (*agen*). Michael would benefit from knowing about the capitalization of proper nouns (*mrs. sault*) and strategies for remembering the spelling of the high-frequency word *again*. All in all, Michael appears to be on the road to becoming a proficient speller.

Jenkins (1999), nevertheless, warns, "Our work as assessors is not to pigeonhole children's orthographic thinking into a discrete point on the continuum" (p. 79). This caution leads to the next important principle of effective spelling assessment—the need to make assessment an ongoing part of your classroom practice.

GATHER INFORMATION ABOUT SPELLING THROUGHOUT THE SCHOOL YEAR

Children make important leaps in spelling development over the course of a school year. Writing portfolios are excellent vehicles for tracing these changes. If students review their drafts from early in the year, they are often amused and surprised by the words they once misspelled. A young child may notice that she or he no longer prints words without spaces between them; an older student may laugh that he or she once spelled *vacation* as *vacashun* before he or she understood the /*shun*/ ending.

The writing portfolio is also a rich source of data for communicating with parents/guardians about their child's progress in spelling. Portfolios can be a starting point in parent-teacher conferences, and can demonstrate the student's growth in a wide spectrum of literacy concepts.

A simple assessment technique is to dictate to a student a journal entry or similar short piece she or he has written. Choose a selection written early in the year, dictate it a few months later, and then a third time toward the end of the school year.

In Figure 3.3, Kelli, age 8, writes a thank-you note to her aunt.

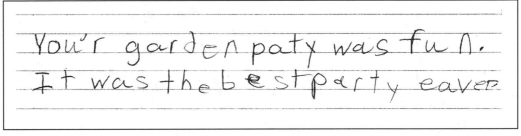

Figure 3.3 Kelli's note translates as follows: "Your garden party was fun. It was the best party ever."

Kelli's note suggests that she is in the Patterns Within Words Stage of spelling development, since she is experimenting with an apostrophe in *your* (*you'r*) and uses a vowel combination in *ever* (*eaver*).

Six months later, Kelli spells *your* and *ever* correctly, but her spelling of *party* is still inconsistent (see Figure 3.4 on page 36). She also has learned that an exclamation mark can be used to express her enthusiasm. A longer dictation would undoubtedly reveal even more information about Kelli's growing understanding of English spelling.

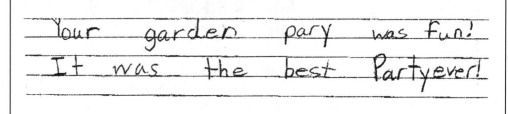

Figure 3.4

EXAMINE STUDENT KNOWLEDGE, USE OF STRATEGIES, AND ATTITUDES

Chapter 1 describes how good spellers share a number of characteristics. They have a knowledge base that includes spelling patterns on a variety of levels; they possess strategies to deal with words they do not know how to spell; and they care about the spelling in their written work and take responsibility for proofreading their drafts. Figure 3.5 outlines some features that can be assessed in each of these areas.

Spelling Assessment

Knowledge

- knowledge of sound–symbol patterns
- knowledge of common letter combinations (e.g., *ough*, *ight*)
- knowledge of structural patterns (e.g., possessives, contractions, adding endings)
- knowledge of meaning patterns (e.g., prefixes, suffixes, and plural and past-tense markers)
- evidence of a growing bank of high-frequency words
- possession of "spelling consciousness"—awareness of the way she or he spells

Strategies

- uses sound strategies for words that fit sound patterns
- employs visual strategies or memory tricks for irregular words
- uses word-building techniques for longer words
- consults other sources (dictionaries, Word Walls, personal dictionaries, and so on) when needed
- demonstrates effective proofreading skills

Attitudes

- possesses a "spelling conscience"—sees correct spelling as a courtesy to the reader and willingly corrects misspellings
- takes responsibility for editing his or her own writing
- views spelling as a system that can be controlled
- interested in words—their meaning, structure, usage, and spelling
- aware of words in the environment—notices new or unusual words

Figure 3.5

Spelling: Connecting the Pieces

INCLUDE THE STUDENT IN THE ASSESSMENT PROCESS

Students are an obvious but often neglected source of assessment information. If given a chance to reflect on their spelling attempts and processes, they can usually provide vital clues about what they know and do not know about the spelling system. Involving students in the assessment process also encourages them to think about themselves as spellers and helps them to develop a "spelling consciousness." It also develops their independence as they self-monitor, self-direct, and self-assess.

"Mrs. Meachum did not tell the truth. She said learning was fun, and it wasn't. At least not all the time. Not when it came to spelling" (Ramona Quimby in Beverly Cleary's Ramona's World, *1999).*

SPELLING INTERVIEWS

Some conversations about spelling will happen spontaneously as you participate with students in writing workshop conferences. At other times, when you want to focus on spelling, you may suggest that students prepare for a "spelling interview." Have them select pieces of writing from their portfolios that are in the draft stage, and explain that you are not expecting error-free work.

During the interview, ask students to look for words that they suspect are misspelled. Have them try a few other spellings of the word and select the one they think is correct. This will tell you how well they are able to locate errors while proofreading, and how good they are at generating possible alternatives. Also ask students to explain their reasoning in making decisions. You may gain valuable information about the strategies they used and their understanding of the spelling system.

SPELLING SURVEY

The Spelling Survey in Figure 3.6 is intentionally open-ended, allowing students to express their opinions about the importance of spelling and their own spelling habits. This tool could be given to students prior to your spelling interview and serve as a basis for further discussion.

Spelling Survey
❶ Do you think you are a good speller? How do you know this?
❷ When is spelling easiest for you?
❸ When is spelling hardest?
❹ What strategies help you to spell words?
❺ If you are not sure whether a word you have spelled is correct or incorrect, what do you do?
❻ Is it important to be able to spell words correctly? Why or why not?
❼ If students want to be great spellers, what should they do?

Figure 3.6

SPELLING CHECKLIST

The Spelling Checklist in Figure 3.7 provides a way of having students assess their spelling processes.

Spelling Checklist	Always	Sometimes	Never
❶ I try to spell words the way they sound.			
❷ I try to use spelling rules to spell words.			
❸ I try to remember the shape of words or where the tricky parts are.			
❹ If I cannot spell a word, I think about the meaning.			
❺ I break words into syllables to spell them.			
❻ I listen for smaller words inside the bigger word.			
❼ I spell a new word by thinking of other words that rhyme with it.			
❽ I use a dictionary, Word Wall, or other type of word list to help me spell.			
❾ I can tell if a word I have written "does not look right."			
❿ I proofread for spelling errors when I write a first draft.			
⓫ I proofread for spelling errors when I edit something I have written.			
⓬ I misspell the same words over and over again.			
⓭ I think that correct spelling in a polished piece of writing is important.			
⓮ I find spelling easy.			

Figure 3.7

"If children are to remain invested in their learning, they need to assess their own progress as readers, writers, and spellers, and to set goals for future learning" (Jenkins, 1999).

SELF-ANALYSIS AND GOAL-SETTING

Students should be encouraged to analyse their spelling difficulties and set goals for themselves. Have them record the correct form of words they have misspelled in their everyday writing or spelling dictations. They should then circle the letters that gave them difficulty and notice any patterns of errors. For younger children, it may be enough to indicate whether these letters were at the beginning, the end, or in the middle of the word. Older students can do a more sophisticated analysis, noticing problems such as homophones, silent letters, doubling consonants, and so on. Spelling goals can then be set that reflect the patterns of errors. Students with similar goals can work together or be clustered together for mini-lessons on specific spelling concepts or strategies.

Figure 3.8 on page 39 gives an example of a Grade 6 student's analysis of errors on a dictated list of words.

Words I Misspelled	Letters I Need to Remember	What Were the Errors?
dinner	di(nn)er	double consonant
customer	c(u)st(o)mer	first and second vowel
their	th(eir)	homophone
cousins	cousins	plural words don't use an apostrophe
someone	someone	*someone* is one word, not two

Figure 3.8 Student analysis of errors

ADD OTHER SOURCES OF INFORMATION TO YOUR ASSESSMENT PROFILES

Although a student's everyday writing should be the main source of information for spelling assessment, other writing contexts are also important. As mentioned earlier, students sometimes mask spelling difficulties in their writing by using only words they are sure of spelling correctly. Dictated words can also add valuable information to your assessment profiles.

DICTATED WORDS

There are various choices for lists of words for word study. The advantage of dictating words from teacher-selected lists is that age-appropriate words can be included. If a spelling text is a source of these lists, the lists are likely to reflect various spelling concepts. Each unit is often based on a concept such as vowel patterns, adding endings, and so on. Other available lists may be made up of frequently used or frequently misspelled words at various grade levels. You can also dictate words related to themes, content areas, or Word Walls compiled with the students.

When you dictate such lists, your students are forced to move beyond the simple words they may choose to use in their writing. They may have to apply spelling strategies for words that they are not sure how to spell.

When you use lists as a source of spelling assessment, it is often helpful to conduct a pre-test in which the words are dictated before the students have a chance to study them. This strategy has a number of advantages. First, it shows you the student's current knowledge of these words and the strategies he or she employs to spell unfamiliar words. Second, it also helps to isolate the words the student needs to study, thereby making the learning period more efficient. The class can then identify difficult parts of each word and brainstorm strategies for spelling them correctly. A post-test can focus on improvements from the pre-test, and identify words still needing to be studied.

Sources of Dictated Words

▶ spelling texts
▶ frequently used words
▶ frequently misspelled words
▶ theme words
▶ Word Walls
▶ appropriate content-area vocabulary

Bear (1996) cautions against dictating words that are too far above a student's spelling level. Children usually abandon their normal spelling strategies when they are at the frustration level and tend to guess rather than apply any systematic strategies.

FOCUS ON WHAT THE STUDENT ALREADY KNOWS ABOUT SPELLING

Developmental research on learning to spell reveals that the quality of a student's spelling attempts is an important indicator of spelling growth. Jenkins (1999) says, "On one level, spelling is delightfully easy to assess—the word is either right or wrong. If we fail to examine children's spelling approximations, however, we close the window on the cognitive strategies that spellers adopt to puzzle out unfamiliar words" (p. 86).

THE BUCKETS

CLOZE STRATEGY

The Cloze Strategy for noting misspellings can help you see patterns in your students' spelling attempts. Instead of marking a response as either correct or incorrect, recopy the correct letters and leave spaces for the others. For example, *ned* (*need*) becomes *ne __ d*, *baskitball* (*basketball*) becomes *bask __ tball*, and so on. By observing a sampling of a student's spelling errors scored in this way, you can see a picture emerging. Questions such as the following can guide these observations:

- Are all sounds represented?
- Are spellings of sounds phonetically acceptable (e.g., *wuz* for *was* is phonetically accurate, although misspelled)?
- Does the attempt contain the correct number of syllables?
- Are there problems with reversal of letters?
- Are errors typically at the beginning, middle, or end of words?

- Are morphemes spelled correctly (e.g., *-ed* for past tense; *-s* or *-es* for plural)?
- Are silent letters routinely omitted?
- Do schwa vowels (vowels in unstressed syllables) create problems (e.g., *helmut* for *helmet*)?

The Cloze Strategy can be used in many aspects of your writing program. In editing conferences, you can point out spelling errors in draft pieces without resorting to circling errors. This approach will help your students focus on the nature of the misspelling. After you dictate word lists in pre-test conditions, applying the Cloze Strategy to misspelled words can help your students isolate the features of the word that need to be studied, and usually reassures them that most of the letters have been spelled correctly.

Figure 3.9 shows a selection of misspellings taken from a Grade 6 student's writing and from spelling dictations. By comparing his attempts with the correct spelling, it seems clear that he spells words as he hears them and uses very few visual strategies to recall what the words look like. This student also has difficulty with the various forms of the homophones *to*, *two*, and *too*, and doesn't realize that by doubling the *t* in *later*, the long vowel *a* becomes short.

If this selection of words were marked in the usual way as a dictation, the student would score zero. If, however, you assign part marks, he actually scores 43 out of a possible total of 52 letters, or 83 percent. This is not to say that close approximations are fine in spelling, but for the student who has a poor self-concept about spelling, knowing how close he or she is can be a wonderful motivator.

Key Word	Attempt	Cloze	Letters Correct
while	wile	w_ile	4/5
heaven	heven	he_ven	5/6
attraction	atraction	at_raction	9/10
nightmare	nightmar	nightmar_	8/9
flirting	flurting	fl_rting	7/8
wheel	weel	w_eel	4/5
to	too	t_	1/2 *
later	latter	la_er	4/5 *
to	two	t_	1/2 *

Figure 3.9   * When an extra letter is added, one point is deducted from the total score.

LINK ASSESSMENT WITH EXPLICIT INSTRUCTION BASED ON IDENTIFIED NEEDS

When you meet your students and begin to assess their knowledge, strategies, and attitudes related to spelling, you can use this information to plan your goals for the year. If you are using a spelling textbook, your assessment data will help you decide which students will likely benefit from grade-level instruction and which should be involved in a modified program. Even if the students seem capable of working at grade level, spelling interviews and student surveys will help you understand how each student learns best. Some students may prefer to work in co-operative groups, while other students may benefit more from independent work.

Vygotsky (1962) used the term "zone of proximal development" to describe how teachers can best facilitate new learning among their students. By interacting with your students and assessing their current levels of performance, you can structure learning situations that will nudge children to the next stage of development.

It is important to present information that will challenge students to move ahead, but not to the point at which they become frustrated. This may mean helping young children understand the concept of a "word" before expecting them to deal with patterns within words. With older students, it may involve helping them to grasp what a base word is before expecting them to cope with longer forms involving prefixes and suffixes. Fountas and Pinnell (1999) echo these concerns: "We waste time when we go over something in a rote way that children already know. We also waste time and risk confusing children by focussing on ideas and concepts that are beyond their current experience. In either case, the learner cannot be active and word study becomes tedious" (p. 67).

Your assessment plan will give you insight into what individual children need in order to progress. It is also crucial to use ongoing assessment to monitor the effectiveness of your spelling program for individual students. You can use evidence both from everyday writing and from more formal spelling tests to help determine whether students are progressing in their spelling development.

INSTRUCTION AND ASSESSMENT: INDIVIDUAL, GROUPS, WHOLE CLASS

You can address the spelling needs of your students using a variety of groupings. A combination of these approaches is most effective.

Individual/Partner Instruction

Editing conferences with your students provide good opportunities to identify spelling difficulties and to provide direct assistance. Students can work with partners and teach each other about spelling patterns or strategies for approaching tricky words. Parent volunteers can also provide one-on-one assistance.

"The words that students consistently spell correctly are those words that have patterns that make sense to them and that fit their current theory of how words are spelled" (Bear and Templeton, 1998).

During formal spelling instruction, whether using a spelling text or teacher-designed materials, students can work independently on exercises geared to their needs. By administering a pre-test before students begin a unit of work, you can assign specific exercises that are appropriate, rather than having every student complete all parts of a unit.

Figure 3.10 provides a means of recording assessment observations over time for each student.

Spelling Profile		Student: _____		
	Sources*	Knowledge	Strategies	Instructional Goals
Date: Sept. 28	writing folder samples	spells short and long vowels accurately	sounds words out well	strategies that will focus on visual memory for irregular spellings
Date:				
Date:	*e.g., writing folder, spelling tests, exercises, notebook, interview			

Figure 3.10 Record of assessment observations in spelling

Mixed-Ability Groups

Students of varying ability levels in spelling can benefit from working in mixed groups. Co-operative activities can give everyone an opportunity to learn new spelling strategies and apply them to difficult words. Word sorts are ideal co-operative activities for detecting spelling patterns and learning spelling rules.

Needs Groupings

If your spelling assessments reveal groups of students at similar stages of development, it makes sense to provide instruction to these clusters. Groups can be formed for specific learning concepts and reconfigured as the needs change.

A spelling text can be adapted for various levels of spelling ability. The pre-test may show that one group of students already can spell most of the words on a list; a second group struggles with a few words; the third group makes many errors. You can assign certain exercises based on the performance levels described. Also, remember that the teacher's guides for many spelling programs offer suggestions for both enrichment and further support.

Figure 3.11 shows a method of recording assessment information and grouping students with similar needs.

Status-of-the-Class Sheet

Teacher Planning / Program Evaluation / Division Planning / Accountability

Comment: Based on retelling of "The Angry Dragon"   • Date: November 1

(Spelling)	Word Study	Capitals / Periods / Commas		Paragraphing	Other:
Holistic	Holistic	Plot	Setting	Writing Organization	Draft	Edit
Punctuation	Writing	beginning, middle, ending	Presentation		Rev.

David W.	4 3 2 1	Benjamin	4 3 2 1	Rahaan	4 3 2 1	Craig	4 3 2 1

David W:
Nicole dainr, danr lat
Nicole's dinner. late
aftre (nit) geting
after night getting
skreemd dont
screemed don't

Benjamin:
coold sneezd tickld
cold sneezed tickled
smild burnd (fot)
smiled burned fought

Rahaan:
* Accurate spelling.
Mostly familiar words
used:
(ie: getting, ready, big,
down, said, because,
nice etc.)

Craig:
happend quite
happened quiet
replyd
replied

| David C. | 4 3 2 1 | Janice | 4 3 2 1 | Spark | 4 3 2 1 | Alex | 4 3 2 1 |

David C:
wery sade im
worry said I'm
hallo becuz than
hello because then

Janice:
drogon on (though)
dragon one thought
* Some familiar words
incorrect but spelled:
ground, snow, dir, joy,
again!!

Spark:
ones uppona burnd
once upon a burned
rober shak wathing
robber shake watching
(rit)
right

Alex:
* accurate spelling.
New words risked:
gigantic, patrol,
* uses familiar words
accuracy and always
extends vocabulary

| Priya | 4 3 2 1 | André | 4 3 2 1 | Nicole | 4 3 2 1 | Cole | 4 3 2 1 |

Priya:
a nother know
another now
dragon's (brogt) (fite)
dragons brought fight

André:
didit no than
didn't know then
biger talest (linch)
bigger tallest lunch

Nicole:
jragon lonley (banch)
dragon lonely bunch
pased happest
passed happist
* needs pronunciation help

Cole:
to lest ferends no
two lets friends know
oter nekt loge
other next long
(bunsh) (thang)
bunch thing

Outcome / Expectation: Students will use 'clusters' as a basis for spelling other words in same family

Student Groupings and Focus	Double letter before suffix	Past is ED, not D, not T	Mentors
Clusters to teach, review: IGHT ING OUGH (UNCH)	David W. Spark Andre Nicole	David W. Benjamin Spark Craig	Rahsaan: Help with familiar words Alex: Help anyone * will work with students at left.

Flip cards for familiar words: DavidC, (ME) Page 1 of 2 / Nov.
Andre

Figure 3.11

A simpler format for tracking groups is found in Figure 3.12.

Status-of-the-Group Sheet

Date: _____

Group Members	Goals/Plans	Notes

Figure 3.12

Whole Class

Throughout the school day you will find chances to examine language patterns with the whole class. New words will arise in every subject area, and your enthusiasm about exploring language can be contagious. Through Shared Reading and Guided Reading experiences, your students can learn about word origins, brainstorm strategies for spelling new words, and savour the sensory qualities of words—the possibilities are endless. Students can brainstorm spelling strategies by means of shared interactive writing. Your assessment observations will also help you determine common spelling errors. You can address these problems and reinforce new learning at every opportunity.

AN ASSESSMENT PLAN SHOULD INCLUDE THE SYSTEMATIC COLLECTION OF DATA

The preceding principles of spelling assessment lead to a clear conclusion—the assessment of spelling must be systematic and planned. Pinnell and Fountas (1998) emphasize this point while stressing that much of the observation will occur during regular classroom activities. "Even though the observation is embedded, it is still systematic. Teachers need to have a classroom assessment plan that includes the systematic collection of data on what children know about letters, sounds, and words. The assessment plan leads directly to instruction" (p. 104).

Chapter 14, "Home Connections," will focus on sharing assessment information with parents and involving parents in their child's spelling development. The rubrics in Figure 3.13 on pages 46–47 represent one way of conveying assessment information. They show, from a variety of perspectives, how the student is performing in spelling relative to grade-level expectations. You will be able to make these rubrics more specific to your grade level through your knowledge of typical grade-level spelling performance, curriculum expectations, grade-based spelling programs, and Figure 2.4 on pages 22–23.

The performance levels of these rubrics indicate the following levels of achievement:

- Level 1: much below the standard for the grade
- Level 2: approaching the standard for the grade
- Level 3: standard for the grade
- Level 4: exceeds the standard for the grade

SPELLING RUBRIC

KNOWLEDGE

	1	2	3	4
* Patterns	• uses phonics or inadequate memory strategies to spell without thought to word structure, meaning, or families of words; often spells the same word different ways	• uses phonics awareness when reminded; needs assistance to understand word structure and meaning as they relate to spelling; uses mnemonics at times to recall words studied	• regularly uses phonics, awareness of word structure, awareness of meaning, and personal mnemonics to spell accurately	• consistently uses phonics, awareness of word structure, awareness of meaning, and mnemonics to spell accurately
High-Frequency Words	• spells few high-frequency words correctly	• correctly spells some high-frequency words	• correctly spells most high-frequency words	• correctly spells a wide range of high-frequency words
Spelling Consciousness	• approaches spelling randomly and not as a system	• simply or incompletely articulates how he or she spells	• can usually articulate how he or she spells	• articulates how he or she spells and views spelling as a system that can be controlled

STRATEGIES

	1	2	3	4
Range	• focuses primarily on a single spelling strategy (e.g., sounding words out)	• uses a limited range of spelling strategies	• usually uses a range of spelling strategies (e.g., sound, visual, meaning)	• consistently uses a range of spelling strategies (e.g., sound, visual, meaning)
Appropriateness	• uses one or two simple strategies for all words regardless of the nature of the word (e.g., sounds out all words; tries to remember what words look like)	• sometimes chooses appropriate strategies to learn the spelling of words (e.g., sounds out patterned words; memorizes irregular words)	• usually uses strategies appropriately (e.g., - sound strategies for words that fit sound patterns - visual strategies or memory tricks for irregular words - word-building strategies for longer words)	• consistently chooses appropriate strategies (e.g., - sound strategies for words that fit sound patterns - visual strategies or memory tricks for irregular words - word-building strategies for longer words)

* Specific patterns will vary with grade level. See Figure 2.4 on pages 22–23 for typical spelling concepts studied at each grade level.

STRATEGIES (continued)	1	2	3	4
Proofreading	• experiences difficulty both in detecting errors and in correcting them	• uses some simple proofreading strategies to detect or correct spelling errors	• usually uses effective proofreading strategies to detect and correct spelling errors	• consistently uses effective proofreading strategies to detect and correct spelling errors
Use of Secondary Sources	• seldom consults other sources in proofreading, or uses them ineffectively	• relies on a small number of sources to aid proofreading	• usually makes appropriate use of sources, such as dictionaries, spell checks, Word Walls, and personal word lists, in proofreading	• independently makes effective use of sources, such as dictionaries, spell checks, Word Walls, and personal word lists, in proofreading

ATTITUDES	1	2	3	4
"Spelling Conscience"	• sees little connection between correct spelling and good writing	• views correct spelling as a requirement set by the teacher	• views correct spelling as a component of good writing	• views correct spelling as an important aspect of clear communication
Responsibility	• proofreads own writing only when required to do so	• proofreads own writing with some direction	• increasingly assumes responsibility for proofreading own writing	• assumes responsibility for proofreading own writing
Views of Spelling	• approaches words randomly without looking for patterns or consistency	• approaches some spelling tasks systematically, but often just tries to memorize words	• demonstrates a growing comfort level with the spelling system; approaches spelling systematically	• views spelling as a system that can be controlled; is confident in ability to become a mature speller
Interest in Words	• shows little interest in words or how they work	• occasionally shows an interest in word-study activities	• often shows an interest in word-study activities that are generated by the teacher	• displays a keen interest in words—their meaning, structure, usage, spelling

Figure 3.13 Spelling rubric

PROVIDE TIMELY FEEDBACK AND OPPORTUNITIES FOR PRACTICE

The insights you glean from ongoing spelling assessment should not be stored in your files and saved for reporting purposes or parent interviews. Your findings should be shared with students so that they can set realistic goals and practise new concepts and strategies related to spelling. These sharing times can take many forms: one-on-one interviews, during writing workshop conferences, whole-class discussions, and small-group interactions.

SUMMARY

This chapter has presented the following main ideas:

1. **Teachers should have an understanding of how children learn to spell before making judgments about their students' spelling abilities.**

2. **Spelling assessment should be ongoing,** combining both formal and informal methods of determining a student's profile as a speller.

3. **Assessment and evaluation of a student's spelling performance should lead to informed decisions about instruction.**

4. **Ten principles should underlie a comprehensive approach to spelling assessment:**
   - Use student writing as the primary source of spelling assessment.
   - Assess spelling within a developmental model of learning to spell.
   - Gather information about spelling throughout the school year.
   - Examine the student's knowledge, use of strategies, and attitudes related to spelling.
   - Include the student in the assessment process.
   - Add other sources of information to your assessment profiles.
   - Focus on what the student already knows about spelling.
   - Link assessment with instruction.
   - Develop a classroom assessment plan that includes a systematic collection of data about your students' spelling development.
   - Provide timely feedback and opportunities to practise new concepts and strategies.

REFLECTIVE THINKING

1. Which of the ten Principles of Spelling Assessment (p. 32) did you find most useful to your classroom situation? Why?

2. What are the advantages and limitations of using writing portfolios as a primary source of spelling assessment?

3. Have you ever conducted a spelling survey or interview with students apart from editing conferences? What might be the benefits or drawbacks to this strategy?

4. What aspects of spelling assessment do you want to know more about? Where might you find the additional information that you require?

5. Pinnell and Fountas (1998) state that "Teachers need to have a classroom assessment plan that includes the systematic collection of data on what children know about letters, sounds, and words" (p. 104). How feasible is this suggestion within the context of your role?

The following chart provides links with other chapters in the book where you will find ideas for translating assessment findings into meaningful instruction:

To learn more about...	see these chapters
Children's spelling development	Chapter 1, page 2
Reading and spelling	Chapter 7, page 85
Writing and spelling	Chapter 8, page 99
Integrating spelling into subject areas	Chapter 9, page 115
Developing a spelling consciousness	Chapter 10, page 130
Spelling strategies	Chapter 10, page 129
Spelling for second-language learners	Chapter 11, page 155
Supporting struggling spellers	Chapter 12, page 170
Challenging skilled spellers	Chapter 13, page 182
Connecting with the home	Chapter 14, page 192

The English Spelling System

Spelling the *sh* Sound

<u>sh</u>oe

<u>s</u>ugar

pa<u>ss</u>ion

ambi<u>ti</u>on

o<u>c</u>ean

<u>ch</u>ampagne

<u>sch</u>mooze

artifi<u>ci</u>al

controver<u>si</u>al

lu<u>x</u>ury

cu<u>sh</u>ion

curva<u>ce</u>ous

ga<u>se</u>ous

qui<u>ch</u>e

con<u>sci</u>ous

Traditionally, spelling has been taught by rules such as "*i* before *e* except after *c*." However, as many people then discover, rules will only take you so far in trying to master the English spelling system. In fact, David Crystal, in his *Cambridge Encyclopedia of the English Language* (1995), states that there are more than 100 exceptions to the "*i* before *e* rule." These include *ei* when it sounds like long *a*, as in *eight*, but also words like *ancient, conscience, height, their,* and *weird.*

English is more difficult to spell than many other alphabetic languages. In Italian and other phonetic languages, there is a one-to-one match between letters and speech sounds. In English, by contrast, the 44 phonemes or speech sounds (the number varies from 40 to 48 depending on the researcher) can be spelled in over 200 ways. There are 15 ways to spell the sound *sh* alone (Bryson, 1990; Payne, 1995).

However, the English spelling system is more logical and more predictable than it would at first seem. Crystal (1995) estimates over 80 percent of English words are spelled by regular patterns. As he puts it:

> There seem to be less than 500 words in English whose spelling is wholly irregular; but several of them are among the most frequently used in the language. Because they are constantly before our eyes, English spelling gives the impression of being more irregular than it really is. (p. 272)

HOW DID ENGLISH BECOME SO COMPLICATED?

The English spelling system has been developing for over a thousand years. As wave after wave of influences swept over the language, each one brought changes to the written word. The process continues as new spellings and new words like *yuppie* and *database* come into the language.

Given its current complexity, it's interesting to note that English started out as a straightforward Anglo-Saxon alphabetic writing system, with roughly 35 phonemes, represented in a left to right match up. We can still see this foundation in words such as *mat* and *stop* (Crystal, 1997).

Problems arose in the sixth century when missionaries from Rome tried to represent those 35 sounds with their 23-letter Latin alphabet, plus a few new symbols to represent non-Latin sounds such as *th*, shown in Figure 4.1 (Johnston, 2001, p. 373). This symbol is called a "thorn."

After the Norman conquest in 1066, French scribes changed many Old English spellings. For example, they substituted *qu* for *cw*, and the old English word *cwene* became *queen*. They also substituted *o* for *u* in words like *come, love, one,* and *son,* simply because the *u* looked too much like other letters in the dense script of the times (Johnston, 2001, p. 377). Figure 4.2 is an example of the similarities in Middle English letters.

English spelling was not standardized until about 1650. Before that, no one worried much about how words were spelled. *Where* was spelled *wher, whair, wair, wheare, were,* or *whear* (Bryson, 1990). Teachers will probably recognize some of their students' misspellings in this list. However, with the introduction of Caxton's printing press in the 15th century, spelling became more rigid. Unfortunately, this happened just as English pronunciation was changing, and, as a result, we often spell words the way people said them 400 years ago. This practice accounts for some of the silent letters in words such as *knight, knee, gnaw, walk, talk,* and *wrong. Knight* would have been pronounced as *kuh-nee-guh-tuh,* and the *l* in *walk* and *talk* were also pronounced (Bryson, 1990).

Later, feeling that English should reflect its classical roots, language experts insisted that *doubt* and *debt* should have a *b* like their Latin roots, and *rime* should become *rhyme.* The word *receipt* gained a *p* and *scissors* a *c*.

Figure 4.1

Figure 4.2

None of this helped make English spelling any easier. However, knowing there are historical reasons for these changes perhaps makes the spelling challenge more interesting. "Teachers of reading and spelling are in a position not only to instruct their students, but also to shape their students' attitudes about language," says Francine Johnston, who teaches in the School of Education at the University of North Carolina (2001, p. 372). Teachers can foster a positive attitude by helping students find reasons why words are spelled the way they are.

HELPING STUDENTS MAKE SENSE OF THE SYSTEM

Since students learn language by searching for patterns, they first need to believe that a system for writing words exists. They then need to explore words, looking for patterns, large and small. Many students become discouraged about spelling at an early age when they perceive that spelling is hard. To take an example from literature, in Beverly Cleary's novel, *Ramona's World*, Ramona is ready to give up on spelling by Grade 4:

> "Mrs. Meacham is *mean*," Ramona explained. "If we get all the spelling words right, she gives us hard words as if they were some kind of treat. They aren't. They are really really hard words like foreign and quarantine, the kind of words where you don't know which letter comes first...I'm tired of spelling." (p. 114)

Even at the earliest stages of learning to write, children are confronted by words such as *one*, *two*, and *you* that seem to have little sound/symbol correspondence. Of the top 100 words on the high-frequency list, approximately one-quarter are words that fit no reliable pattern, or, like *come* and *have*, seem to break a pattern. The difficulty is not that students will fail to learn *you* or *have*. These words are of such high frequency, students will learn to spell them by reading and writing them many times. The problem is that students may give up trying to make sense of English spelling because it seems so random and unpredictable.

Students confronted by the challenges of learning to spell may well ask, "Why does almost every pattern have exceptions: hat, mat, bat, what?" "Why do so many important words have no pattern at all?"

Top 100 List Words That Break Patterns				
are	from	one	some	what
as	have	our	their	would
because	know	people	there	you
come	of	said	two	
could	once	school	was	

Figure 4.3

The instability of the English spelling system has even frustrated some of our great writers. George Bernard Shaw was among those who advocated a complete reform of English spelling. He claimed English spelling was so nonsensical that *fish* could just as easily be spelled *ghoti*:

fish = ghoti

gh as in *enou**gh***	**gh_ _ _**
the short sound *i* as in *w**o**men*	**gho_ _**
the *sh* sound as in *ac**ti**on*	**ghoti**

However, Shaw's example actually demonstrates the "sense" of the English spelling system: the *gh* letter combination never spells the *f* sound at the beginning of words—only at the end of words such as *tough*, *rough*, and *enough*. Similarly, the *ti* spelling of *sh* never occurs at the end of a word unless it is part of the suffix *-tion*. These "positional constraints," as they are called, are an important feature of the English spelling system.

As educators, it is not essential that we have a complete knowledge of all the complexities of the spelling system, but we must believe the system exists and help students to explore its logic and patterns. In guiding students' exploration and learning, here are six important principles to follow:

Principals of the English Spelling System

❶ The Alphabetic Connection. There is a connection between spelling and sound. English spelling is not highly phonetic, but there are many strong patterns based on sound/symbol relationships.

❷ Positional Constraints and Orthographic Patterns. Many letter combinations are restricted to certain positions in words (e.g., *ck* at the end of words, but never at the beginning). English also has orthographic or written patterns that tend to be consistent (e.g., *light*, *night*, *bright*, and so on).

❸ The Historical Connection. Since historical factors have influenced the spelling of words, old letter combinations are kept even when the pronunciation has changed (e.g., *knee* and *gnat*).

❹ The Meaning Connection. Word meaning is a key element in the English spelling system. Two words related in meaning will often have similar spellings (e.g., *sign/signal*). Spelling also helps the reader establish meaning (e.g., *for/four*).

❺ New Words. People invent new words at a great pace and fit them into the spelling system (e.g., *e-mail*, *skateboard*).

❻ Borrowed Words. People borrow words from many languages and have done so over time. English tends to keep the spelling of the borrowed word as it was in the original language (e.g., *café*).

The following sections describe these six principles and their applications in more detail:

1. THE ALPHABETIC CONNECTION

As we noted earlier, in true phonetic languages such as Italian, one sound is always spelled with one letter. In these phonetic languages, learning to spell is not difficult. In English, however, correct spelling is a major task that lasts a learner's lifetime. A newspaper editor recently commented, "I never refuse to hire a writer who can't spell, but I never hire one who won't look up the correct spelling."

Although there is not a one-to-one match between sound and spelling in English, there are many words that fall into groups with the same sound and spelling pattern. As Patricia Cunningham says, "Currently, research from several areas supports the long-standing practice of word family/phonogram/spelling pattern instruction" (1994, p. 1). The following list contains the most important of these vowel-consonant rhyming patterns, sometimes called *rimes*. Not only do these rhyming families help us with short words, but they are also useful for spelling longer words such as *lipstick* and *pumpkin*.

Common Vowel-Consonant Rime Patterns

a	**e**	**i**	**o**	**u**
ack (back)	ed (bed)	ick (pick)	ock (clock)	uck (tuck)
ad (dad)	eg (peg)	id (kid)	ob (rob)	ub (rub)
ag (bag)	en (hen)	ig (dig)	od (cod)	ug (mug)
am (jam)	et (get)	im (him)	og (dog)	ump (bump)
an (can)		in (pin)	op (hop)	unk (bunk)
ap (map)		ip (lip)	ot (not)	up (pup)
at (sat)		ish (fish)		ut (cut)
		it (sit)		

Figure 4.4

Unfortunately, as every writer knows, English spelling does not always follow such simple patterns. A student discovers a pattern for *cut, hut, but,* and *rut*—but what about *put*? It has a different vowel sound. With your encouragement, students can learn that it can be interesting and fun to look for words that do *not* match the pattern. This principle of *dissonance*—looking for the items that don't match—can be as useful as constructing the predictable list.

2. POSITIONAL CONSTRAINTS AND ORTHOGRAPHIC PATTERNS

POSITIONAL CONSTRAINTS

Children begin to internalize the positions of certain letters and letter combinations in words as they learn to read. (See Chapter 5, "Listening and Speaking.") Consider the spelling of /k/ in a final position. Good readers and spellers know that *ckip* cannot be an English word, but *zick* could be. They have noticed that there is a large group of words following the *-ick* pattern (*brick, flick, kick, lick, pick, quick, sick, stick, trick,* and *wick*); however, *ck* is never seen at the beginning of English words.

What students may find more difficult is making a decision about whether to use *k* or *ck* at the end of a word. Johnston (2001) suggests that students examine two lists: one where a short vowel sound is followed by *ck,* and another where a long *e* is followed by a single *k*. She encourages students to read the words aloud, to speculate on why the final letters are different, and then to look for other examples of the pattern and add them to the list.

In saying the words aloud, students will recognize that a short vowel is followed by *ck*, while a long vowel sound, represented by two vowels together, is followed by a single *k*.

In contrast, look at a letter combination that only occurs at the beginning of words. *Wr* spells *r* at the beginning of around 30 common words, such as *wrap* and *write*, but never spells *r* at the end of words. The idea that they can learn these words, and that *there will be no more* gives students the confidence to know when to use *wr*. They will be unlikely to write, as one student did: "I *rapped* the present."

To teach this to students, you can start with the most common words beginning with *wr*, such as *write* and *wrap*, and ask them to search the dictionary for more words that begin with *r* spelled *wr*. Once they have found the list in the dictionary, talk about the meanings of the words and how they can use them in writing.

Positional Constraints

A *positional constraint* is a restriction placed on letters that can spell a specific sound. For example, it describes the fact that *ck* can never appear at the beginning of a word, but it can appear at the end and in the middle of a word.

ck or k	
__ck	__k
back	beak
slick	sleek
wick	weak
rack	reek
speck	speak
chick	cheek

Wr Words			
wraith	wreckage	wretched	writhe
wrangle	wren	wriggle	written
wrap	wrench	wring	wrong
wrath	wrest	wrinkle	wrote
wreath	wrestle	wrist	wrought
wreathe	wrestler	write	wrung
wreck	wretch	writer	wry

Figure 4.5

Another positional constraint in English is that the *v* sound is usually spelled *ve* at the end of words. There are abbreviations such as *nav* for *navigation* and *Nov.* for *November*, but all other words end in *ve*. This explains the *ve* at the end of words such as *have* and *give*. Normally, the final silent *e* signals a long vowel, but in words that end in the *v* sound, it simply rounds out the word.

You can encourage students to look for other positional constraints as they examine words in their reading and writing. It may be useful to create lists with students and keep them posted in the classroom for reference. Other positional constraints include the following:

/g/ is spelled with one *g* at the end of words, not two. The only exception is *egg*.

/h/ does not occur at the end of English words. *Gh* and *th* are common.

/j/ is not spelled *j* at the end of words, except borrowed words such as *raj*. The sound /j/ is usually spelled *ge* as in *age*, or *dge* as in *edge*.

/n/ is usually spelled with one *n* at the end of words, except for *inn* (Payne, 1995).

ORTHOGRAPHIC PATTERNS

English also has orthographic or writing patterns. These patterns complement the alphabetic sound–symbol connections to give students another level of information about how sounds are spelled. Some of these patterns are old habits that die hard. For example, the *-ight* pattern for long *i* plus *t* comes from Old English when the *gh* was pronounced (Johnston, 2001).

Students can learn the large family of *-ight* words as a group, expand them, and then look for words such as *bite* and *white* that don't fit the pattern (see Figure 4.6 on page 57).

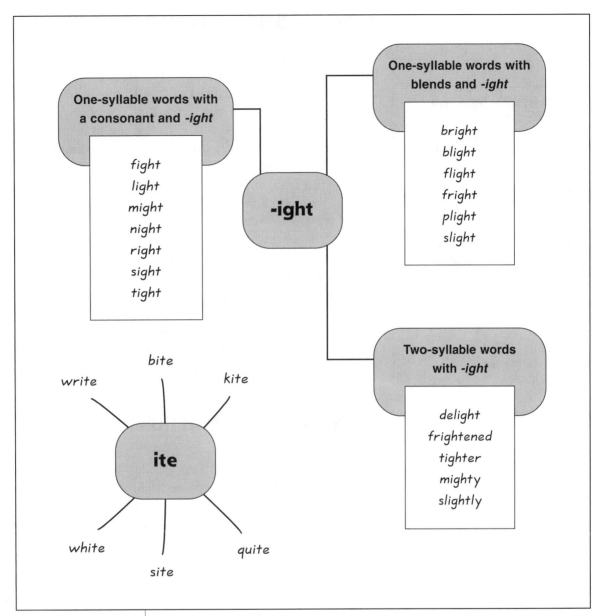

Figure 4.6 Word webs based on *-ight* and *-ite* patterns

There are many other examples of orthographic patterns in English spelling. Some operate within syllables, as in *hope,* where the final *e* signals a long *o.* There are hundreds of words in English with this long vowel-consonant-*e* pattern. Other patterns operate between syllables, such as the doubling of letters to indicate that the preceding vowel is short, as in *hopping* or *zapped.* Once students grasp these patterns, they can begin to spell words they don't necessarily know by sight (Templeton, 1999).

3. THE HISTORICAL CONNECTION

Since the 18th century, when spelling was more or less codified, there have been few changes in the spelling of existing words. Despite calls for spelling reform, the peculiarities of English spelling have remained.

This conservative approach to spelling is probably a good thing. The history of a word contains clues to its spelling, as many words follow spelling rules from their original languages. For example, *s* is always spelled *s* in old English words, such as *sent*, but it is spelled with a *c* in words with a Latin origin, such as *cent* (Payne, 1995).

One result of all the changes in English before it was codified is that we still spell many words the way they used to be pronounced; for example, there is still a *k* in *knight* (which was pronounced /k/*night*) and a *t* in *castle* (which was pronounced *cas*/*t*/*le*).

Students might ask why we don't change the spelling to fit the sound. One answer is that in a language spoken and written by over 400 million people worldwide (and by roughly the same number as a second language), consistency in spelling is probably wise. Although we speak in different accents, we all spell the same way. Also, spelling is important for establishing meaning in English.

Alternate Spelling	
American	**British/ Canadian**
▶ omelet	omelette
▶ check	cheque
▶ center	centre
▶ color	colour
▶ theater	theatre
▶ traveled	travelled

4. THE MEANING CONNECTION

ROOT AND BASE WORDS

Say the words *photograph* and *photography* in a natural cadence and note how the second *o* in *photography* is stressed, while in *photograph* the stress is on the first *o*. It is hard to hear whether that second vowel in *photograph* is an *o*, *i*, or *u*. But if you're used to spelling *photo*, it is clear that *o* is the correct letter in both words. Similarly, the *ph* spelling of the *f* sound is repeated in all the words having to do with *photos* (which comes from the Greek root *photos*, meaning "light"). In English, meaning and spelling are often connected. Therefore, errors such as *oppisition* and *compisition* can be corrected if the student relates them to their base words *oppose* and *compose* (Templeton and Morris, 1999). In the same way, *sign*, *signal*, and *signature* are all spelled with *g*, even though the *g* is silent in the word *sign*.

GRAMMAR: WORD ENDINGS

Whether a verb means the action is happening right now (*raining*) or yesterday (*rained*) influences its spelling. When students develop a morphosyntactic awareness—that is, an awareness of how words fit into grammatical patterns—their spelling takes a great leap. It is one of the major steps in the transitional stage between sound-based spelling and mature spelling. Current research by Nunes, Bryant, and Bindman (1997), suggests that between six and eight years of age, children take five steps towards the awareness that past-tense verbs end in -*ed*:

Step 1: They spell word endings unsystematically.

Step 2: They phonetically transcribe the -*ed* ending (e.g., *kist, slipt*).

Step 3: They spell some -*ed* endings, but overgeneralize to irregular verbs and other words (*kised, sleped,* and *sofed* for *soft*).

Step 4: They use -*ed* spellings on past-tense verbs, but not on other words (e.g., *kissed, sleped, soft*).

Step 5: Their -*ed* spellings are confined to regular past-tense verbs (*kissed, slept, soft*).

Nunes, Bryant, and Bindman say that as children develop, grammar helps them spell words such as *kissed* and *tricked*, which end in a *t* sound instead of *ed*, as well as *poured*, which sounds as though it ends in *d*. They are paying attention to meaning as well as sound.

This research supports the idea that developmental sequence is very important in teaching spelling patterns. (See Chapter 2, "What Does the Research Mean for the Classroom?") There is not much point in teaching the doubling of final letters to make words such as *getting* and *hopped* until students have grasped the reasons for adding -*ed* and -*ing*, about two years after they first begin to write.

Their study also found that 12-year-olds were often completely "at sea" when it came to the use of the apostrophe to indicate possession, as in *kids'* and *John's*. "This supports our claim that learning about the grammatical basis for spelling continues for most of the school years" (Nunes et al., 1997, p. 168).

HOMOPHONES

Words that sound alike but mean something different are the basis of puns, jokes, riddles, and all kinds of wordplay: "What do you call a naked grizzly? A *bare bear*!" Visual strategies, as in the box below, can help students remember the differences in meaning:

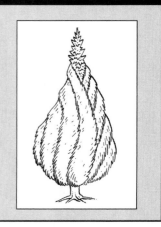

> **apostrophe**
>
> Errors abound in the use of the apostrophe. On a recent trip we saw "Fresh Blueberry's" on several roadside signs. The words *its* and *it's* are so often confused that some people believe the *it's* form will eventually be dropped.

Homophone Pairs

You can display the cartoons and ask students to discover the homophone pairs.

    a fur fir

    a hoarse horse

    a bored board

    a bare bear

Homophones such as *rode/road* and *know/no* can be a challenge for students learning to spell, but our written language would be difficult to read without them. Imagine signs such as the ones in the margin.

You can help students explore homophones using jokes, riddles, and word games. Point out homophones in literature, media headlines, and advertisements, as well as in the students' own writing. It may be useful to post homophone lists in the classroom for students to refer to when writing. (See Appendix C.)

5. NEW WORDS

As teachers of English, we continually face the challenge of spelling new words that come into the language. For example, how do we spell *e-mail*, when it appears as *E-mail*, *e-mail*, and *email*? A few years ago, we received a letter from an irate teacher. She complained that we used the spelling *looney* for a one-dollar Canadian coin in a book published in the 1980s. By this time, the spelling *loonie* was well established and our spelling was in error.

We responded that when the text was written, loonies were new. No definitive spelling of the word had been established. Both the *ie* and the *ey* endings could be found in newspapers, magazines, and other print sources. At that time, *looney* seemed the most favoured. Now, of course, the loonies in our pockets are well worn, and the spelling, *loonie*, has become established.

The spelling of *loonie* illustrates three important principles of English spelling:

1. The meaning principle is important (**loon—loon**ie).

2. There are many ways to spell the same sound (e.g., *ie*, *ey*, *y*, and *ee* all spell long *e* at the end of a two-syllable word).

   cook**ie**

   monk**ey**

   pon**y**

   coff**ee**

3. Spelling is often based on usage and may evolve over time.

When the two-dollar coin was introduced, there was no such confusion about the spelling. People automatically labelled it the "toonie" and spelled the word to match *loonie*. This illustrates the principle in English spelling of *spelling by analogy*.

Loonie and *toonie* are only two examples of the new words that continually flood into English. They illustrate one of the reasons English is so difficult to spell—it has a huge vocabulary. The *Oxford English Dictionary* lists 615 000 words.

Some experts estimate that with scientific and technical words, the total is over two million. Even the ordinary, everyday English vocabulary is larger than other commonly spoken and written languages, and offers more flexibility and versatility to its speakers (Lederer, 1991).

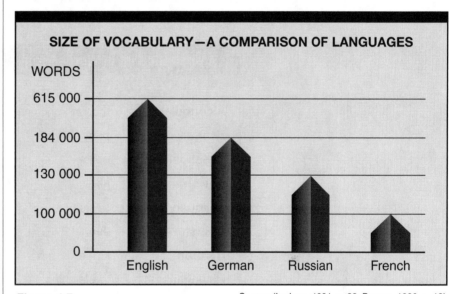

Figure 4.7

Source: (Lederer, 1991, p. 22; Bryson, 1990, p. 13)

6. BORROWED WORDS

Borrowing words is an old habit of the English language. By the 16th century, English had already borrowed words from over 50 other languages (Bryson, 1990). English is a "magnet" language—it welcomes words from every corner of the globe, and with them their spellings; for example, *café* and *fete*. A large number of these borrowed words come from three languages: Greek, Latin, and French (approximately 20 percent come from French alone).

Although most students will not study Greek or Latin, drawing their attention to Greek and Latin roots can help them remember some of the anomalies in English spelling. To illustrate this, you can have them highlight the *ph* in words of Greek origin. Older students can spin word wheels, adding more words containing the Greek roots *graph* and *photo*.

More recently borrowed words, from *gyro* to *calzone*, continue to flavour English with vocabulary from other languages. It is a feature of the English language that the original spelling changes as little as possible, even when it causes confusion. Bryson gives as an example the French word *buffet*, meaning "a meal spread out on a long table," or "a piece of dining-room furniture." It comes from French and is pronounced in the French way, with a silent *t* and the stress on the final syllable. However, we already have a word with exactly the same spelling—*buffet*, pronounced *buffit* and meaning "to hit" (Bryson, 1990).

Students may enjoy putting together an alphabetical list of borrowed words. If students speak Urdu, Vietnamese, or Kurdish, they could be asked to suggest words from these languages to complete the list below.

Alphabetic List of Words From Other Languages

Algonquian	moose	**Maori**	kiwi
Bengali	bungalow	**Norwegian**	shingle
Czechoslovakian	polka	**Ojibwa**	wigwam
Danish	skill	**Portuguese**	molasses
Egyptian	oasis	**Russian**	vodka
Finnish	sauna	**Spanish**	rodeo
German	kindergarten	**Tagalog**	boondocks
Hawaiian	ukulele	**Urdu**	?
Icelandic	whisk	**Vietnamese**	?
Japanese	tycoon	**Welsh**	flannel
Kurdish	?	**Yiddish**	kibitzer
Lapp	tundra		

Figure 4.8   Source: (Lederer, 1991, p. 23)

Teachers do not need to be language experts, or know all the intricacies of English spelling. It is more important that we model for the students the belief that order can be found. You can start with the easiest and most common words and patterns, and broaden the field of exploration to words whose spellings are unusual, intriguing, or downright diabolical.

As well, it is important that the sequence of discovery mirrors the developmental readiness of the students. Grade 2 students will probably not benefit from examining longer words with prefixes and suffixes, but they will be happy exploring longer compound words made up of two familiar shorter words, such as *sunshine*.

SUMMARY

This chapter has presented the following main ideas:

1. **English has a spelling system, although it is complex and challenging to learn.**

2. **Students need to perceive that there is order to English spelling, even though many of the high-utility words they learn first (*love, you*) do not follow patterns.**

3. **Sorting words by patterns, large and small, is an important spelling strategy.**

4. **There are six important keys to unlocking the spelling system of English:**
    *   Although there is not a one-to-one match between letters and sounds, English spelling has many patterns based on sounds.
    *   Letter combinations are often restricted to certain positions in words (e.g., no words in English begin with *ff* or *bs*). Positional constraints and orthographic patterns determine the spelling of many high-frequency words (e.g., *back*, *right*).
    *   English spelling is conservative. Old pronunciations of words are preserved in their spellings. Words of classical origin are spelled to match their Greek and Latin roots (e.g., *phone*, *science*).
    *   English spellings are often related by meaning (e.g., *resign*, *resignation*).
    *   New words are continually being added to the language.
    *   Words borrowed from other languages are common in English and usually retain their original spelling.

5. **Teachers don't need to be spelling experts.** They do need to believe there is a system to spelling and to help students to explore it.

REFLECTIVE THINKING

1. How many new words can you think of that have entered the language in the past 20 years? It may help to think of categories, such as media, technology, food, politics, and entertainment.

2. In reference to the English language, Richard Lederer says, "Sometimes you have to believe that all English speakers should be commited to an asylum for the verbally insane" (1990, p. 15). Do you think the authors agree with his opinion? Do you? Explain.

3. How can you help your students to make sense of the English spelling system? Make a list of ideas from this chapter that you would like to try in your classroom.

4. The "Simplified Spelling Society" advocates reforming the English spelling system so that words are spelled exactly as they are pronounced. What are some drawbacks to this idea? (Hint: Consider how Newfoundlanders and Labradorians, Ontarians, and Albertans would spell the word *Toronto* in this phonetic system.)

5. Make a list of interesting facts about the English language that you would like to share with your students.

The following chart provides links with other chapters in the book:

To learn more about...	see these chapters
The developmental sequence for spelling	Chapter 2, page 15
Listening and speaking	Chapter 5, page 66

PART

2

Spelling In Your Literacy Program

Listening and Speaking: Oral Language and Spelling

• •

Oral language is spoken language: the conversations children have, the stories they listen to and tell, the songs they sing. Current research shows strong links between oral language, reading, and spelling. Good teachers have always known that this linkage exists. Immersing children in a rich oral-language environment is the foundation for language growth in all areas: listening, speaking, reading, and writing. In this chapter, we provide suggestions for making your classroom a place where students can explore and discover the sounds, patterns, rhythms, and rhymes of words. Getting children "hooked on words" is the foundation for successful spelling instruction.

ORAL LANGUAGE IN THE EARLY YEARS

THE ASSOCIATION BETWEEN SOUNDS AND LETTERS

While children learn to speak at home in a family setting, their written language develops primarily at school (Ehri, 1997). Researchers agree that the connection between spoken and written language must be taught: it can't be learned "by osmosis." Making the connection begins with what curriculum documents call "phonological awareness," which begins with phonemic awareness.

A *phoneme* is a speech sound, such as the *m* in mother. When children begin to distinguish one speech sound from another and hear the different sounds within words, they are developing phonemic awareness. Once they are able to isolate speech sounds, children can begin to learn the connection between these sounds and the letters of the alphabet.

> **phoneme**
>
> A *phoneme* is the smallest unit of speech that distinguishes one word from another. For example, the *t* of *tug* and the *r* of *rug* are two English phonemes.

We know that knowledge of the letter–sound connection is a good predictor for how well children will read and write (Adams, 1990; Nunes, Bryant, and Bindman, 1997). When children make the link between the *m* sound that they hear at the beginning of *mom* and the letter *m*, they are on their way to becoming readers and writers.

Children need a great deal of experience with oral language to make this association between sounds and letters. They also require interaction with parents and teachers that reinforces the connection. Fortunately, young children have an appetite for repetition. They like to sing, chant, or say the same phrases over and over. They love oral-language games with repeated sounds. Listen to the lively *m* sounds in the following chant:

> Five little ⓜonkeys juⓜping on the bed.
> One fell off and buⓜped his head.
> Ⓜaⓜa called the doctor, the doctor said…
> "No ⓜore ⓜonkeys juⓜping on the bed!"

Children enjoy chanting this rhyme over and over, working their way from five little monkeys down to one little monkey. The chant can be repeated slowly or quickly, softly or loudly. It can be accompanied by movement or clapping to emphasize the rhythm of the language. Chanting the rhyme clearly and forcefully also helps children hear the two syllables in *monkeys*.

Once children know and delight in a rhyme or chant, it's a natural next step to print it on chart paper and highlight *m* or print it in a second colour. Children can talk about how the *m* sound feels in their mouths, how they hold their lips together when they make the *m* sound, and how they say *mmmm* when something looks, smells, sounds, or feels very good. In all these ways, they are reinforcing their awareness of the letter–sound connection.

Teaching TIP

Children may not hear the *m* when it is followed by *p*, as in *jumping* and *bumped*. You can help them hear it by chanting aloud with emphasis on the *m,* or pointing to the letter as you are saying it aloud.

IMMERSING CHILDREN IN THE SOUNDS OF ENGLISH

The more children are sung to, read to, and told stories, the more readily they make the transition from listening and speaking to written language. Some children come to school with a rich oral-language background; others need enrichment in this area. One primary teacher, who has many second-language learners in her Grade 2 class, takes every opportunity to have her students sing or chant their favourite poems, songs, and skipping rhymes. They sing or chant aloud when they

- come together in a circle
- are cleaning up after activities
- are lining up to leave the classroom
- have any transition time to fill.

They are having fun, their attention is engaged, and they are reinforcing oral-language skills. The group chant or song gives the second-language learners an opportunity to join in and practise without embarrassment. For them, it provides both a language model and group support.

When the children are learning to make the all-important association between letters and the beginning sounds in words, the teacher focuses on one particular sound. For example, she might emphasize the *p* sound by selecting children in the class whose names begin with *P*, reading aloud a picture book such as *Pig in the Pond*, or having the class make a poem about some of their favourite things that begin with *p*.

P
P is for ponies,
P is for pop,
P is for popcorn,
Pop. Pop. Pop.

Use chants and rhymes that have lilting rhythms and predictable rhymes. Skipping rhymes such as "Teddy Bear, Teddy Bear" are excellent, and children will have heard them on the playground.

A classroom rich in oral language should have many resources. For an extended list of poems, picture books, chants, and rhymes to support making the connection between oral language and print, see Appendix B, page 205.

Teaching TIP

A supportive oral-language environment where children chant or sing together can help ESL students learn the rhythms of English.

USING CHILDREN'S LOVE OF ALLITERATION TO TEACH BEGINNING SOUNDS

Young children are particularly sensitive to alliteration—words beginning with the same consonant sounds—as in *many monkeys*. You may wish to develop a rhyme or chant to associate beginning sounds with letters; for example, "Silver slipper starts with S" or "Bouncing ball starts with B." Children can often see and hear this connection in their own names: "My name is Tyler and it starts with T." Although there is not a one-to-one match, many English phonemes are related to the names of letters of the alphabet. For instance, the sound *t* is heard when we say the word for the letter *t*. It makes sense to teach these letter–sound connections first, and leave the more difficult ones, such as *y* and *q*, until later.

Letter–Sound Connections: Teaching Sequence

Sequence	Consonants	Vowels
1st Group	m s b t	a
2nd Group	c r l p	o
3rd Group	d n f j	i
4th Group	k g w h	e
5th Group	q v z x y	u

Figure 5.1 Letter–sound connections

USING CHILDREN'S LOVE OF RHYME TO TEACH SPELLING PATTERNS

As well as a love of alliteration, young children also have a natural appreciation of rhyme. A humorous TV commercial shows a woman who rhymes everything for her baby: *cutsey-wutsey, sleepy-weepy, dressy-wessy*. She can't break the habit even in her adult conversation, thus demonstrating what every parent and every teacher of young children knows: rhyme is addictive and contagious.

You can make good use of this addiction to rhyme to teach spelling patterns. *Cat* and *hat* not only sound the same, they both end in *at*. As Cunningham says, "Finding out that rhyme, words that begin alike, words that can all be changed into other words just by moving around the letters, and other patterns, is like solving a riddle or a puzzle" (Cunningham, 1992, p. 112–113).

Chapter 10, "Spelling Strategies and Word Study" discusses strategies for exploring rhyming patterns in detail; here the emphasis is on developing a sense of rhyme through oral language. Research has shown that children who cannot hear or write rhyming words are often poor spellers (Scott, 1991). They have missed the vital connection that *splat* rhymes with *hat*, and will also be spelled with an *at*.

Poems with rhyming words that have the same spelling pattern can be written on chart paper to help children understand that they can use rhyme to predict how words are spelled. For example, in the following poem, rhymes with -*atter*, -*at*, and -*ad* can be highlighted:

Billy Batter

Billy <u>Batter</u>,
What's the <u>matter</u>?
How come you're so **sad**?
I lost my <u>cat</u>
In the laundro<u>mat</u>,
And a dragon ran off with my **dad**,
My **dad**—
A dragon ran off with my **dad**!

By Dennis Lee

Supplying rhyming words at the ends of lines can be a shared activity that even very young children enjoy, and once a sense of rhyme is developed, children can make the connection between the letter combinations they see and the rhyming sounds they hear. These can be highlighted, sorted, and used for word-building activities.

My cat can <u>stalk</u>
My cat can <u>walk</u>
Oh how I wish
My cat could
<u>TALK!</u>

By Sonja Dunn

ORAL LANGUAGE IN THE LATER GRADES

Listening will continue to be important as children's oral vocabulary expands. With longer words, it is necessary to hear each syllable clearly, even though it may be glossed over in speech. Often, the words we misspell as adults are those we don't hear correctly. For example, for many years one person spelled *asphalt* as *ashphalt*, and *dilapidated* as *dilapitated* because she heard the words that way. Many students have similar problems with other multisyllabic words. A good strategy for learning the spelling of longer words is to overstress or say aloud the unstressed syllables or silent letters; for example, *parallel* or *Wednesday*. (See Chapter 10, "Spelling Strategies and Word Study," for a longer discussion of this strategy.)

Talking about the history of commonly misspelled words (*rough* was pronounced with a throaty *gh* at the end, *said* rhymed with *braid*) can help children remember the unusual spellings. Cheryl Mahaffey Sigmon (2001) recommends having students snap, clap, stomp, or tap each letter of a commonly misspelled word as it is spelled aloud by the whole class.

RHYME AND RHYTHM

Although other strategies will replace the early emphasis on rhyming word patterns, rhyme, alliteration, and rhythm continue to be an important part of word study in the junior and intermediate years. Many rhyming words (but not all) follow a similar spelling pattern. Students can work in groups to expand lists of rhyming words with similar patterns.

ORAL POETRY

Read aloud, or shared as a group, poetry can reinforce the exploration of word patterns at a more advanced level. Students can take turns reading lines or stanzas and then join in the chorus. They can create their own rap poetry or song lyrics with internal rhymes. This poem by Arnold Sundgaard explores four different patterns:

"A language-rich classroom enables children to hear and say many varieties of language, experiencing word play, rhyme and repetition for themselves" (Booth, 1998, p. 91).

The Elephant

The elephant is quite a **beast**.
He's rather large to say the **least**.
And though his size is most **impressive**
The elephant is not **aggressive**.
He never throws his weight **around**,
Still he always holds his **ground**.
He only wants to feel **secure**.
Long may the elephant **endure**!

By Arnold Sundgaard

More complex vowel patterns such as *beast/least* and *around/ground* can be compared, as well as the *-essive* ending in *aggressive* and *impressive*. Students can brainstorm orally and then spell other words, using each pattern.

-east	-ound	-essive
feast	sound	excessive
yeast	bound	possessive
	pound	expressive
	mound	successive
	found	
	hound	
	round	
	astound	
	profound	

Figure 5.2 An example of rhyming words with vowel patterns from "The Elephant"

WORD STORMING

Expanding students' vocabulary can be an ongoing group activity as part of Shared Reading, read aloud, and writing activities. You can challenge students to create lists of synonyms in their writing for overused words such as *said, ran,* or *happy*. A teacher in Regina has a "banned word of the week," for words such as *nice* that students tend to use too frequently. She challenges her students to find interesting alternatives in literature or the thesaurus to use in their speech and writing.

Lists of synonyms can be displayed in the classroom for quick reference or written in a personal thesaurus. At the same time as they are expanding their vocabulary, students can reflect on the spelling patterns they observe; for example, the *-ful* and *-y* endings of adjectives such as *joyful* and *gloomy*. For more about vocabulary-building and thesaurus activities, see Chapter 8, "Writing and Presenting."

TALKING ABOUT WORDS

Students can develop their capacities as word explorers by discussing the shades of meaning of synonyms and using them orally in context. An effective activity for stimulating such discussion is to use a photo from a newspaper or magazine, and have students search for a word that exactly describes the expression on someone's face.

WORD OF THE DAY

A "word of the day" or "word of the week" list is another strategy to expand oral and written vocabulary. Students can bring in favourite or unusual words. Or they can brainstorm words to match particular criteria; for example, words with sounds that match the meaning.

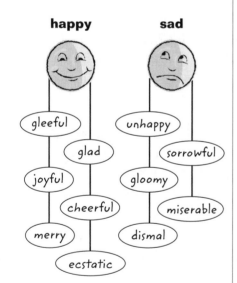

happy   **sad**

gleeful   unhappy
glad   sorrowful
joyful   gloomy
cheerful   miserable
merry   dismal
ecstatic

TALKING ABOUT SPELLING PATTERNS

Students can work with a partner or in a small group to sort word patterns from the written versions of poems. For example, by reading aloud and discussing the word patterns in the following poem, students will begin to develop a sense of when to double a final consonant, or drop a final *e*:

Monday Morning

Moaning, groaning,
mumbling, grumbling,
glowering, showering,
rubbing, scrubbing,
washing, sploshing,
groping, soaping,
howling, towelling,
splashing, dashing,
muttering, buttering,
crunching, munching,
sighing, tying,
brushing, rushing,
cramming, slamming
and off to
school.

By John C. Head

After enjoying the sound of the poem orally, and talking about onomatopoeic words such as *sploshing* and *crunching*, students can sort the words into categories based on how different words add endings.

No change	Drop *e* before adding *-ing*	Double last consonant before adding *-ing*	Change *ie* to *y* before adding *-ing*
moan—moaning	mumble—mumbling	rub—rubbing	tie—tying
groan—groaning	grumble—grumbling	scrub—scrubbing	
glower—glowering	grope—groping	cram—cramming	

Figure 5.3 Word sort from "Monday Morning"

Each category of words can be expanded, and students can discuss which categories are most common. You can challenge them to develop generalizations for the spelling patterns; for example, *"A word with a short vowel followed by one consonant usually doubles the consonant before adding -ing."* A search for exceptions to the generalizations (such as *towelling*) then becomes meaningful, and it will be easier for students to remember words that "don't fit the rules."

WORDPLAY

Students of all ages enjoy wordplay, such as jokes based on multiple meanings and homographs:
- "Why can't an elephant go around the world? It only has one trunk."
- "What has four wheels and flies? A garbage truck."

You can challenge students to invent their own wordplay jokes, perhaps by having a class contest.

Wordplay can also help students explore words that have slightly different meanings in different contexts. Remember the old joke, "Have you ever seen a horse fly?" Here is an entire poem based on that idea. *Plot* and *bark* are actually homographs, but that doesn't spoil the fun.

> **homographs**
>
> *Homographs* sound and look alike, but have different meanings, and often different origins (e.g., *dove, dove*).

Have you ever seen a sheet on a river bed?
Or a single hair from a hammer's head?
Has the foot of a mountain any toes?
And is there a pair of garden hose?

Does the needle ever wink its eye?
Why doesn't the wing of a building fly?
Can you tickle the ribs of a parasol?
Or open the trunk of a tree at all?

Are the teeth of a rake ever going to bite?
Have the hands of a clock any left or right?
Can the garden plot be deep and dark?
And what is the sound of the birch's bark?

Anonymous

In the preceding activities, the focus has been on the sound–spelling connection. Learning to spell in English is a life-long process. An important and necessary part of the process is learning to listen to the sounds of words, comparing them to other words, playing with words, and sorting them into patterns.

SUMMARY

This chapter has presented the following main ideas:

1. **Listening and speaking are the foundation of students' language.** Effective teachers immerse children in a rich oral-language environment.

2. **English is an alphabetic language.** The association between speech sounds and letters must be taught, and this requires focused talk and listening.

3. **Chanting, rhyming, and singing are all activities that reinforce a first-language speaker's sense of rhyme and rhythm,** and support students who are learning English as a second language.

4. **Beginning sounds can be linked to the letters that spell them in words children hear and speak,** such as their names, favourite toys, or words in a familiar song or chant.

5. **Students familiar with rhyme will make the transition from listening and speaking to spelling word parts with similar letters, such as *splash*, *dash*, and *crash*.**

6. **Listening and speaking in the junior and intermediate years can help reinforce spelling skills by**
    - continuing to emphasize the rhythm and rhyme of longer words
    - expanding students' oral vocabulary through brainstorming words with similar meanings and discussing their differences
    - talking about spelling patterns and sharing discoveries about spelling

7. **Wordplay—enjoying puns, plays on words, and multiple meanings—is an important part of exploring language through listening and speaking.**

REFLECTIVE THINKING

1. The authors state, "The more children are sung to, read to, and told stories, the more readily they make the transitions from listening and speaking to written language." What features of your classroom program highlight oral language?

2. Make a list of your students' favourite poems or chants. What spelling patterns can be explored through one or two of these poems?

3. If you had a list of "banned words," or words used too frequently by your students in their oral and written vocabulary, what words would be on the list?

4. How can wordplay activities facilitate spelling growth? Give specific examples.

5. What would you do to help a student who has a limited background in oral language?

The following chart provides links with other chapters in the book:

To learn more about...	see these chapters
Writing and Presenting	Chapter 8, page 99
Spelling Strategies	Chapter 10, page 129

6

Viewing and Representing: The Media and Spelling

••

WORDS IN THE ENVIRONMENT

A three-year-old spells out the letters on a sign: S-T-O-P. "Daddy," she shouts, "I know what that means—stop!" Signs on stores or print on a cereal box attract children's attention. These big, bright letters in a child's environment are often a first link to written language. Words in the mass media and in the world around them can help children see the connection between sound and symbol. This chapter will explore the connection between media and word study and suggest ways to engage children in the exploration of words through viewing and representing.

NEW WORDS—NEW SPELLINGS

Commercial interests often invent words for brand names. Many of these, such as nylon, rayon, laundromat, and escalator, eventually become part of the language. Others, like Kleenex and Rollerblade, are still written as proper nouns to recognize their brand status (*The Globe and Mail Style Book*, 1996). In activities on page 78, students can explore the associations evoked by a brand name.

What's in a Name?

1. Have students investigate the pronunciation of NIKE (nīkē). Ask them to think about why Nike doesn't rhyme with *bike* and *hike*. (It is the name of the Greek goddess Nike, who was the goddess of victory, usually portrayed with wings.) Discuss why the manufacturers chose this word for athletic shoes.

2. Invite students to explore how the printing of the word *NIKE*, the shape, and the swipe underneath convey an emotion or idea.

3. Challenge students to invent a new brand name for sports equipment and to design a matching logo. Encourage them to use a common word with a different spelling or pronunciation as their brand name.

Using Brand Names

The Globe and Mail Style Book suggests that you should always use a capital to recognize that a brand name has commercial value and not reduce it to the status of an ordinary word (e.g., *Coke*, *Kleenex*, *Jell-O*).

By investigating these brand names, students can explore the conventions and rules that guide the spelling of English words. For example, syllable juncture—the ways words break into smaller units—can be examined by looking at longer brand names. Patricia Cunningham and Barbara Hall (1998) use an activity they call "Brand Name Phonics" with older students. Using a brand name like Sprite, students spell words such as *quite*, *spite*, *ignite*, *polite*, and *campsite*.

Students can also invent brand names that match the spelling patterns of longer words, as in the following activity:

What's Your Brand?

Encourage students to design a product name that matches a multisyllabic word in English. Provide examples like the following:

lem on ade—Gat or ade
tom a to juice—Clam a to juice
cran ber ry—Cran tas tic

OLDE WORDS SPELLED IN NEW WAYS

Engage students in looking at ways marketers adapt English spelling to create a new message. For example, high-risk activities, such as rock-climbing or skydiving, are sometimes called extreme sports. The spelling is routinely changed to *X-treme* to "punch up" the idea that a sport is so dangerous it should be prohibited.

In the same way, *light* spelled *lite* has become almost synonymous with low-calorie or low-alcohol content. In time, this spelling may be accepted as a new word that means "low, in the positive sense" to differentiate it from the other meanings of *light*.

Media Watch—New Spellings for New Meanings

Have students conduct a media watch to look for print, TV, and movie ads containing words with altered spellings that create new meanings. Invite them to create a group collage of their findings. Discuss how changes in spelling can change meanings.

lite   *brite*

x-treme

Advertisers often use unconventional spellings to convey something

- old-fashioned

- expensive

- casual or fun

Have students go on a media hunt for signs and ads, such as "Ye Olde Hyde House," "Olde-Thyme Fiddler's Contest," "The Art Shoppe," "Restaurante," and "The Hitchin' Post." Adding an *e*, subtracting a *g*, or using the archaic word *ye* conveys age and/or wealth, and may hark back to an older form of English where many common words were spelled with a final *e*, or a long *i* was spelled with *y*. Students can represent their findings in a collage, an ad for an upscale restaurant, or a poster for an old-fashioned event.

SPELLING ERRORS IN THE ENVIRONMENT

In Beverly Cleary's novel, *Ramona's World*, Ramona Quimby, age nine, has been made very much aware of spelling by a zealous teacher. Poor Ramona grumbles about learning to spell, but when she and her friend Daisy spot a bogus letter in a newspaper ad, they are moved to write to the company. Ramona is surprised when she recieves a reply praising her for her attention to spelling.

Receiving this letter is a turning point for Ramona. Her spelling self-esteem has been resurrected. After she takes the letter to school and the teacher reads it to the whole class: "Ramona felt good, better than she had felt since the first day of fourth grade" (Cleary, 1999, p. 121).

Spelling errors are also part of a student's wider world. The ability to spot them can help students understand the importance of correct spelling to get a point across. It is one thing to change the spelling of a word for a purpose and another to make an obvious mistake. Challenge students to become "sign detectives," watching for misspelled words on signs and deciding which are intentional and which are real mistakes.

Such investigations are fun and interactive. More importantly, the discussion around errors in the environment can reinforce the idea that spelling matters, and that mistakes may send a message that was not intended, as in the following example:

MEDIA AND WORDPLAY

A love of wordplay—puns, double meanings, homophones, alliteration, and catchy references to past language—typifies media headlines, ads, and brand names. Fun with words is everywhere in media land, and students can learn much about spelling from looking at how society plays with words in their environment. For example, have students watch for and collect store-front signs.

The owners of these businesses clearly have a way with wordplay.

Puns and plays on words are beloved by marketers in every medium. Ocean Spray Cranberries, for example, has developed a product name that plays on the words *cranberry* and *fantastic*. *Crantastic* manages to combine the idea of cranberry, plus fantastic, with the shape of the package. The drink box is tall and thin, a convenient shape for children's lunches. The sound of the word *crantastic* makes the consumer think "fantastic cranberry sticks."

WORDPLAY IN THE NEWS

Newspaper headlines make use of wordplay, puns, homophones, alliteration, and media references to develop catchy headlines that will attract the reader's eye. On any given day, students using two or three daily newspapers will be able to find examples of wordplay in headlines and create a "catchy-headline" collage.

Wordplay Headlines

Dark days descend on Daisy the diabetic dog

Lotta hoopla in Beijing

The first headline uses alliteration of the letter *d*. The second headline, a report on a women's basketball team's victory, plays on the words *hoop* and *hoopla* and takes advantage of rhyme.

Watching for words in the environment is part of drawing students' attention to the way words work. Students should be encouraged to make a link with the patterns they are examining in their spelling program. Being aware of the words around them can also illuminate how the media use words to attract our attention. Viewing and representing words is an important component of becoming a wise consumer of the media. It can also help make the connection between the outside world and the classroom. In addition, it benefits those learners in the class who learn best visually. For more on visual learners, see Chapter 10, "Spelling Strategies and Word Study" and Chapter 12, "Supporting Struggling Spellers."

SUMMARY

This chapter has presented the following main ideas:

1. **Many students first spell words they see on signs, such as EXIT, STOP, and Tim Hortons.** Words in the world around them help children become conscious spellers and, for some children, make the first link between letters and sounds.

2. **Media, particularly advertising, use visual style to emphasize word meanings and convey messages.** Students can learn to be alert to these messages and create their own.

3. **Media invent new words, (e.g., *slurpee*, *bungee*) and new spellings for old words to express new meanings:** lite foods (low calorie), x-treme sports (high risk). Spelling variations can provide messages such as "old-fashioned" or "expensive."

4. **Spelling errors affect a media message.** Students can write down misspelled words viewed in store windows, billboards, and ads, and discuss what effect poor spelling has on the intended message.

5. **Media makes much use of wordplay.** Students can collect puns and double meanings in headlines, slogans, and ads, and create their own.

6. **Viewing the media for messages conveyed in the spelling, visual style, and wordplay can prepare students for their role as wise consumers.**

REFLECTIVE THINKING

1. Conduct a media hunt through magazines or newspapers to find a variety of brand names. Consider where these words came from (e.g., Greek gods), the spelling patterns they represent, and the message conveyed by each name.

2. Words are often misspelled by advertisers as a way of making a product's name "catchy" (e.g., *Foto*, *Lite*). Do you believe this form of wordplay influences the spelling development of children? Should it be allowed?

3. Apart from gathering examples of misspelled signs in the community, what can you and your students do to let businesses know that careless spelling matters to consumers?

4. Choose one of the wordplay strategies in this chapter and discuss how you might use it in your writing program.

5. Why is it crucial to teach children to carefully watch words in the media? For example, why is *large* often the smallest size drink?

The following chart provides links with other chapters in the book:

To learn more about...	see these chapters
Writing and Presenting	Chapter 8, page 99
Supporting Struggling Spellers	Chapter 12, page 170

CHAPTER

7

Reading and Spelling

••

HOW ARE READING AND SPELLING CONNECTED?

The connection between reading and spelling at first seems obvious; they appear to be two sides of a coin. Spelling converts speech to print and reading converts print to speech. Spelling conveys meaning through the use of letters and reading is a process of making meaning through print.

Perfetti (1997) argues that spelling and reading are always intertwined. When children spell a word, they usually check it to "see if it looks right." This ongoing proofreading is a form of reading. Likewise, when children encounter a word in print, they check their spelling vocabulary (the store of words in the brain) to confirm that the word matches its spelling in that context. For example, students who understand the spelling of *their* and *there* will stop when they read, "The dogs lost there bones..." because they realize that this spelling does not fit this situation.

Considering the connections between reading and spelling, it is often surprising to encounter students who love to read, but who are poor spellers. Research shows that at least 10 to 15 percent of students show a marked discrepancy between their reading and spelling skills. So reading and spelling, though related, are not mirror images of each other. In this chapter, we explain the connections between spelling and reading and offer suggestions for helping students to improve their spelling through word-solving activities in reading.

SPELLING IS MORE DIFFICULT THAN READING

The fact that spelling a word is usually more difficult than either decoding or comprehending it in reading often comes as a surprise to teachers and parents. They are surprised because spelling has traditionally been viewed as a simple memorization task. While it is true that visual memory plays an important role in spelling, particularly for the irregular parts of words, the spelling process goes far beyond memorization and requires a sophisticated set of thinking skills. The following example may

help to explain why teachers often encounter students who are better readers than spellers, but rarely encounter those who are good spellers but poor readers (Scott, 1991).

If students see the word *boat* in a story, they may use one or a combination of strategies to read it. They may

- recognize the word as a sight word
- sound it out
- compare it with a word they know that looks similar (e.g., *coat*)
- guess its meaning from its use in the sentence (e.g., The *boat* sailed down the river). In doing so, they bring their knowledge of the world to the text.
- guess its meaning from picture clues

This constellation of reading clues does not only apply to simple reading tasks but to more complex words as well. Longer words often provide further meaning clues if the reader isolates the base or root words from prefixes and suffixes, as in *multi-nation-al.*

When we turn to *spelling* the word *boat*, however, the options decrease. Unless the word is in the students' spelling vocabulary, they can only sound it out or try linking it with a similar word they might know. If that word happens to be *coat*, their guesses will be accurate. But if they think of the rhyming word *vote*, they will spell it as *bote*, a response that is phonetically accurate but still misspelled. They will not have the advantage of context or picture clues that text often provides.

There Are Often Several Ways to Spell a Given Sound in English

The example of spelling and reading the word *boat* highlights another reason that spelling is usually more difficult than reading. When a student sees the letters *b-o-a-t* in print and tries to apply phoneme/grapheme rules to them, there is only one phonetically correct response /bōt/. On the other hand, when the student thinks of the concept *boat* and tries to spell it phonetically, a correct response could be *boat*, *bowt*, or *bote*. In the earlier stages of spelling development, another possibility arises when students try to link each sound with the letter of the alphabet whose name "says" the sound. This stage, the Phonetic Stage, results in *boat* being spelled *bot*, since the long *o* sound matches the name of the letter *o*.

These differences in spelling possibilities come about because written English does not have a one-to-one mapping of letters to sounds. There are often several ways to spell any given sound, and a good speller needs to know which way is correct for a specific word.

Figure 7.1, on pages 87–88, shows the possibilities for spelling English sounds. These choices differ depending on whether the sound is at the beginning, middle, or end of a word. For example, the sound /f/ can be spelled with *f* or *ph* at the beginning of a word, *f*, *ff*, *gh*, or *ph* in the middle, and *f*, *ff*, *gh*, or *ph* at the end.

Common Spellings of English Sounds

Sound	Beginnings of Words	Middles of Words	Ends of Words
a	and, aunt	hat, plaid, half, laugh	—
ā	age, aid, eight	face, fail, straight, payment, gauge, break, vein, neighbour	say, weigh, bouquet, they, café, matinée
a̍	art	barn, bazaar, heart	hurrah
b	bad	table, rabbit	rub, ebb
ch	child	cappuccino, richness, nature, watching, question	much, catch
d	do	lady, ladder	red, used
e	any, aerial, air, end	many, said, says, let, bread, leopard, friend, bury	—
ē	equal, eat, either	metre, team, need, receive, people, keyhole, machine, believe	algae, quay, acne, flea, bee, key, Métis, loonie, pity
f	fat, phone	after, coffee, often, laughter, gopher	roof, sniff, cough, half, epitaph
g	go, ghost, guess	ago, giggle, catalogues	bag, egg, rogue
h	help, who	ahead	—
i	enamel, in	message, been, pin, sieve, women, busy, build, hymn	—
ī	aisle, aye, either, eye, ice, island	height, line, align, might, buying, type	aye, eye, lie, high, buy, sky, dye
j	gem, jam	educate, badger, soldier, adjust, tragic, exaggerate, enjoy	bridge, rage, hajj
k	coat, chemistry, kind, quick, quay	record, account, echo, lucky, acquire, looking, liquor, extra	back, seek, walk, tuque
l	land, llama	only, follow	coal, fill
m	me	coming, climbing, summer	calm, hum, comb, solemn
n	gnaw, knife, nut	miner, manner	sign, man, inn
ng	—	ink, finger, singer	bang, tongue
o	all, almond, author, awful, encore, honest, odd, ought	watch, palm, taut, taught, sawed, hot, bought	Ottawa, paw

Figure 7.1 Common spellings of English sounds

Common Spellings of English Sounds

Sound	Beginnings of Words	Middles of Words	Ends of Words
ō	**o**pen, **oa**th, **ow**n	Ge**o**rge, s**ew**n, h**o**me, b**oa**t, f**o**lk, br**oo**ch, s**ou**l, fr**ow**n	chat**eau**, s**ew**, potat**o**, t**oe**, th**ough**, bl**ow**
ȯ	**o**rder, **oar**	b**o**rn, b**oar**d, fl**oor**, m**our**n	—
oi	**oi**l, **oy**ster	b**oi**l, b**oy**hood	b**oy**
ou	h**our**, **ou**t, **ow**l	b**ou**nd, dr**ough**t, h**ow**l	pl**ough**, n**ow**
p	**p**en	pa**p**er, su**pp**er	u**p**
r	**r**un, **rh**ythm	pa**r**ent, hu**rr**y	bea**r**, bu**rr**
s	**c**ent, **ps**ychology, **s**ay, **sc**ience, **sw**ord	de**c**ent, loo**s**en, mu**sc**le, ma**ss**ive, an**sw**er, e**x**tra	ni**ce**, marvellou**s**, mi**ss**, la**x**
sh	**ch**auffeur, **s**ure, **sh**irt	o**c**ean, ma**ch**ine, spe**c**ial, un**s**ure, con**sc**ience, nau**se**ous, ten**s**ion, i**ss**ue, mi**ss**ion, na**t**ion	ca**che**, wi**sh**
t	**pt**armigan, **t**ell, **Th**omas	dou**bt**ful, la**t**er, la**tt**er	dou**bt**, crash**ed**, bi**t**, mi**tt**
th	**th**in	too**th**ache	ba**th**
TH	**th**en	mo**th**er	smoo**th**, ba**the**
u	**o**ven, **u**p	c**o**me, d**oe**s, fl**oo**d, tr**ou**ble, c**u**p	—
ū	**oo**ze	n**eu**tral, m**o**ve, f**oo**d, gr**ou**p, r**u**le, fr**ui**t	thr**ew**, sh**oe**, carib**ou**, thr**ough**, bl**ue**
u̇	—	w**o**lf, g**oo**d, sh**ou**ld, f**u**ll	—
yū	**Eu**rope, **u**se, **you**, **Yu**kon	b**eau**ty, f**eu**d, d**u**ty	qu**eue**, f**ew**, c**ue**, **you**
v	**v**ery	o**v**er	o**f**, lo**ve**
w	**w**ill, **wh**eat, **o**ne	**ch**oir, q**u**ick, t**w**in	—
y	**y**oung	opin**i**on, can**y**on	—
z	**x**ylophone	rai**s**in, sci**ss**ors, e**x**act, la**z**y, da**zz**le	ha**s**, ma**ze**, bu**zz**
zh	—	mea**s**ure, divi**s**ion	mira**ge**
ə	**a**lone, **e**ssential, **o**blige, **u**pon	sp**a**ghetti, fount**ai**n, mom**e**nt, penc**i**l, bott**le**, critic**i**sm, butt**o**n, caut**i**ous, circ**u**s	sof**a**
ər	**ear**ly, **ur**ge	sal**ar**y, t**er**m, l**ear**n, f**ir**st, w**or**d, j**our**ney, t**ur**n, syr**up**	li**ar**, det**er**, st**ir**, act**or**, f**ur**, b**urr**, meas**ure**

Figure 7.1 Common spellings of English sounds (continued)

As you can see, reading and spelling, though related, are not the flip side of each other, and we should not assume that reading will guarantee growth in spelling. Most students need systematic, direct instruction in spelling principles and strategies as part of a rich literacy environment.

READING CAN ENHANCE SPELLING

Although reading by itself is unlikely to produce good spellers, reading can aid spelling growth if the teacher builds directed word study into the reading process. Cramer (1998) says, "Background information about letters, sounds, meaning, and word structure can be efficiently obtained from reading. When this base of information is rich, the likelihood of developing spelling power is increased" (p. 127). By encouraging students to be "word explorers" in the context of Guided or Shared Reading, teachers can help them to generalize their findings to other words and to gradually understand the written system of English.

Classrooms that focus on explicit instruction using quality literature are fertile ground for exploring words in ways that are exciting and productive. Both reading and spelling benefit as a result. Fountas and Pinnell (2001) emphasize the reciprocal links between these two skills:

> Solving words—taking words apart while reading for meaning and spelling words while writing to communicate—sustains reading and writing. Readers use a range of strategies to recognize, decode, and understand the meaning of words. Writers select words to convey precise meaning, and they use a range of strategies to spell them accurately. (p. 370)

1. USING VISUAL MEMORY

Word-solving strategies related to reading can include the following:

Irregular Words

The more students see a word in print, the better their chances of spelling it correctly. Think how much harder it would be to spell an irregular word such as *said* if you had never seen it in print. No amount of sounding out would produce the correct spelling. Many high-frequency words that students encounter do not fit common spelling patterns, as shown in Figure 7.2 on page 90.

High-Frequency Words			
among	do	move	said
answer	does	nothing	some
any	done	of	sure
are	from	one	was
build	gone	once	who
come	have	people	work
could	hour	put	

Figure 7.2 Irregular words

Borrowed Words

Other words that don't fit common spelling patterns are those borrowed from other languages. Think how difficult it would be to spell the borrowed words in Figure 7.3 if you had never seen them in print.

English Word	Language of Origin
cipher	Arabic
ghoul	Arabic
plaid	Scotch Gaelic
yacht	Dutch
beige	French
biscuit	Middle French
kindergarten	German
dinghy	Hindi
cappuccino	Italian
bazaar	Persian

Figure 7.3 Words borrowed from other languages

Visual Features of Words

Because of the importance of visual memory in spelling, especially for irregular features of words, students should be encouraged to look at words carefully during Shared and Guided Reading activities. Students who are good readers but poor spellers often read extensively but skim the pages of text and make excessive use of context. As a result, their visual memory of the words is vague and often will not include tricky or irregular features. As a teacher, you can call attention to visual features, such as those in Figure 7.4, during pre-reading activities. During reading, strategies can be modelled for noting tricky words without slowing down the reading. Finally, after reading, you can draw attention more systematically to some of the features you have outlined, and extend these concepts to other words with similar letter combinations.

Visual Features	Examples
letter shapes and direction	*p/d; p/q; d/b*
silent letters	*lim**b**; scissors*
letter clusters	*th**ough**; ei**ght***
double consonants	*sheriff; cappuccino*
schwa vowels (vowels in unstressed syllables)	*independent; dependant*
sequence of letters	*angel; angle*

Figure 7.4 Visual features of words

Students also learn over time that certain letter combinations are acceptable in English while others are not. This knowledge usually develops because of exposure to print through reading, rather than through any direct teaching. Good spellers, if asked to identify which of these pseudo-words could be an English word, usually pick the correct options: a) *glick*, b) *zepl*, c) *phrist*, d) *earmzk* (correct answers: a and c). This linguistic knowledge can then be applied when the student is faced with spelling an unknown word.

2. SOUND PATTERNS

Students who are good readers and good spellers use their knowledge of the relationships between letters and sounds to chunk words into parts when decoding, and to generate words while writing. Increasing students' understanding of how the sound level of language works in reading can help them to develop their ability to decode words in their reading and to generate words with correct spelling in their writing. During Shared Reading, you will find many opportunities to note sound patterns such as those in Figure 7.5 on page 92. Of course, this type of analysis should never destroy the flow of the passage or detract from an appreciation of its meaning. Word study in the hands of a skilled teacher can enhance reading, spelling, and writing fluency, and encourage greater independence among students.

Sound Features	Examples
Phonological awareness: that is, the awareness of the sounds that make up words	• feeling the production of consonants in the mouth • hearing the sounds in words from left to right • listening for beginning, middle, and ending sounds
Letter clusters	• blends (**brown**) • digraphs (**chick**, **then**, **thick**, **fish**) • diphthongs (**house**, **toy**)
Short vowel sounds	• *back*, *best*, *bitter*, *bond*, *butter*
Long vowel sounds	• *same*, *seem*, *side*, *soak*, *super*
Phonograms (onset and rime)	• *can*, *send*, *mind*, *found*, *brush*
Rhyming patterns (not always spelled the same)	• *blow*, *sew*, *go*, *foe*, *though*

Figure 7.5 Sound patterns

Poetry

Good children's literature provides rich opportunities to appreciate the sounds of the English language. Poetry, of course, is the most natural context in which to experience patterns of rhyme and should be a component of all classrooms. Children of all ages love the rhyming gymnastics of Dr. Seuss books or the playful antics of Dennis Lee. Pattern books, often available as big books, also highlight sound patterns and make it easier for children to link sound and letter combinations.

Some children's authors capitalize on linguistic elements and make them the topic of poetry. Shel Silverstein's poem, "The Gnome, the Gnat, and the Gnu," for example, is a delightful play on the sometimes frustrating feature of silent letters.

The Gnome, the Gnat, and the Gnu

I saw an ol' gnome
Take a gknock at a gnat
Who was gnibbling the gnose of his gnu.
I said, "Gnasty gnome,
Gnow, stop doing that.
That gnat ain't done gnothing to you."

He gnodded his gnarled ol' head and said,
" 'Til gnow I gnever gnew
That gknocking a gnat
In the gnoodle like that
Was gnot a gnice thing to do."

By Shel Silverstein

3. USING MEANING PATTERNS

Morphology

Creating meaning is the fundamental purpose of reading. One of the basic elements of this process is determining the meaning of specific words. Words contain meaning cues on a variety of levels as part of the system known as the *morphology* of language. The smallest units of meaning, which cannot be divided, are called *morphemes*. A morpheme can be a single word such as *house*. This type of morpheme is known as "free" because it can stand on its own as a word. In the early stages of reading and writing, students tend to focus on learning free morphemes. As their reading and writing vocabularies expand, however, they encounter *bound morphemes*, which are meaning cues that must be used with words. Units such as *-ed*, signalling past tense, *-s* and *-es* for plural, and *-ing* and other prefixes and suffixes are typical bound morphemes.

It is often easier for students to recognize morphemes in print than to spell them. The case of plural markers is one such example. When students see *s* at the end of the word *friends*, they are likely to recognize the letter *s* as a clue for "more than one." The use of *friends* in the context of the sentence would also confirm this conclusion, as in "My friends are coming over tonight."

Spelling *friends*, however, is more challenging. If students simply sound out the word, they will spell the final /z/ sound as *z*. It is only when they make the cognitive leap and realize that meaning clues, or morphemes, are not always spelled as they sound, that students can spell the /z/ at the end of some words as *s* if it signifies "more than one." In this instance, *meaning takes precedence over sound*, a fundamental principle in written language.

In a similar fashion, the past-tense morpheme *-ed* is spelled this way even when it sounds like /t/, as in *jumped*. Students who sound words out as their primary spelling strategy will likely continue to spell *jumped* as *jumpt*. Older students may have grasped the past-tense marker, but they will often spell the suffix /shun/, as in the word *vacation*, as *vacashun*. The following poem by Shel Silverstein seems almost designed to take advantage of this particular spelling pattern:

ATIONS

If we meet and I say, "Hi,"
That's a salutation.
If you ask me how I feel,
That's consideration.
If we stop and talk awhile,
That's a conversation.
If we understand each other,
That's communication.
If we argue, scream, and fight,
That's an altercation.
If later we apologize,
That's reconciliation.
If we help each other home,
That's cooperation.
And all these ations added up
Make civilization.

(And if I say this is a wonderful poem,
Is that exaggeration?)

By Shel Silverstein

Guided Reading and Shared Reading are ideal times to bring these morphemes to the attention of students who may not grasp them simply through exposure to print. It is through these "teachable moments" of word study that reading can reinforce and encourage spelling development.

4. USING WORD BUILDING

Many students do not realize that in both reading and writing, long words are often base or root words to which morphemes have been added. Taking the time to help students understand the concept of *word building* during reading activities will pay off in both reading and spelling skills, as well as in oral language development. Many teachers use Word Walls to encourage systematic word building.

Compound Words

Students in the early grades will find they can read and spell many words if they understand how compound words are formed. You can draw their attention to the two free morphemes (or base words) in compound words. This can be done by noting a compound word that appears in a story or other forms of print and showing its component parts, either using the base words themselves or picture illustrations.

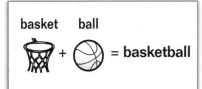
basket   ball
+ = basketball

It is important to distinguish between compound words, in which there is usually a meaning connection between the two parts (as in *houseboat*, *baseball*, and *popcorn*), and a longer word that simply has smaller words in it (as in *carpet*). There is no meaningful connection between *car* and *pet*.

Derived Forms

Older students will benefit from learning word-analysis strategies for "solving" unfamiliar multisyllabic words in reading. A word such as *unnecessarily* may seem to be just a jumble of letters to struggling readers until they systematically break the word into the base word *necessary*, the prefix *un-*, and the suffix *-ly*. While showing the meaning connections among the prefix, base, and suffix, you should also point out the spelling features that pertain to the word. Show that the double *n* near the beginning of the word is logically the result of *un-* being attached to *necessary*, and the *y* at the end of the base word changes to *i* when *-ly* is added.

A root is similar to a base word, but a root is often a bound morpheme unable to stand on its own as a word. Many root words in English are derived from Greek and Latin. Even the most basic knowledge of some common roots can tremendously expand a student's oral, reading, and writing vocabularies.

When a new word is encountered in classroom reading, you can work with students to explore its roots. Then try to create a root web containing many forms of the word by adding a variety of affixes (beginnings and endings). Figure 7.6 shows a number of words that share the common Latin root *port*, from *porto, portare*, meaning "to carry."

An etymological dictionary or a book of word origins would be a valuable addition to your classroom library, particularly in the middle and later grades, to assist students in this type of word-solving activity.

un	necessary	ly

= unnecessarily

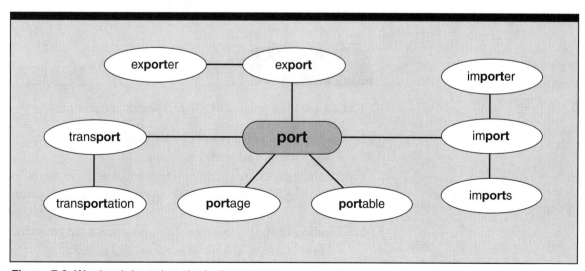

Figure 7.6 Word web based on the Latin root *port*

The Meaning Principle

As noted earlier, an important principle underlying written English is that *meaning takes precedence over sound*. In other words, words that are related in meaning are usually related in their print form, even if they do not sound the same. This aspect of English is very beneficial to readers, since by recognizing a common base or root word in print, it is often possible to guess the meaning of an unfamiliar word. For example, a student could hypothesize that the word *unrecognizable* means "cannot be recognized" by isolating the base word *recognize*, the prefix *un-* (meaning "not"), and the suffix *-able* (meaning "to be able to").

un	recognize	able

= unrecognizable

While the meaning principle has great advantages in reading, it also creates challenges in spelling for students who rely too heavily on the sounding-out strategy. One of the examples often used is *resign/ resignation*. Since the two forms are related in meaning, they share a common spelling of *sign*, even though in the base word *sign* the letter *g* is silent, but it is pronounced in *resignation*. The student who tries to sound out the word *resign* will likely spell it *resine* or *rezine*.

Mature spellers use this knowledge to their advantage. They do not rely solely on sounding out words, but they also apply the meaning principle as a strategy for spelling. They realize that if they can spell one form of a word, they can likely spell another form of it even if the sound has changed. For example, they may remember the spelling of *muscle*, with its silent *c*, by relating it to *muscular*, in which the *c* is pronounced. The term *derivational constancy* means that there is a consistency in the spelling of words that are derived from the same base or root.

You can make students aware of the meaning principle by pointing out derived forms of words encountered in reading, and exploring both the base and root words and other derived forms. You can quickly sketch root webs with students, similar to Figure 7.6 on page 95. This form of word study will help to enhance students' oral, reading, and spelling vocabularies.

SUMMARY

This chapter has presented the following main ideas:

1. **Spelling and reading are closely connected:**
    - Both are meaning-making processes.
    - Spelling seeks to convey meaning through the use of letters.
    - Reading is a process of making meaning through print.

2. **Reading in itself, however, does not guarantee growth in spelling:**
    - Many students are better readers than spellers.
    - The two processes, though related, are not mirror images of each other.

3. **Spelling is usually a more difficult skill to acquire than reading:**
   - There are more clues available when reading a word than when spelling it.
   - There are often several ways to spell a given sound in English.

4. **Reading can enhance spelling development if teachers build word study into classroom reading instruction.** Word study can take place in both planned and spontaneous fashion through
   - Guided Reading
   - Shared Reading
   - Shared/Interactive Writing
   - Guided Writing

5. **Reading can improve a student's visual memory for words, especially for**
   - irregular words
   - words borrowed from other languages

6. **Looking at sound patterns during reading instruction can benefit spelling.** These patterns may include
   - listening for the sounds that make up a word, including beginning, middle, and ending sounds; letter clusters such as blends, digraphs, and vowel sounds; and rhyming patterns
   - relating letters and sounds

7. **Patterns of meaning are crucial to both reading and spelling.** Teachers can increase student awareness of meaning patterns during reading activities.

8. **Morphology refers to the meaning system of language:**
   - Morphemes are the smallest units of meaning that cannot be divided.
   - Free morphemes can stand on their own as words (e.g., *house*).
   - Bound morphemes cannot stand on their own (e.g., *-s* and *-es* for plural).

9. **Bound morphemes can cause spelling problems because they are not always spelled as they sound** (e.g., *-s* at the end of *buses*; *-ed* at the end of *jumped*). Teachers can help students understand these "markers" when they are encountered while reading and writing.

10. **Meaning takes precedence over sound.** Words that are related in meaning tend to be spelled alike even though they may not be pronounced the same (e.g., *nation/national*).

11. **Systematic word building will help develop a student's oral, reading, and spelling vocabularies.** There are many opportunities through reading to examine how words are built. Words can be analysed for
    - base and root words
    - compound words
    - prefixes and suffixes
    - word origins

REFLECTIVE THINKING

1. What arguments do the authors give for asserting that spelling is more difficult than reading? Does your experience confirm or contradict this position?

2. This chapter outlines four areas in which word-solving strategies in reading can contribute to growth in spelling: visual memory for words; sound patterns; meaning patterns; and word building. Which area seems most pertinent to the age group you teach? Explain.

3. Examine a story, poem, or other form of reading that you plan to use with your class. What spelling concepts or strategies could be introduced or reinforced during Shared or Guided Reading activities?

4. The authors stress the significance of the "meaning principle" in written English, that words related in meaning are usually related in print, even if they do not sound the same (p. 96). Why is the meaning principle an advantage in reading but often a challenge in spelling?

5. What ideas or information would you add or delete from this chapter if you were the author? Explain.

The following chart provides links with other chapters in the book:

To learn more about...	see these chapters
How children learn to spell	Chapter 1, page 2
The English spelling system	Chapter 4, page 50
Spelling strategies	Chapter 10, page 129

CHAPTER

8

Writing and Presenting

One of the most contested areas of language teaching is the question of how to connect the teaching of spelling and the teaching of writing. There are those who believe there is little if any transfer from words on spelling lists to students' writing. Therefore, they see no point in formal spelling instruction (Graves and Stuart, 1985). Abandoning the teaching of spelling, though, seems a case of "throwing the baby out with the bath water." A more useful approach is to ask, "How can we effectively teach spelling in the context of writing?" In this chapter, we hope to provide some answers to this question.

HOW DO WRITING AND SPELLING INTERCONNECT?

Very early in the process of learning to read, children discover that spelling does not have a one-to-one match with sounds. At five, Teagan asked, "What does 'o-f' say?" "Of," her mother replied. "No, Mommy," she remonstrated. "It's not o-v! It's o-f!" This anecdote demonstrates what researchers have been telling us: **writing is harder than reading** (Bosman and Van Orden, 1997). This is especially true in English where there are over a thousand ways to spell 40 speech sounds. Hughes and Searle (1997) found that good spellers usually enjoyed writing, but the reverse is also true. Many children dislike writing because they are poor spellers. Writing tasks reveal their inadequacies for all to see.

In the last 25 years, hundreds of books have been written about teaching children to write. Some of the best (Calkins, 1983; Atwell, 1988) make important contributions in advocating authentic communication as the foundation of good student writing. However, they also advocate teaching spelling as a follow-up to writing through mini-lessons that address spelling deficiencies in children's written work. The difficulty is that research shows that teaching spelling so unsystematically does not give children the foundation of alphabetic, pattern, and meaning elements that they need to be good spellers (Templeton and Morris, 1999). In the context of balanced literacy, a sizable helping of word study, including spelling, should be part of a child's literacy diet (Willows, 2002).

INTEGRATING SYSTEMATIC SPELLING INSTRUCTION WITH AUTHENTIC WRITING

How can we best teach spelling effectively without sacrificing spontaneity and authenticity in the young writer? How can we best ensure the transfer of spelling knowledge to writing?

One approach is to integrate a systematic study of words with meaningful writing experiences. This allows students to consolidate using words in context at the same time as providing the motivation for developing a "spelling conscience." In fact, this is how writers function in real life. Authors who write for a living find no contradiction between writing creatively and writing correctly. They have learned to proofread their final drafts, use reference books, and consult editors. They take care that nothing leaves their desks until it is correct. They have a "spelling conscience," a sense of responsibility to their readers.

Spelling instruction, as a means to effective communication, doesn't have to stifle young writers. On the contrary, confident spellers will take risks and use a wider vocabulary and more complex sentence structure as they gain mastery over the tools of writing. Students unsure of their spelling skills are likely to take refuge in the words they already know.

THE ROLE OF INVENTED SPELLING

Young children, given the opportunity at home or at school, write freely, using their own best guesses at the spelling of words. Does this invented spelling delay or disrupt learning to spell correctly?

The simple answer is no. Ronald Cramer and Charles Read, among others, have studied the long-term effect of invented spelling. As Cramer says, "There is neither permanent nor temporary damage or delay in learning standard spelling. On the contrary, literacy achievement tends to be accelerated and superior" (2001, p. 332).

Look at this writing sample (Figure 8.1) by five-year-old Safiya, at play with a friend.

Figure 8.1 Safiya's writing translates as follows: "I want some food. I am so happy. I think you like me."

Safiya has portrayed herself juggling words. Look at what she already knows: words are organized from left to right; most of the words she writes begin and end with the right consonant; and some sight words are correct (*so*, *I*, *you*, *me*). She is already at the Phonetic Stage, even when she is writing for fun.

In the school context, trying out, guessing, or inventing spellings provides the freedom to explore the connection between oral vocabulary and writing. In a workshop with Grade 1 children, one author always asks, "What foods do you dislike?" as a response to a story about a girl who refuses to eat dinner. The author received the letter on page 102 in a package from one class:

Figure 8.2 Bernard's writing translates as follows: "I hate Brussels sprouts and liver and tomatoes, but my mom makes me eat it."

Bernard has rubbed out *brosos*, *libr*, and *eat* in his writing, unsure of the words' spelling. It is wonderful that he tries these hard words.

In the same batch of letters came one from a girl who said she disliked apples most of all.

Figure 8.3 The sample translates as follows: "Dear Mrs. Siamon. Thank you for coming. My unfavouritist food is apples."

This student was probably writing a word she saw on a classroom chart, especially since the short vowel *a* in *apple* was marked. In this case, the teacher had been asked not to correct the children's spelling, but this young student was already concerned about spelling correctly.

When should invented spelling end? Cramer (2001) says we continue to invent spellings for words we don't know in rough drafts all our lives. However, he also advocates organized spelling instruction "focused on words, strategies, and principles of English spelling" (p. 315).

Children usually phase out invented spelling themselves as they become more competent spellers (Templeton and Morris, 1999). We can support this transition by encouraging invented spelling for more difficult words balanced by demanding correct spelling of core words. It's difficult to put an age or grade marker on this process, but the student in Grade 3 or Grade 4 who is still breezily "guessing" at words, and whose inventions show little recognition of spelling patterns throws up a red flag. He or she may need more concentrated work on high-frequency words and simple spelling patterns.

INSTILLING A SPELLING CONSCIENCE IN YOUNG WRITERS

How can we encourage students to feel it is their responsibility as writers to use correct spelling out of respect for their readers? How can we make certain that students transfer the patterns explored and words studied to their final drafts? Current research supports the use of an instructional model based on the following:

- Develop a love of words.
- Link writing to students' interests and experiences.
- Create meaningful and authentic writing tasks.
- Link spelling skills to writing situations systematically.
- Foster responsibility for spelling through shared writing activities.
- Model writing and revising, using real examples.

DEVELOP A LOVE OF WORDS

A love of words starts with oral language as students learn to enjoy the sound of words. Learning to write those words is more meaningful if students already appreciate their power to "punch up" meaning. This word awareness is best accomplished through experience with oral language. Picture books such as *Where the Wild Things Are* or a novel such as *The Hobbit* read aloud will introduce students to the rich possibilities of language.

To get students working with words, you can challenge them to come up with words to describe the sound and the feel of skating or skateboarding, or the look and taste of a ripe strawberry. If they can't find the words, encourage them to invent some.

Besides brainstorming word lists and playing with words informally, introduce students to a writer's best friend, the thesaurus. The word *thesaurus* means "treasure," and a good thesaurus is a treasure chest of words. Here young writers can find the exact word they need to express an idea, or a shade of meaning. If they look up a simple word like *ran* (which they can spell), they will find a list of synonyms that they can probably read and understand but whose spelling may be unfamiliar: *scurry, race, tear, gallop, dash, sprint,* or *hurtle.* From these words, students can choose a synonym whose meaning best matches the action they want to describe. Try some of the following thesaurus activities with students to help them become familiar with this valuable tool:

Taking a Word's Temperature

Ask students to put these synonyms in order from least to most intense:

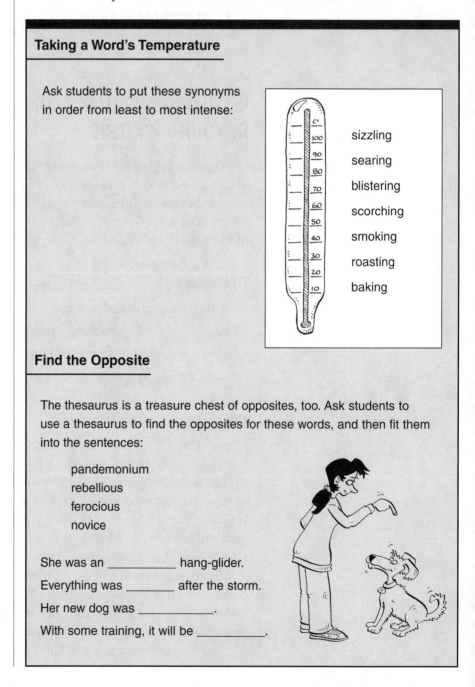

sizzling

searing

blistering

scorching

smoking

roasting

baking

Find the Opposite

The thesaurus is a treasure chest of opposites, too. Ask students to use a thesaurus to find the opposites for these words, and then fit them into the sentences:

  pandemonium
  rebellious
  ferocious
  novice

She was an _____ hang-glider.

Everything was _____ after the storm.

Her new dog was _____.

With some training, it will be _____.

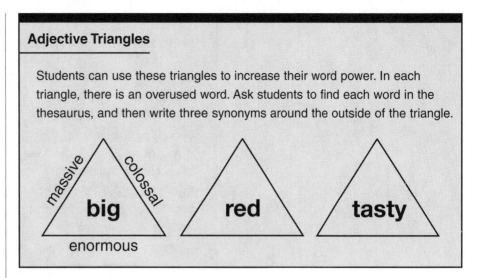

Adjective Triangles

Students can use these triangles to increase their word power. In each triangle, there is an overused word. Ask students to find each word in the thesaurus, and then write three synonyms around the outside of the triangle.

LINK WRITING TO STUDENTS' INTERESTS AND EXPERIENCES

Adults like to write about subjects that deeply engage them, whether it's a shopping list for a special meal or a personal memoir. Children are no exception. In fact, writing projects that relate closely to students' own experiences and interests are the best predictor of writing competence (Allal, 1997). Attempt to adapt writing assignments to your students' situations. If you're using a published spelling program, check to see whether writing assignments are sufficiently open-ended to allow this.

In the examples below, students are given two choices for writing procedural text. In each one, the imperative voice is used, sentences are sequenced carefully, and the writing is brief and simple. Use samples such as these to help students become familiar with this form of writing and to use as models.

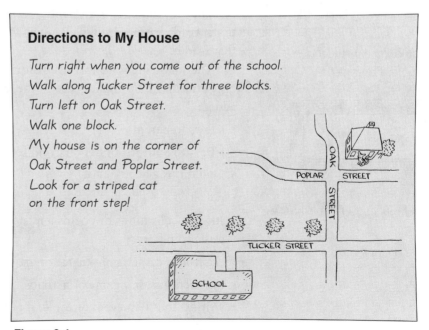

Directions to My House

Turn right when you come out of the school.
Walk along Tucker Street for three blocks.
Turn left on Oak Street.
Walk one block.
My house is on the corner of
Oak Street and Poplar Street.
Look for a striped cat
on the front step!

Figure 8.4

How to Make a Paper Airplane Fly

- Look at the plane from the back. Make sure the wings and tail rudder are straight.
- If your plane DIVES and crashes, bend the back edge of each wing slightly up.
- If your plane STALLS, bend the back edge of each wing slightly down.
- If your plane TURNS right or left or SPIRALS, make sure the wings are even and the tail is straight.

Figure 8.5

CREATE MEANINGFUL AND AUTHENTIC WRITING TASKS

Students can't be expected to care about their writing if the writing task is forced or artificial. At the same time, writing tasks such as "just write whatever you want in your journal" can become boring and open-ended. Again, the cognitive load can become too great if students decide to write a novel instead of a paragraph. Some scaffolding and interactive planning can make writing more fun and satisfying. It is vital that the occasion is real and the audience is authentic. As many teachers know, responsibility to the reader comes into play only if the writer knows and cares about that reader.

The following is a short list of some of the authentic writing opportunities that might occur in the classroom. Many others could be added:

- letters to parents
- letters to authors, presenters, and school helpers
- invitations
- posters
- student collections of poems and stories for the classroom library
- classroom displays of science or art
- instructions for a game or activity
- writing about an event or topic of personal importance
- thank-you notes

LINK SPELLING SKILLS TO WRITING SITUATIONS SYSTEMATICALLY

If spelling skills are to be linked to the writing process in a meaningful way, teaching them must reflect knowledge of the English spelling system and the developmental nature of learning to spell. Ideally, skills should build from Grade 1 to Grade 8 in a logical sequence, and this sequence should be consistent, at least within a school (and even better, within a jurisdiction such as a school board or district). The developmental sequence should also reflect the curriculum expectations of the region. See Figure 2.4 in Chapter 2 for a summary of spelling concepts by grade level organized into the developmental stages of spelling.

In a well-thought-out program, whether school or board generated or published, the spelling and grammar skills to be taught should fit the writing form. In this way, students can explore forms and styles of writing at the same time that they are gaining control of the spelling system. They will also have individual control over the content of what they write.

For example, Grade 1 students learning simple rhyming families, such as *-an* could brainstorm words that rhyme with *fan*, then make a simple folding fan and write one word on each section. Later, group or individual poems could be made with the words.

Dan, Dan, the funny old man,
Washed his face in a frying pan,
Dried it off with a paper fan,
And drove to work in his purple van!

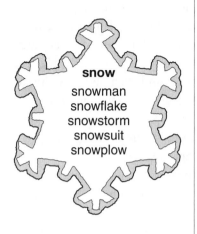

snow
snowman
snowflake
snowstorm
snowsuit
snowplow

Grade 2 or Grade 3 students could generate compound words to match seasonal or weather conditions and create shape poems in the shape of the sun, a snowflake, or raindrop.

Grade 3 or Grade 4 students could explore the past tense, both the regular *-ed* forms and the irregular, high-utility past-tense forms such as *went* and *heard*. This word-study objective combines spelling, grammar, and vocabulary building. It fits well with a writing workshop on narrative writing or memoir or journal writing where students relate a personal event from their past.

Older students can write news bulletins, using the present continuous *-ing* forms. These could be in the form of an eyewitness report, sports broadcast, or a "What's New in Our Neighbourhood" bulletin.

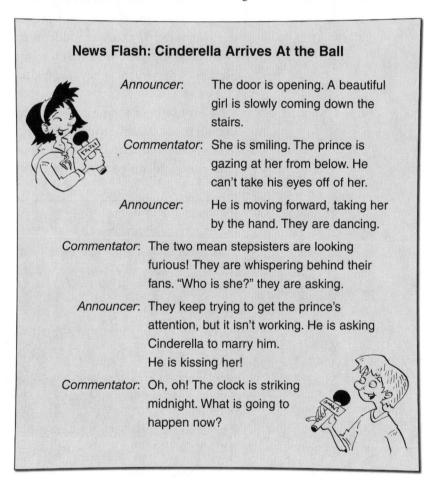

News Flash: Cinderella Arrives At the Ball

Announcer: The door is opening. A beautiful girl is slowly coming down the stairs.

Commentator: She is smiling. The prince is gazing at her from below. He can't take his eyes off of her.

Announcer: He is moving forward, taking her by the hand. They are dancing.

Commentator: The two mean stepsisters are looking furious! They are whispering behind their fans. "Who is she?" they are asking.

Announcer: They keep trying to get the prince's attention, but it isn't working. He is asking Cinderella to marry him. He is kissing her!

Commentator: Oh, oh! The clock is striking midnight. What is going to happen now?

With careful planning, a spiral writing curriculum with word-study objectives of increasing complexity can be built. For example, in Grade 2, teachers can have students use simple adjectives like *slim*, *big*, or *tall* to describe family and friends in a "Family Album." In Grade 4, comparative and superlative adjectives such as *biggest*, *most interesting*, or *taller than* could be used for descriptive writing, and in Grade 6 to Grade 8, students can explore words with adjectival endings such as *impressive*, *expensive*, or *luxurious*.

FOSTER RESPONSIBILITY FOR SPELLING THROUGH SHARED WRITING ACTIVITIES

Writing activities can lend themselves to students working in small groups or with partners. Reading work aloud to the group or revising with an editing or proofreading partner can help students focus on correct spelling as part of their responsibility to the reader, an essential part of communication. The rigid Writing Process model of pre-writing, writing, and post-writing activities has fallen out of favour with some teachers as they realize that there is more than one way to approach the writing task. However, it can be a useful organizing principle as long as students are not locked into a three-step process.

Before Writing—Planning is the Key: Although there is much to be said for "free-writing" to prime the creative pump, before writing is ready to be published, extensive planning and discussion needs to take place. When students do this planning in a group, it can reduce the cognitive load, creating a scaffold to support the writing task. Before students start to write, they plan the communication as a group. They talk about what they want to communicate and who their audience is. They discuss the form their writing will take and make lists of words they might need to create the text. It is a good idea to provide a model of the kind of writing they will do, identifying the key features. The following graphic organizers can help students to develop their ideas:

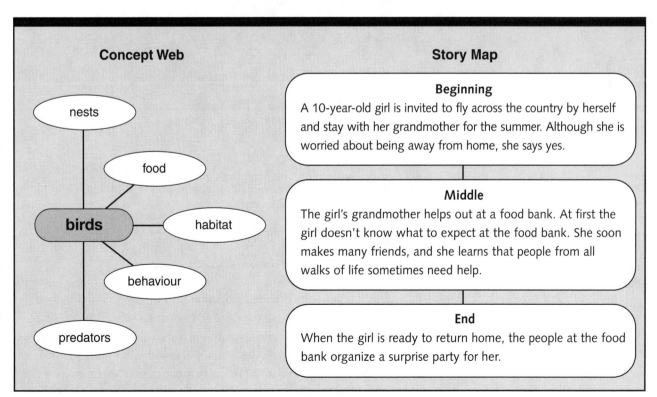

Figure 8.6 Graphic organizers

Children internalize strategies and skills that come out of interacting with a network of peers and teachers. This is sometimes referred to as *Shared Writing*.

During Writing—Creating a Workshop Environment: You can assist students by providing writing and editing aids in a Writing Centre: word lists, students' own personal word lists, and reference materials, such as dictionaries and thesauruses. You can also encourage young writers to seek help from peers. Work for positive team solutions, not competitive, esteem-breaking papers covered in red ink.

After Writing—Modelling the Process: Following revision and editing, proofreading is a vital stage in text composition and one that is particularly relevant for spelling. Jan Turbill talks about two stages in the proofreading process: recognizing errors and correcting errors. You can display the following proofreading guidelines in the Writing Centre and encourage students to pay attention to them when they reach this stage in their writing projects. In this way, spelling becomes an integral part of the whole writing process:

Tips for Identifying Spelling Errors

- Focus on one word at a time.
- Read aloud, slowly!
- Use a pencil to touch each word, or hold a ruler under the line of text.
- Read from bottom to top or right to left.
- Read with "fresh eyes." Have someone proofread who has never seen the piece before.

Tips for Correcting Spelling Errors

- Sound out the word in syllables.
- Write the word several different ways and decide which one "looks right."
- Compare it with spelling words you know.
- Check books, charts, and word lists where the word is written.
- Use a dictionary.
- Ask others.

Proofreading is a sophisticated skill that you need to model before students form proofreading partnerships or small groups. You can display a piece of writing, both uncorrected and corrected (be sure not to use one from the current class) to show the impact of spelling and grammar mistakes on the reader. Then, establish a protocol, such as the one on page 111, for correcting errors.

Proofreading Tips

- Model the strategies for proofreading (tapping individual words, reading backward, and so on).
- Proofreading partners should "switch hats," acting as editors for each other.
- Copies of the proofreading guidelines can be sent home, or teachers may want to involve family members by including a proofreading workshop at a parents' meeting.

When students proofread each other's writing, have them do the following:

- Provide cloze for errors, putting the number of errors at the end of the line, or at the end of a paragraph.

  > sho__d,   veg_tables
  > We shood eat vegtables every day.

- Avoid circling or underlining errors in red ink. Use a dot to indicate errors, or a rainbow of colours.

The overall goal is to develop a publishing standard for the classroom or school, and promote the idea that "nothing leaves this classroom that is not up to that standard." Naturally, these standards vary from class to class. For example, samples of Grade 1 words with invented spelling can be displayed.

MODEL WRITING AND REVISING

We are constantly asking students to write. We know that writing fluently and well is a vital skill for school success as well as career success later on. The skill is not just in correct spelling and grammar, but in the ability to organize thoughts, summarize information, and develop hypotheses. Students will be asked to write—and judged on their writing abilities—throughout their lives. As teachers, we've gone through writing term papers, examinations, résumés, job applications, and reports. We have valuable experience to share with our students, and we can do this by modelling writing behaviour in a workshop environment.

At the end of a graduate writing course for teachers, one professor sends the teachers off to conference with each other. In the meantime, she sets up the classroom as a coffee house with plastic gingham tablecloths, coffee, and cookies, and a copy of the "published" anthology of their best writing at each place. During discussion and "readings" in a coffee-house atmosphere, they shared the following insights:

- Writing down your thoughts and feelings requires trust in your fellow writers and a willingness to take risks. The transactional writing tasks we undertake daily (writing lists, reports, and lesson plans) are easier in this respect than personal writing.

- Getting feedback from other writers engaged in the same task is important. All writers need to know if their story engages, moves, or delights their readers. It is very hard to judge for yourself if what you've written is any good.

- There is a huge emotional investment in personal writing. It is not easy to do, and we should not ask children to try it if we are unwilling to model the risk and commitment ourselves.

- There are also great rewards in personal writing. The satisfaction of having others appreciate your work, of seeing it "published," of reading it aloud is worth the risk and the hard work.

Many of these insights would apply if the group had written transactional or nonfiction pieces. Any kind of writing benefits from group feedback and reflection. If we take students through the steps we take to develop our own thoughts and feelings, we can help them become better writers. Modelling the writing and revision processes for students helps them to put responsibility for spelling into its proper context.

SPELL CHECKS AND WRITING

Students may ask: "Why do I need to proofread? I'll just run my work through the spell check." The new tools that come with computers to help turn out error-free communications are useful and will probably become more so. Personally, we love the wiggly red line that points out spelling errors, typos, and missed spaces. There is no doubt it saves time. However, we have learned not to rely on it when accurate communication matters.

A spell check does not catch homophone errors, of course (*coarse*). It doesn't care if the writer uses *their*, *there*, or *they're*. It will not tell the writer that he or she has written *you* instead of *your*, or *hi* instead of *his*. More seriously, it will not let the writer know that he or she put a space in the wrong place (as was evident in a newspaper article where *so that* became *sot hat* and the writer's very serious quote was ruined). It will not tell the writer if he or she left out a *not* so that the message says "*yes*" instead of "*no*." The following list of spell-check errors is illuminating (Igo, 2001):

Correct	Incorrect	Spell Checker
definitely	definantly	defiantly
infinitely	infinitly	infinity
a lot	alot	allot
surprised	surpised	surpassed
sponsor	sponcer	spencer, sponger, spanker

Figure 8.7

Students need to see the spell check as another tool in their arsenal of proofreading devices. But they also need to remember that a computer doesn't have a spelling conscience. It doesn't care if we look foolish or send the wrong message. Ultimately, it's the writer's responsibility to see that the spell check hasn't missed an embarrassing or confusing error.

SUMMARY

This chapter has presented the following main ideas:

1. **Learning to write is more difficult than learning to read.** Some students avoid writing because they feel they are inadequate spellers.

2. **Teaching spelling as incidental to writing is inadequate for many students.** They need a systematic, developmentally appropriate spelling program.

3. **At the same time, spelling instruction needs to be integrated into an authentic writing program.** Teaching spelling as a separate entity does not provide students with the motivation for spelling correctly in their written communication. To accomplish this integration, it is important to do the following:

- Develop students' love of words and fluency. Encourage them to explore the thesaurus.
- Link writing to students' interests.
- Work with students to create authentic writing opportunities.
- Link spelling skills to forms of written expression (e.g., adjectives with descriptive paragraphs).
- Foster the development of a spelling conscience through group activities.
- Emphasize proofreading and revising, using real examples.

4. **Technology has changed the way we proofread and revise, but spell-check programs cannot substitute for spelling and proofreading skills.**

REFLECTIVE THINKING

1. What did you learn from this chapter to enhance the transfer of your students' spelling knowledge to their writing?

2. Invented spelling is not wild guessing but a thoughtful application of the sound–letter relationships that students have. How might you explain this perspective to parents who are concerned that invented spelling may hamper their child's spelling development?

3. The list on page 106 presents some authentic writing ideas. Add other writing opportunities to the list that would appeal to your students.

4. Does your province or school district provide a sequence of spelling skills that builds logically through the grades? If so, to what degree is it consistent with the developmental stages of spelling described in Chapter 2, Figure 2.4 on pages 22–23?

5. Has this chapter modified any of your beliefs about the link between spelling and the writing process? Explain.

The following chart provides links with other chapters in the book:

To learn more about...	see these chapters
Spelling concepts by grade level	Chapter 2, pages 22–23
The English spelling system	Chapter 4, page 50

Integrating Spelling Across the Curriculum

In Chapters 5 to 8, we described the importance of connecting spelling with other areas of literacy—listening and speaking, viewing and representing, reading, writing, and presenting. In this chapter, we will be stressing the importance of integrating spelling into all areas of the curriculum. As a teacher, you provide the crucial link between the formal, systematic study of spelling patterns and strategies, and the application of this knowledge in every subject area encountered by your students.

The challenge of providing this link extends well beyond the time that is traditionally thought of as "language time" to include the entire school day. Cross-curricular links with spelling don't simply reinforce spelling knowledge. By applying the skills they have acquired in word-study activities, students will be better prepared to tackle new vocabulary encountered in reading and writing across the curriculum. The quality of the students' written work in these subjects will also improve as they use spelling rules and generalizations, and learn important vocabulary related to the topic.

A few cautions are in order, however, when integrating spelling into themes and various subject areas.

1. Spelling embedded in content-area study is only one aspect of a comprehensive spelling program. It should enhance but not take the place of formal systematic spelling instruction. It is tempting to say that all necessary spelling issues and patterns will be addressed as they arise in students' reading and writing. In reality, however, such an approach often sacrifices the coverage of important concepts needed for normal spelling growth.

2. Spelling instruction in content areas should reflect careful attention to spelling patterns, strategies, and meaning. A list of theme- or content-related words that is simply posted on a theme chart or sent home for study has little chance of improving students' spelling performance in the long term. Students are likely to see the value of

"All too often, spelling instruction within themes has simply repeated the mistakes of outmoded texts in a slightly more meaningful context" (Scott, 1994, p. 58).

learning these words only while they are engaged in a given topic, and only if they are reading and writing them daily.

Instead of requiring students to memorize long lists of theme words, select words containing patterns that can be generalized to other words they will encounter. For example, in doing a unit on "Communities Around the World" with younger children, the word *globe* can be used to show the *o-consonant-e* pattern for the long *o* sound. Other word families such as *-ome, -one, -ote, -ose,* and so on can be studied in the same manner.

When important terms do not reflect common spelling patterns, place the emphasis on brainstorming effective strategies for learning to spell these words. In the same communities unit, for example, the word *sign* may be present. Call attention to the silent letter *g* and present the visual–spatial strategy of configuration boxes to help students remember the shape of the word.

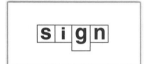

This configuration approach can then be applied to other words with ascending and descending letters that do not fit sound patterns. In later years, this same feature can be taught through meaning connections by referring to the related words *signal* and *signature.* In the early grades, however, a simple visual–spatial approach is more appropriate.

3. Decide the level on which content-area words should be studied. Many terms that appear in curriculum documents and textbooks are important as working vocabulary but are too advanced for students' level of spelling. When you begin a unit of study, consider these questions:

- Which terms are important for students to know and understand?

- Should students be able to write this word with the support of charts, personal lists, or other references?

- Is this a word that is used so frequently that students need to spell it without hesitation?

Words that fit the third category should be the focus of your spelling instruction for the unit. Rather than frustrate young children with dictated lists of words such as *photosynthesis,* teach the meaning of this term, and deal with the root *photo,* meaning "light."

Plant Words: Grade 3

Words to Understand	Words for Reference	Words to Spell
characteristics	blossom	bark
conservation	energy	branch
environment	fibrous	bulb
erosion	herbs	flower
germinate	minerals	food
investigation	orchard	fruit
life cycle	oxygen	garden
reproduction	pistil	ground
terrarium	pollen	leaf
	stamen	leaves
	structure	light
	vegetable	plant
		root
		seeds
		soil
		stem
		sunlight
		trunk
		water
		wetlands

Figure 9.1

Brainstorm other words containing this root (*photograph*, *photocopy*, *telephoto*) and show how "light" is related to these terms. This process sends a vital message to students; it shows students that they can often understand and spell longer words by looking for common word parts within them.

Figure 9.1 on page 116 shows a sample breakdown of words for a Grade 3 science unit on plants.

4. Evaluate spelling as a component of polished work for content areas. By including conventions such as spelling, grammar, and punctuation as a category on writing rubrics for all subject areas, you are giving students the message that these features are important in everyday contexts, not only in "language time." Correct spelling in a published work is a mark of respect for the reader and an important aspect of communicating one's message.

5. Spelling in content areas can be part of a wide variety of word-study activities. Figure 9.2 illustrates the range of word-study concepts that can be addressed through themes and specific subject areas. Your choice of concepts and activities will be determined by the nature of the vocabulary in the unit, the needs and interests of your students, and the expectations or outcomes for your grade level.

Word-Study Concepts

Spelling Patterns	Vocabulary Concepts	Language Usage	Grammar
• vowel/consonant patterns • abbreviations • base words • capitalization • compound words • contractions • homographs (e.g., *wind/wind*) • homophones (e.g., *horse/hoarse*) • irregular spellings • multisyllabic words • past-tense endings • plurals • possessives • prefixes and suffixes • rhyme • silent letters	• antonyms • denotation and connotation • dictionary skills • euphemisms (e.g., *downsized*) • inclusive language • multiple meanings • new words in the language • portmanteau words (e.g., *situation + comedy = sitcom*) • synonyms • word origins	• acronyms • alliteration • clichés • expressions • idioms • jargon • metaphors and similes • onomatopoeia • puns	• parts of speech • sentence structure • punctuation • word usage

Figure 9.2 Word-study concepts

SAMPLE UNITS IN SOCIAL STUDIES

The following three sample units show how word study can be integrated across subject areas on a variety of levels. Many opportunities to study spelling and vocabulary will present themselves incidentally, but you should also build word-study components into a unit in a systematic way.

For example, if your students have difficulty dealing with longer words in reading or writing, use content-area terms to show that multi-syllabic words are often just simple base words that have been extended through prefixes and suffixes. Compound words are also a good way of demonstrating word building, even to young children.

Concepts taught through a formal spelling program can be reinforced through theme-related activities, as shown in the communities unit that follows. Proofreading skills will be practised when students know that "spelling counts" in subjects other than language arts.

When you link formal word study with every subject area throughout the school day, you are telling students that word study is crucial to their success as learners. They will see that decoding skills will help them decipher new terms in science, and spelling patterns and strategies will enable them to tackle unfamiliar words in their content-area writing. In short, literacy is not bound to any one subject area.

Early Years: Communities

The community theme can encompass the school community, the students' local community, and communities around the world. This sampling of word-study activities shows how vocabulary and spelling principles can be integrated into this topic.

Community Alphabet

Students can be challenged to supply words in a chart or list related to their community for each letter of the alphabet. You can have the students add to the chart or list throughout the unit, and post it in the classroom as a separate set of words related to the community theme.

Word Sort: Long e

For this activity, you can have students sort the words in the box into three categories for spelling the long *e* sound: *y*, *ea*, *ee* (see Figure 9.3 on page 119). If you provide the three patterns, it is a closed sort. Alternatively, you can use an open sort and have the students decide among themselves what the patterns will be.

Provide each group of students with a set of cards containing the words. They can sort them into three categories on their desks, or you can provide circles in the form of paper cutouts, craft hoops, or Hula Hoops.

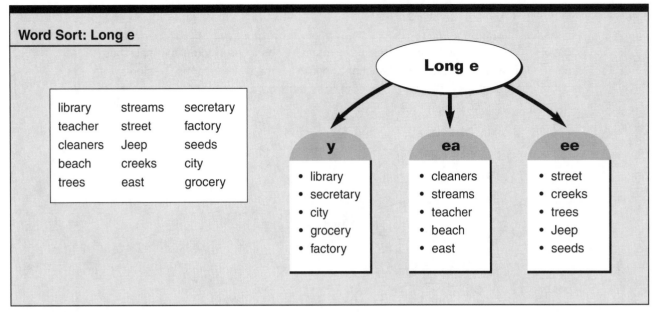

Word Sort: Long e

Long e

library	streams	secretary
teacher	street	factory
cleaners	Jeep	seeds
beach	creeks	city
trees	east	grocery

y
- library
- secretary
- city
- grocery
- factory

ea
- cleaners
- streams
- teacher
- beach
- east

ee
- street
- creeks
- trees
- Jeep
- seeds

Figure 9.3

Word Sort: Singular and Plural

The word sort on page 120 moves away from sound–symbol patterns and deals with patterns for making words plural (see Figure 9.4). The words in the box relate to the theme of Community and are selected by the teacher to represent different patterns for plurals. Students can sort the words in the box into singular and plural categories. The plural words then can be sorted further using a word web divided into two categories: plurals formed by adding -*s* and plurals formed by adding -*es*.

Note that *stores* simply adds -*s* to the singular form to create the plural. Students might place *stores* in the -*es* category if they do not isolate the singular form first. This is a good check to determine if some students are just sorting words visually.

Other plural words related to community can be added throughout the unit.

Compound Words

It is important for students to learn that long words are often just smaller words combined in meaningful ways. Compound words are an ideal tool for demonstrating this feature of language.

You can present the individual words in the word web in Figure 9.5 on page 120 on cards and work with students to combine as many pairs of cards as possible to form compound words. Another approach is to help students follow the arrows in the word web to create the new words. In each case, encourage students to analyse and state the meaning connection between the compound word and its parts. For example, a student might say, "*lunchtime* is the time we set aside for lunch," or "a *bathtub* is a tub we use for having a bath."

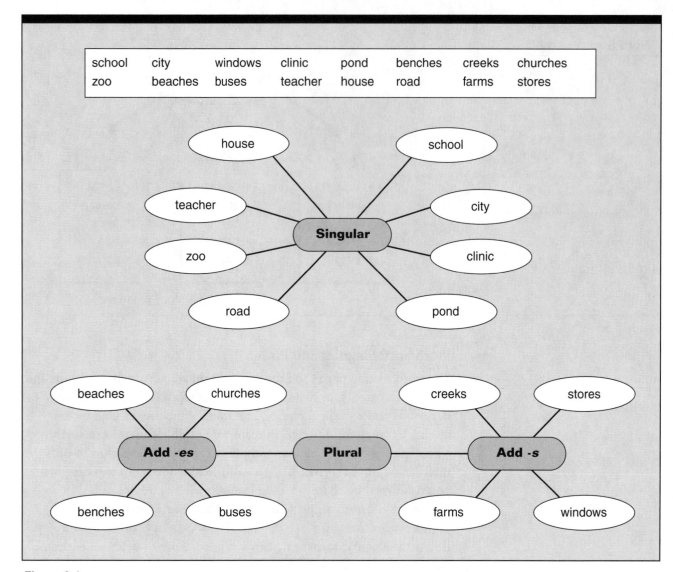

Figure 9.4

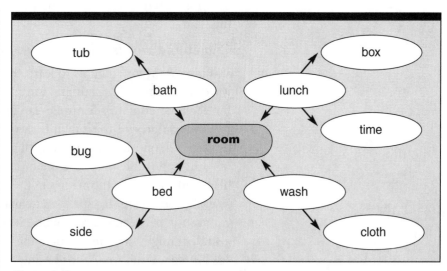

Figure 9.5

Middle Years: Early Civilizations

Word Building

A study of early civilizations is an ideal way of introducing students to the origins of the English language. This information is not just of historical interest; understanding how our language came to be will help students decipher new words, especially those containing Latin and Greek roots, prefixes, and suffixes.

Most of the activities in this unit are designed to show how words that may seem long and complex are actually just simple word parts that have been built systematically. For example, while studying Greek myths, you might discuss the myth about Arachne, a woman who challenged the goddess Athena to a contest in weaving and was changed by her into a spider. You could print the word *arachnophobia* on the board and encourage students to find the root word *arachn*. Discuss the connections between the name Arachne and the word part *arachno*, and then ask students to examine the other word part *phobia*.

The intent is not for students to spell words, such as *arachnophobia* independently. Rather, it is to see that the word *arachnid*, a class that includes spiders, and the word *phobia*, meaning "fear," combine logically in *arachnophobia* to describe "an abnormal fear of spiders."

Word building can be used to help students understand that words with the same roots are related in meaning. Challenge students to read the types of phobias in Figure 9.6, and predict what the phobia means. Students can look up the meanings of the phobias presented and add others to the web (see Figure 9.6). They could also write about or discuss any phobias they have, and then create a mind map of their phobia with words and images to describe it.

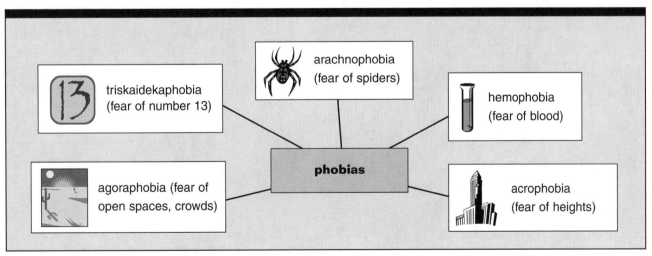

Figure 9.6

Word Origins

Etymology dictionaries are sources of fascinating information on word origins. In using these dictionaries, students will see how learning about the Greek or Latin roots of words can help them figure out the meanings. Students can find the origins of a variety of everyday objects or animals whose names have Greek or Latin origins, such as *arachnid*.

Word Origins Chart

English Word	Root	Meaning of Root	Translation
insect	sect (Latin)	cut; "that which is cut into"	ancients believed that the bodies of the bugs they examined appeared to have been divided by slicing
terrier	terra (Latin)	earth	a hunting dog that is able to dig out animals that are hiding in holes in the ground
salmon	sal (Latin)	leap	a type of fish that actually leaps upstream to spawn
hippopotamus	hipp potamus (Greek)	horse river	river horse

Figure 9.7

Word Sort

Another activity you can have students do is sort vocabulary by topic. Give them a master list of words associated with an early civilization, and ask them to sort the words into categories. In an open sort, students will decide on their own classifications. Figure 9.8 is an example of a closed sort, where the categories are provided for students. The words can also be given as a deck of cards to sort.

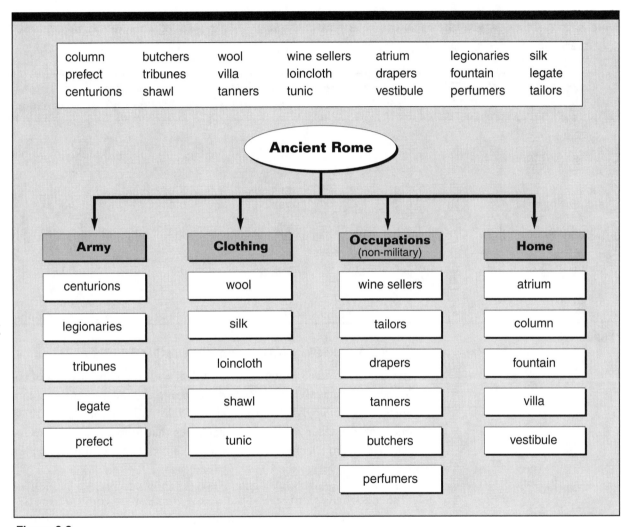

Figure 9.8

Latin Mottoes

An interesting activity is to have samples of mottoes for students to examine and analyse. These mottoes can come from sources such as schools, family crests, and provincial and federal buildings. Students will quickly see that many of these mottoes are written in Latin. Have them search for other mottoes—on money, for example—and attempt to find the translation. Students can also create a motto for the class using English, French, or a language of their choice. Challenge students to design a crest and include the motto in the finished product.

Spelling Feature Grid

Students can compare words for spelling characteristics. This chart (Figure 9.9) should be given to students with just the key words and categories. Students can complete the chart by comparing the words under each category. They can then analyse the grid and discuss any patterns noted. The categories can be tailored to match spelling concepts you have covered in your curriculum.

Ancient Egypt					
Word	Number of Syllables	Which Syllable Is Stressed?	Sound /k/ Spelled ch?	Sound /f/ Spelled ph?	Double Consonants?
immortal	3	2	no	no	yes—mm
sphinx	1	1	no	yes	no
archaeologist	5	3	yes	no	no
hieroglyph	3	1	no	yes	no
chemicals	3	1	yes	no	no
irrigation	4	3	no	no	yes—rr

Figure 9.9

LATER YEARS: CANADA'S NATURAL RESOURCES

In the later grades, students need to deal with the complexities of spelling longer words, as well as with understanding the meaning of new terms, such as *technology, distribution, sustainable,* and *renewable,* that they encounter in their reading. The activities that follow deal with spelling patterns, word meanings, and strategies for dealing with irregular words.

Word Chains

Students often fail to realize that many words share common roots. During a lesson about how technology has affected natural resources, for example, you might write the word *technology* on the board, point out the root *techn,* and discuss its origins. The example in Figure 9.10 on page 125 shows that the Latin root *techn,* meaning "art" or "skill," forms the basis of many English words. Challenge students to complete the web using words with the root *techn.*

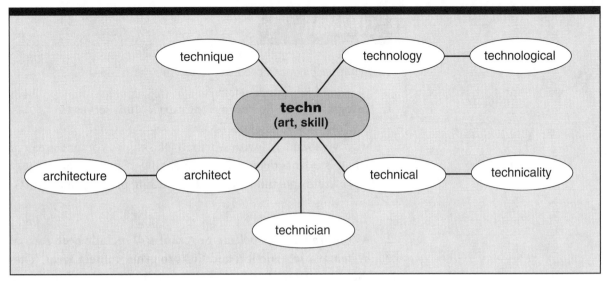

Figure 9.10

Syllable Scramble

Students can be encouraged to attend to the sequence of syllables in long words by unscrambling the syllables and writing them in order. This can be done on a work sheet (Figure 9.11), or each syllable can be written on a separate card and scrambled (Figure 9.12). Syllable scrambles are particularly useful for kinesthetic learners or struggling spellers. Challenge students to make their own syllable scrambles and to share them with a partner.

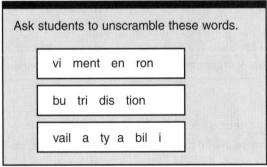

Figure 9.11

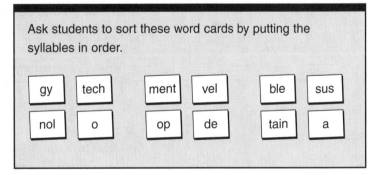

Figure 9.12

Cloze

Cloze helps to highlight letters that are best learned visually. Students can fill in the blanks with the correct letters. It may help to go over these letters with a highlighter pen, or write the letters in a different colour or size. These strategies should make the tricky letters stand out in the students' minds. The Cloze Strategy is effective at all grade levels since it encourages students to focus on the tricky parts of words.

SUMMARY

This chapter has presented the following main ideas:

1. **Integrating spelling across the curriculum serves to**
   - reinforce spelling knowledge
   - provide students with word-attack skills in content-area reading
   - help students determine the meaning of new terminology
   - present opportunities for proofreading practice in content-area writing

2. **A comprehensive spelling program will include both formal, systematic instruction and links to other subject areas.** These links should reinforce but not replace systematic study of spelling patterns and strategies.

3. **Spelling instruction in content areas should reflect careful attention to spelling patterns, strategies, and meaning.** Some words can be selected with patterns that can be generalized to other words. Irregular words can be approached through spelling strategies. Meaning connections among words should be emphasized in reading, writing, and oral vocabulary. The rote memorization of content-area vocabulary has little long-term benefit.

4. **Teachers need to decide the level on which content-area words should be studied.** These may include
   - for meaning, but not for spelling
   - for use in writing with the support of charts, Word Walls, and so on
   - for independent spelling

5. **Spelling should be a component of evaluation of the writing process for content-area work when an opportunity has been given to proofread.** This practice reinforces the principle that correct spelling enhances communication.

6. **Spelling is one component of word study in content areas.** Most thematic studies provide rich opportunities to explore reading strategies, vocabulary, grammar, language usage, spelling patterns, and spelling strategies.

REFLECTIVE THINKING

1. How would you answer a student who complains, "This is a science report, not language arts? Why does spelling count?" How would you answer a colleague who poses the same question?

2. Select a subject area and topic that you currently teach. Prepare a chart as in Figure 9.1 on page 116 that includes the following:

Words to Understand	Words for Reference	Words to Spell

3. Examine the chart you prepared in Question 2. Using Figure 9.2 on page 117 and your own curriculum documents, outline outcomes or expectations that could be addressed with the words in your chart. Classify the concepts under these headings:

Spelling Patterns	Vocabulary Concepts	Language Usage	Grammar

4. Which activities in the sample units (pages 118–125) can be adapted for use in your classroom? Would you use these activities for all your students or specific groups? Explain.

5. What impact can word-solving activities in spelling have on students learning to read and spell content-area vocabulary? Try to use specific examples to explain your thinking.

The following chart provides links with other chapters in the book:

To learn more about...	see these chapters
Spelling assessment	Chapter 3, page 32
The English spelling system	Chapter 4, page 50
Spelling strategies	Chapter 10, page 129

PART 3

Meeting a Range of Student Needs

CHAPTER 10

Spelling Strategies and Word Study

In earlier chapters, we discussed how important it is for students to become strategic learners when it comes to spelling. The English spelling system is highly complex, and students need a wide range of strategies to acquire all the words they will need to write. The best spelling strategy suits the learner and the word to be learned. While young learners may focus on phonological strategies, older students need to broaden the range to include morphological (meaning) strategies and special strategies, such as mnemonics for the most difficult words.

It is critical that students have enough support in the classroom and at home so that they acquire these strategies. Otherwise, they may decide that spelling is random, incomprehensible, or just plain too hard. In this chapter, we provide the background for this support, dividing spelling strategies into the following six areas:

1. Auditory Strategies
2. Visual Strategies
3. Tactile/Kinesthetic Strategies
4. Meaning Strategies
5. Memory Tricks and Mnemonics
6. Using the Dictionary

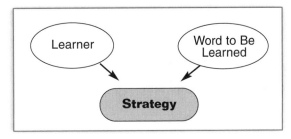

Figure 10.1

DISCUSS STRATEGIES WITH STUDENTS

Research tells us that students learn to spell by paying attention to patterns (Treiman and Cassar, 1997). However, when words break the patterns, students need to make a conscious, personal effort to remember their spelling. Children use a combination of spelling strategies from their earliest days as writers. While they may begin by matching letters to sounds (a phonological strategy), they also employ visual and meaning strategies from an early age. For example, one five-year-old attempted to spell *sing*, and ended up with *sagge*. She was trying to match the consonant and vowel sounds, but she also threw in an extra *g* and a silent *e* because she had seen these features in other words.

As growing "wordsmiths," students need to see themselves as strategic learners and to take responsibility for selecting strategies to learn new words. Part of this spelling growth is students' ability to reflect on their development as spellers and to talk about how they learn. The excerpt that follows is from a discussion with a Grade 4 student. In it, the student discusses her spelling strategies, and reflects on how she learns and the difficulties of English spelling:

> **S:** How about the sound of words? Does that help you?
>
> **B:** Yes, it does, but not always because some of the words are really weird. For example, when I had to spell North Carolina, I spelled it North *Care a line a* which makes a lot more sense than Carolina!
>
> **S:** How did you know how to spell "North," for example.
>
> **B:** Well, after you learn that the "th" sound is *th*, you can sound out the *nor*. The older you are, the more you know how to spell, not because you're smarter or anything, but because you've done it before. (Siamon, 1991)

Strategy checklists can be displayed in writing centres, and there can be ongoing discussion about the *why*, *how*, and *when* of using these strategies. These discussions could include questions such as the following:

- Which spelling strategies might be useful for this word?
- Which strategy did you choose?
- Why did you choose it?
- How did it work for you?

Spelling Strategies Checklist

- ☐ I say the word carefully.
- ☐ I draw a shape around the word.
- ☐ I think of a memory trick to remember the word.
- ☐ I write the word in syllables.
- ☐ I write the word with spaces for the hard letters.
- ☐ I think of the other words with the same spelling pattern.

Figure 10.2

AUDITORY STRATEGIES

While it's true, as Richard Lederer says (1998, p. 142), that the problem with English orthography is "the considerable distance that stretches between the sounds of our words and their spelling," sound-based or phonological strategies are still very important across the span of learning to spell. We may have "two languages, one spoken, and one written" (Lederer, p. 142); still, English is an alphabetic language, and we always begin with the attempt to link sound to symbol.

Younger children in particular use auditory strategies like sounding-out to spell a word they want to write. Older learners still find auditory strategies useful for spelling unknown words. The following auditory strategies offer a range of ideas to try with students:

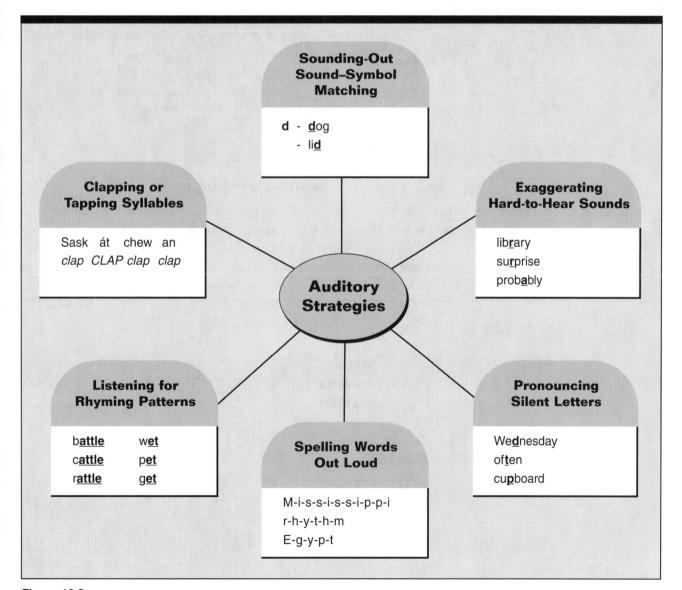

Figure 10.3

SOUNDING-OUT

For young students, or those learning English as a second language, it is useful to use pictures to reinforce the relationship between the sounds they hear and the letters used to symbolize the sounds. Some students may have difficulty distinguishing between sounds such as *b* and *p*, *d* and *t*, as well as vowel sounds. For sounding-out, it's essential that students hear and enunciate speech sounds clearly, so that they don't spell *bastek* instead of *basket* or *pasgetti* instead of *spaghetti*. You can use picture cards or objects, and a series of questions such as the following to focus students' attention on the sounds of words:

dog

What do you see in the picture?
Say the word *dog* carefully.
What sound do you hear at the beginning?
What sound do you hear at the end?

EXAGGERATING HARD-TO-HEAR SOUNDS

In words such as *library* and *surprise*, the first *r* is difficult to hear. Most people said *libary* before they learned to say *library* and *Febuary* before they learned to say *February*. Many spellers exaggerate the *r* to help them remember the spelling of these words.

You may want to display in the classroom a list of words with hard-to-hear sounds. Alternatively, have students begin personal word lists, with the tricky letters highlighted:

Words With Tricky Letters

lib<u>r</u>ary
su<u>r</u>prise
Feb<u>r</u>uary
prob<u>a</u>bly
enviro<u>n</u>ment

PRONOUNCING SILENT LETTERS

English words are full of silent letters. When these are part of a spelling pattern, like the silent *e* in *cake*, they usually don't pose a problem. However, when they seem to be "just thrown in" as in *Wednesday*, it is difficult to remember them.* Many good spellers use a strategy of pronouncing these silent letters as they write the words. For example, they pronounce the highlighted letters in these words: *parli**a**ment*, *sci**s**sors*, *ju**d**ge*, and *comb**e**d*.

SPELLING WORDS OUT LOUD

Sometimes saying the entire sequence of letters for words such as *rhythm* and *rhyme* assists with the spelling of these words. Some of us may remember learning to spell a word like *Mississippi*, when it was fun to chant the sequence of letters for their repetition and rhythmic sound:

> M-i-s-s,
> i-s-s,
> i-p-p,
> i

LISTENING FOR RHYMING PATTERNS

You can reinforce the idea of rhyme by reading rhyming verses to students and putting special emphasis on words that rhyme. Dennis Lee's "Alligator Pie," for example, is good for this purpose.

> "Alligator **pie**, alligator **pie**,
> If I don't get some I think I'm gonna _____."

You then pause while students chime in with the rhyming word. Later, write the lines on chart paper, and highlight the rhyming words to show their similarity in spelling.

It is important to provide students with enough experience listening to rhyme so that they can generate rhyming words easily. (See sources for rhyming poetry in Appendix B.)

CLAPPING OR TAPPING SYLLABLES

In many languages, each syllable is spoken with the same stress and duration. In English, though, there are strong and weak stresses on syllables, and the weak ones are said quickly. Clapping or tapping the syllables of longer words such as *restaurant*, *family*, or *probably* helps students, particularly those learning English as a second or third language, to hear these unstressed syllables.

Clapping or tapping syllables is also a useful way to help students hear the syllable boundaries in words. You can begin with their names, then go on to words from subject themes or place names:

Cal	gar	y		ther	mom	e	ter
CLAP	*clap*	*clap*		*clap*	*CLAP*	*clap*	*clap*

Teaching TIP

In Canada, we frequently see the alternate spelling of *traveled* instead of *travelled*, *center* instead of *centre*, and *color* instead of *colour*. This can provide "interference" for the visual learner.

VISUAL STRATEGIES

Some students are fortunate—they are naturally visual spellers. They see a word and remember what it looks like. For non-visual learners, visual strategies have to be learned and practised.

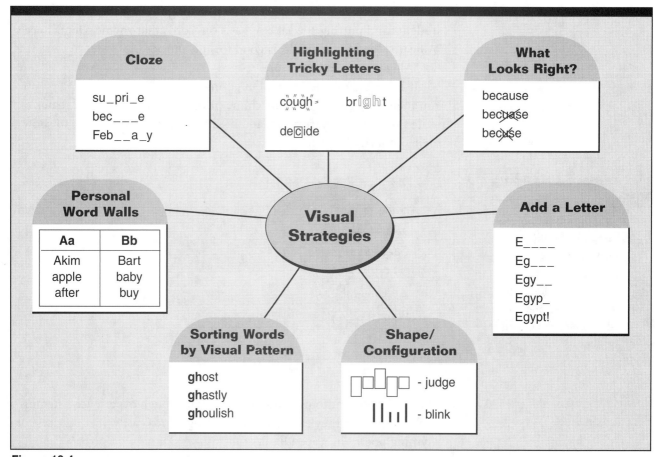

Figure 10.4

Visual strategies are very important for beginning spellers, as a high percentage of the top 100 most frequently used words do not follow sound patterns (as in the numbers *one, two, four,* and *eight*). For this reason we talk about a bank of "sight words" that beginners will see often in their reading and need to write often as well. For example, in "I love you," which is the first sentence many children learn to write, only the word *I* is spelled phonetically!

CLOZE

In the Cloze Strategy, students learn to "close" the blanks with the correct letters. For example, if they have written *becuase,* they would be presented with **b e c __ __ s e**. Only the two misspelled letters need to be added. This strategy works well because it directs the students' attention to the part of the word that needs to be studied. It also shows students that they already know five of the seven letters, and have only two to master. Instead of the teacher or editing partner crossing out or circling an incorrectly spelled word, cloze provides a scaffold for the learner to write it correctly.

With practice, students can learn to write words with missing "tricky" letters for themselves as a study guide.

HIGHLIGHTING TRICKY LETTERS

Using a similar strategy, students can highlight tricky letters in a number of interesting ways. The point here is for students to highlight the letters that they find difficult to spell, and to choose a highlighting technique that works for them and will leave a visual impression. For example:

Highlighting Difficult Letters

Students can

- use a highlighter pen — light

- write the letters in a different colour — success

- write the letters much larger or on a slant — lib**r**ary

- use capital letters — frIEnd

- shade or box the letters — Tues day

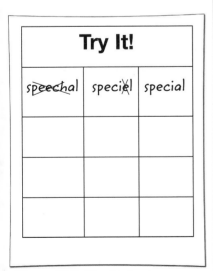

Try It!

speechal	speci x l	special

Figure 10.5 "Try-it" sheet

WHAT LOOKS RIGHT?

The What-Looks-Right? Strategy should be familiar to most adult spellers. When uncertain about the spelling of a word, adults write it several ways and then pick the one that "looks right." Encourage students to use this strategy by having them complete "try-it" sheets during writing activities.

ADD A LETTER

The Add-a-Letter Strategy works well for those words a person has the most trouble learning to spell (sometimes referred to as "spelling demons"). It is a way of visually reinforcing the sequence and number of letters. The student writes the first letter of the word and leaves blanks for the others. Each time the word is written, a letter is added.

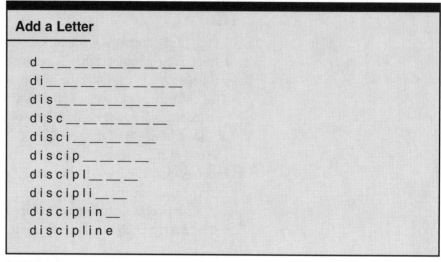

Figure 10.6

SHAPE/CONFIGURATION

Shape/Configuration Strategies can help students to create a sharp picture of a word. These strategies will be particularly useful as students encounter words that don't have regular spelling patterns. Drawing shapes around the words, boxes for each letter, or lines to suggest the height of the letters are effective techniques for students who respond to the overall form of the word rather than letter-by-letter sequences.

SORTING WORDS BY VISUAL PATTERN

In this strategy, students are given sets of word cards to sort according to visual patterns. For example, students can sort words according to whether they double a consonant or drop the final *e* when adding *-ing*, and then discuss what these words have in common (see Figure 10.8).

Figure 10.7

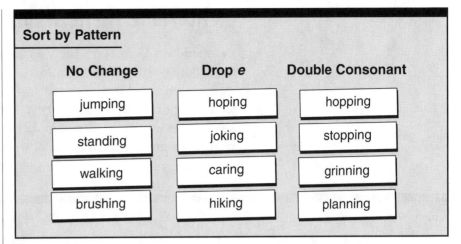

Sort by Pattern

No Change	Drop *e*	Double Consonant
jumping	hoping	hopping
standing	joking	stopping
walking	caring	grinning
brushing	hiking	planning

Figure 10.8

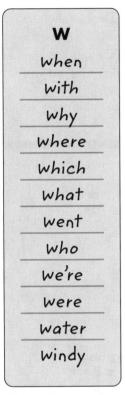

W

when
with
why
where
which
what
went
who
we're
were
water
windy

Figure 10.9

PERSONAL WORD WALLS

Just as a classroom Word Wall can be a good reference for writing, Personal Word Walls that students keep in a writing folder or in a separate notebook can reinforce visual learning. Words can be listed under letters of the alphabet, and new words can be added later on. Once again, the emphasis is on students taking personal responsibility for words that they need to learn. One Grade 2 student, for example is pleased with the nice long strip of *w* words she has acquired over the year (see Figure 10.9).

Words sorted by pattern can also be displayed on cans used to hold pencils (Pinnell and Fountas, 1998), in mobiles, or on shapes such as leaves or stars.

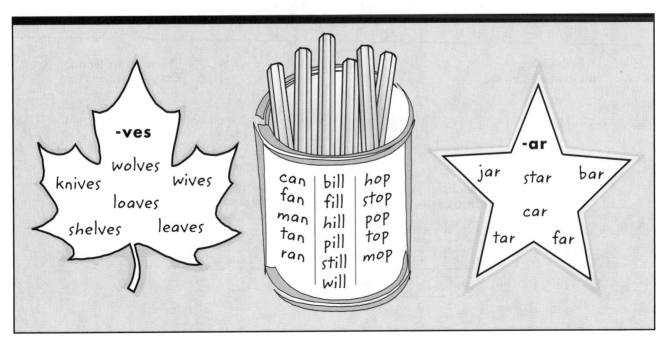

Figure 10.10

TACTILE/KINESTHETIC STRATEGIES

Many students learn best when they can make a mind–body connection. Tactile/kinesthetic learners require hands-on learning. They enjoy moving things around, and they are good at remembering the sequence of actions; for example, the sequence of letters used on a keyboard to spell a word. Letter tiles or cards, manipulative word games, or trying out words on an individual chalkboard are all strategies that appeal to the tactile learner.

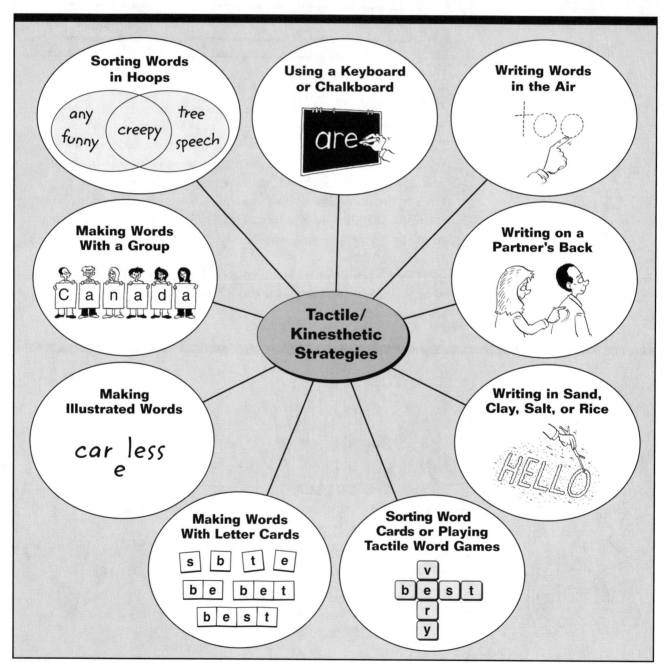

Figure 10.11

WRITING WORDS IN THE AIR

Large muscle movements, such as drawing huge letters in the air, appeal to learners who like to use their bodies. For very young students, you can model making letters with a pointing finger and large swoops of the hand to indicate direction and shape before students wrestle with fine motor control on paper.

WRITING ON A PARTNER'S BACK

Figure 10.12

Guess the Word is a game students enjoy playing with a partner. They use their fingers to "write" a letter or word on a partner's back, and the partner tries to guess what has been written. (This often leads to many repetitions!) To make it easier, students can choose words from a spelling list or a category such as animals, food, or names.

WRITING IN SAND, CLAY, SALT, OR RICE

Figure 10.13

Writing in sand, clay, salt, or rice is an activity suitable for the primary grades. It has the same principle as writing in the air; students practise "writing large" before they have to "write small." A classroom sandbox can be used, you can make individual salt boxes by painting the inside of a low box black and adding the salt, or students can inscribe modelling clay that they have rolled flat. They will enjoy using unusual writing tools—a stick, a feather, or a modelling tool. Young children can also roll modelling clay into a long roll and shape these into letters.

Older students can paint or print words using a variety of media, or draw shapes around words (see Figure 10.13).

SORTING WORD CARDS AND PLAYING TACTILE WORD GAMES

Sorting word cards and playing tactile word games are suitable activities for primary, junior, and intermediate students. Decks of word cards help students to observe and to explore words while they move the cards around in sorting activities. You can provide cards for open sorts where students decide the sorting principle and look for words that fit, or closed sorts that look for a special pattern. Students can also move around the room in word sorts. Each student has one card and puts herself or himself into the correct group, for example, silent *e* words.

MAKING WORDS

Games such as Scrabble, Boggle, or Spill and Spell also invite students to move letter tiles or cubes around to spell words. Using a variation of Patricia Cunningham and Barbara Hall's "Making Words" (Cunningham and Hall, 1994), you can supply students with the letters of a longer word, such as *tornado,* and have them make as many words as possible, anything from two letters to seven letters. Moving the letter cards around in different sequences helps students to explore the different ways words go together in patterns. (See Figure 10.14 on page 140.)

Making Words

n o t r a o d

two-letter words

d o   t o   n o   a n   o n

three-letter words

d o t   n o t   r o t

r o d   n o d

t a n   D a n   r a n

D o n   t o n   R o n

five-letter words

a d o r n

r a d o n

d o n o r

four-letter words

d o o r   r o o t

t o r n   d a r n

r o a d   t o a d

seven-letter words

t o r n a d o

Figure 10.14

Figure 10.15

MAKING WORDS WITH A GROUP

Having students move large letter cards into position as a "life-size word" can reinforce difficult concepts such as contractions, where letters must be dropped and apostrophes put in their place.

Provide students with large 11 x 17 cards with the letters of the contractions and a brightly coloured apostrophe. Ask students to line up so that they spell a word combination such as *do not,* and then have them squeeze together until the *o* in *not* is pushed out of place and replaced by another student holding an apostrophe (see Figure 10.15).

MAKING ILLUSTRATED WORDS

A strategy that combines the tactile and visual modalities and is fun for older students is portraying words in a way that says something about their meaning, as in the examples below.

Figure 10.16

SORTING WORDS IN HOOPS

Sorting word cards into large hoops on the floor is a good strategy for students who like to learn while they are in motion. For example, they can sort short vowel words with *a*, *o*, and *i*. You can provide students with picture cards representing words with short vowels *a*, *o*, and *i*, as well as three large hoops for sorting. As a follow-up, students could make word cards to match some of the pictures.

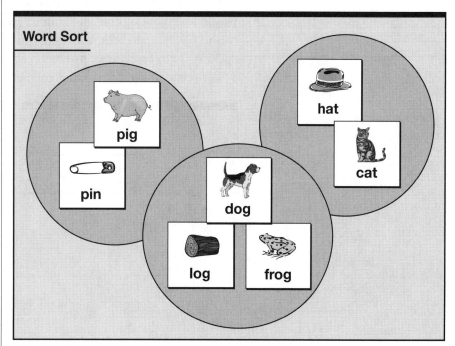

Figure 10.17

Just as a musician learns a sequence of notes on a piano, our fingers "remember" the sequence of letters that form words. Practising on a keyboard or individual chalkboard will help many students internalize the sequence of letters in a word.

Teaching TIP

If you are using a published spelling text with students, choose one that includes a variety of activities for learning words: visual, auditory (sound), tactile (feel), and morphological (meaning).

MEANING STRATEGIES

Learning to spell English words is a process with three main strands:

- alphabet
- pattern
- meaning

With the alphabet strand, students learn that the language is an alphabetic system. They discover that letters, arranged from left to right, represent speech sounds.

With the pattern strand, students become aware that words can often be grouped together by spelling pattern. The *night, sight, light, right* pattern is one of these. So is the vowel-consonant-consonant-vowel pattern of two-syllable words, such as *hopping* and *skipping*, where the vowel in the first syllable is short.

The meaning strand weaves in and out of the other two; it expands words in an ever-widening pool as students understand that the spelling of many words is linked to meaning.

Families of words such as *sign* and *signal* can be related in meaning. Suffixes and prefixes are parts of words that change meaning and have predictable spelling (but not sound) patterns, as do plural and verb forms. Greek and Latin roots often connect words by meaning as well as spelling, as in *psychology, psychiatry, psychic,* and *psychotic*. All these words relate to the Greek word *psyche*, meaning "mind or soul."

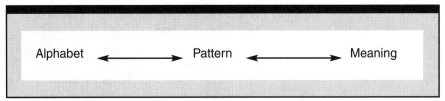

Figure 10.18

Source: (Bear, Invernizzi, et al, 2000, p. 5)

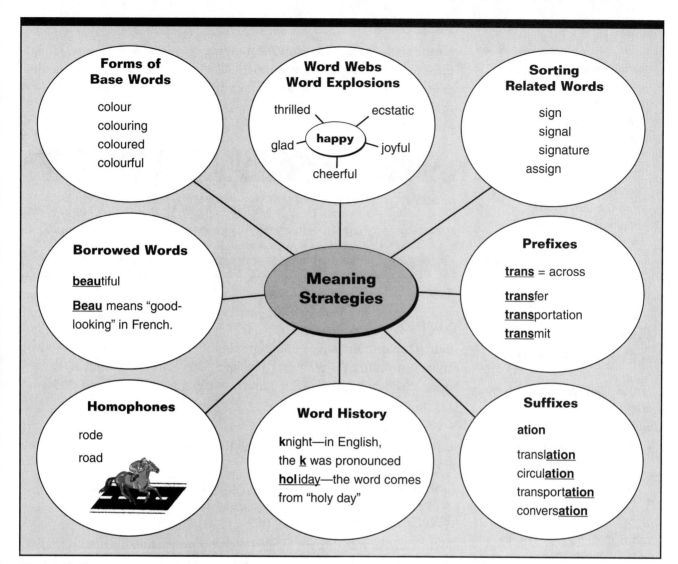

Figure 10.19

SORTING RELATED WORDS

The concept of related words is one key to unlocking the logic behind longer words. You can either provide students with a variety of base words and have them write the related or derived forms, or you can offer students word lists that represent base and related words. For example:

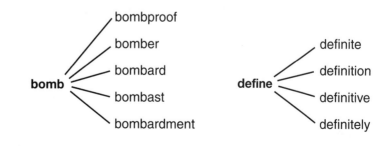

Figure 10.20

PREFIXES

Encouraging students to learn the meaning of common prefixes will help them to read and spell many multisyllabic words. They will realize that no matter what the pronunciation of the vowel in a prefix, the spelling is consistent (e.g., ri jois̀—*rejoice*; rē māk—*remake*). Students can group prefixes by meaning. For instance, *in*, *il*, *ir*, *im*, *un*, and *non* all mean "not."

in-	il-	ir-	im-	un-	non-
inactive	illegal	irregular	immature	unhappy	non-profit
incapable	illegible	irrelevant	improper	unknown	non-resident
inexpensive	illiterate	irresponsible	impure	unpopular	nonsense

Figure 10.21 "Not" prefixes

SUFFIXES

Suffixes that sound alike but are spelled differently can be confusing for students to learn; for example, *-sion* and *-tion*. Encourage students to make the meaning and spelling link between the base verbs and their noun extensions:

- **confuse/confusion**
  Don't *confuse* me. He got lost in all the *confusion*.

- **tense/tension**
  She is very *tense*. There's a lot of *tension* before a performance.

WORD HISTORY

Many English words have changed their pronunciation over the centuries, but not their spelling (Johnston, 2001). Some of these words have silent letters that were once pronounced. Others have letter combinations that have changed in sound. For example, the *kn* in *knight* was once pronounced, as was the *gn* in *gnaw* and the *gh* in *rough* and *high*.

There are many words that are linked to their historical meaning. Why is there an *h* in the middle of *shepherd*? Because a *shepherd* used to **h**erd sheep. Why is the first syllable in **break**fast spelled as *break*? Because it originally meant "to *break* the night's *fast*." Students can search their dictionaries for the historical reasons behind the spellings of interesting words.

-*sion* and -*tion*

/*sh*/ is often spelled *si*, usually after *l*, *n*, or *r*:

- expulsion   convulsion
- dimension   extension
  suspension   mansion
  tension
- conversion   diversion
  subversion

/*sh*/ is most often spelled *ti*, after a consonant, a long *a*, or a short *i*:

- action   election
- association   station
  education
- position   competition

BORROWED WORDS

More than a quarter of English words come from the French language. Many other languages have also provided English with a variety of new words, and the original spelling of these words is usually retained. Knowing the etymology of these borrowed words can greatly help students understand their spelling. The word *study*, for example, originally comes from the Latin word *studium*, meaning "to apply oneself with zeal" or "to study." *Studio*, *student*, and *studious* all relate to the Latin root.

INTERESTING ORIGIN

When short stories became popular in the 14th to 16th centuries, they were called, in Italian, *storie novelle*, meaning "new stories."

Words	Meaning
Dutch—**cookie**	from *koekje*, meaning "little cake"
Algonquian—**caribou**	from *xalibu*, meaning "one who paws or scratches," like a caribou in the snow pawing for grass
Arabic—**al**	the word for *the* in Arabic appears in many words adopted from this language: *al*gebra, *al*cohol, *al*falfa, *al*cove
German—**kindergarten**	a garden (*garten*) for children (*kinder*)

Figure 10.22 Borrowed words

FORMS OF BASE WORDS

It is important for students to understand that many multisyllabic words are inflected forms of base words. You can have students create word webs and charts that show these word relationships, as in the examples below:

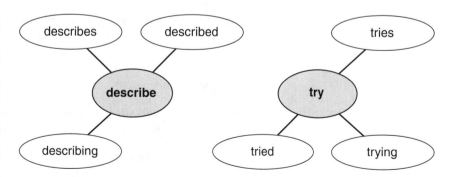

Figure 10.23

WORD EXPLOSIONS

The concept of related words can be applied to many words from other curriculum areas. Have students create word explosions for topics they are studying. For example, in history or social studies, the word *nation* can be extended in many directions:

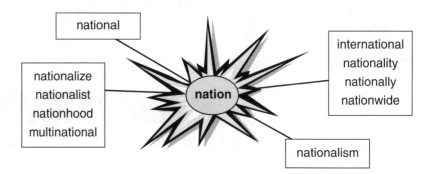

Figure 10.24 Word explosion: building on the base word *nation*

HOMOPHONES

Words that sound the same but are spelled differently are difficult for any speller. Most of us have tripped up on *their*, *there*, and *they're*, or on *it's* and *its*. Recently, in a large bookstore, a sign for a Mother's Day exhibit read "**Your** the best Mom in the world!" An annoyed customer had corrected the mistake, adding an apostrophe and an *e* to write *You're*.

Homophones

Focusing on meaning is the key to spelling homophones. Lists can be displayed in the classroom, and students can use activities like those that follow to link words to meanings:

- Have students write sentences and paragraphs in which they leave blanks for homophone pairs and challenge a partner to fill them in.
  (Your, You're _____ beautiful, _____ brother)

- Suggest to students that they brainstorm homophone pairs, and then use mime to demonstrate the differences in meaning.

- Encourage students to play homophone word games. An excellent selection can be found in *Hey, Hay! A Wagonful of Funny Homonym Riddles* by Marvin Terban.

- Suggest that students draw pictures to illustrate homophones (e.g., *pair*, *pear*, *pare*). Visual representation assists many students in remembering the differences in meaning.

Mnemonics comes from the Greek word *mnemonikos*, meaning "remember."

MEMORY TRICKS AND MNEMONICS

The word *mnemonic* means "aiding or intending to aid memory." (It certainly requires a special effort of memory to remember how to spell the word itself!) While spelling research has shown that people don't memorize by rote all the words they need to spell, for some words, attention to sound, patterns, or meaning cues is insufficient. For such words, students need to develop individual memory strategies or tricks that work for them.

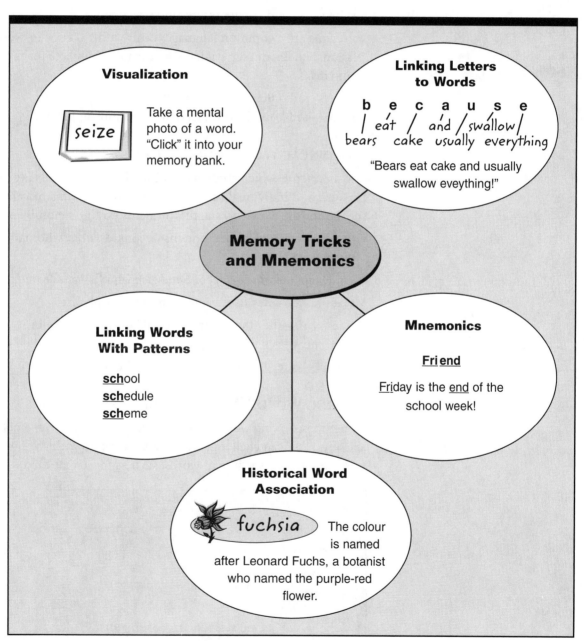

Figure 10.25

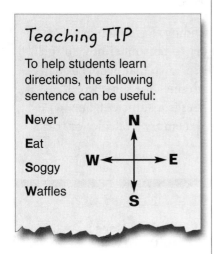
LINKING LETTERS TO WORDS

Letter-to-word connections have traditionally been used by students to learn complex concepts and formulas. The first letter of each word stands for a letter or a word to be memorized. For example, to learn the planets and their order out from the sun, a sentence such as following might be helpful:

- **M**y **v**ery **e**nergetic **m**other **j**ust **s**wam **u**nder **n**ine **p**iers!
- Mercury, Venus, Earth, Mars, Jupiter, Saturn, Uranus, Neptune, Pluto

The same strategy can be used to learn difficult-to-spell words:

- skiing—**S**ix **k**ids **i**nvite **i**nteresting **n**ew **g**uests.

Acronyms are a common language feature of this letter-to-word relationship. Encourage students to learn the complete form of different acronyms:

- radar—**ra**dio **d**etecting **a**nd **r**anging
- scuba—**s**elf-**c**ontained **u**nderwater **b**reathing **a**pparatus

HISTORICAL WORD ASSOCIATION

The manner in which students associate ideas and words is a very personal and individual matter. However, there are historical associations, such as for the word *fuchsia*, that students do find helpful. For example:

- fuchsia—after a German botanist, Leonard *Fuchs*, who named the purple-red plant
- sandwich—after the Earl of *Sandwich* who first made one
- saxophone—after its inventor, Antoine Joseph *Sax*
- sideburns—after the American Civil War general, Ambrose Everett *Burnside*, who had them
- derrick—after *Derrick*, a 17th century London hangman

LINKING WORDS WITH PATTERNS

Sometimes, linking words in a sentence can help you remember unusual spellings. You can challenge students to come up with their own sentences to remember the spelling of words, such as those that follow:

scheme **sch**ool **sch**edule	(I have a ***sch***eme for a ***sch***edule at ***sch***ool.)
scissors **sc**ience	(I need ***sc***issors in ***sc***ience.)
sure **su**gar	(You ***su***re eat a lot of ***su***gar!)

VISUALIZATION

There are a variety of visual strategies students can use to help them reinforce memory. Some examples follow:

Visual Strategy Activities

- Have students close their eyes and visualize themselves writing a word, letter-by-letter, on a mental screen. Then have them take a mental photo of the word to store in their memory banks.

- Invite younger students to paint words using a variety of media, including sponges, finger paint, brushes of various sizes, and vegetable prints. Students could add illustrations to link meaning to words.

- Ask students to make drawings that illustrate the different meanings of words.

green house

greenhouse

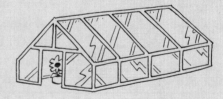

USING THE DICTIONARY

Some students may ask, "How do you check the spelling of a word in a dictionary if you don't know how to spell it?" This is a good question. Students need strong dictionary skills to use a dictionary as a tool for spelling. They need to be skilled at using guide words and alphabetizing to the second and third letter. These basic dictionary skills are an essential part of a word-study program. Other dictionary-related skills, which are beneficial for students to acquire, include the following:

1. Use the chart in the front of the dictionary, often labelled "Common Spellings of English Sounds," to help locate words.

2. Use the entry itself as a source of the spellings of variant forms of a word.

1. USING "COMMON SPELLINGS OF ENGLISH SOUNDS"

If a student looks up *psychology* under *s*, or *wrench* under *r*, his or her search will be fruitless. Many students who rely on sound cues give up on dictionaries without realizing this is a resource to help them. Usually, at the front of the dictionary, students will find a "Common Spellings of English Sounds" chart that can be a valuable resource for spelling. (See Chapter 7, "Reading and Spelling," for an example of this chart.)

Dictionary Activities

Have students use a dictionary to complete the activities that follow, which will give them practice using the "Common Spellings of English Sounds" chart:

- Ask students to find three ways to spell *s*, *r*, and *k* at the beginning of words, and write the words.

- Have them look for three ways to spell *f*, *ch*, and *sh* in the middle of words, and write an example for each.

- Have them find three ways to spell the *j* sound at the end of words, and write the words.

---

2. USING THE DICTIONARY ENTRY

A dictionary entry is a treasure-trove of information. Aside from the definition of a word, it also provides a great deal of spelling information. In Figure 10.27 on page 151, from the *Gage Canadian School Dictionary*, many of these elements and features are present: related words, irregular plurals, and inflected verb forms. In this dictionary, some homophones are listed as "confusables," while in the *Gage Canadian Intermediate Dictionary* (see Figure 10.26), homophones appear at the end of the entry, sometimes accompanied by an etymological note.

> **role** or **rôle** (rōl)   **1** a performer's part in a play, opera, etc.: *the leading role.*   **2** a part played in real life: *She played an important role in Canadian history.*   *n.*
> ☛ *Hom.*   ROLL.
> ☛ *Etym.*   From F *rôle,* earlier *roule,* originally the roll of paper, etc. on which an actor's part was written. 17c.

Figure 10.26

Ensure that students become familiar with the useful tools that dictionaries provide in the front matter. Students should note that regular forms of the plural, verb tenses, and adjective forms, such as *flowers, watching,* or *longest,* are not usually given in the dictionary. However, when there is a spelling change, these forms are often listed, as in *tired, happier,* and *described.*

Teaching TIP

Although the "Common Spellings of English Sounds" chart is useful for spelling the middle and endings of words, it's the first column, the beginning spellings, that will help students to avoid frustration when using a dictionary. Think of the word *chaos* for example—is it spelled *kaos* or *caos*? No, it's *chaos,* like *chemistry* or *chasm.*

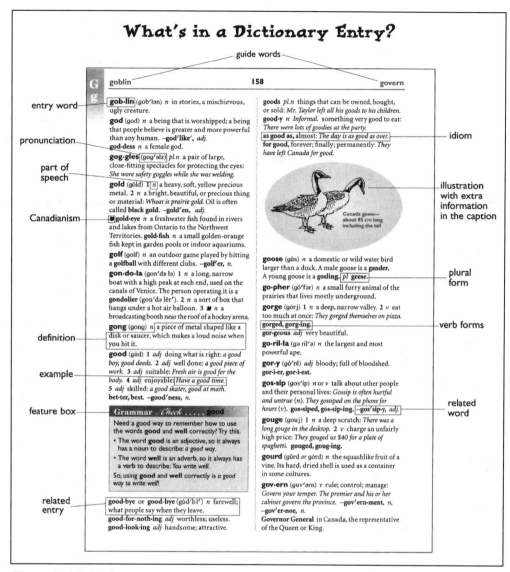

Figure 10.27 Dictionary entry key

Dictionary Entries

Have students complete an activity such as the one below that focuses on helping them to read dictionary entries with ease:

- Ask students to write the entry word they would look for to find these words:

terrified	parties
largest	children
funniest	geese

- For practice with homophones, have students look up homophone pairs and use each word in a sentence that shows its meaning:

rode—road	council—counsel
plain—plane	principal—principle

STRATEGIES TO SUIT THE LEARNER

Howard Gardner's theory of multiple intelligences (1983) proposes that the brain has many ways of learning. Gardner, using ideas derived from neurobiology, psychology, anthropology, philosophy, and history, suggests that there are seven distinct types of intelligence (Gardner has since added an eighth intelligence, the Naturalist). If we apply this idea to spelling, we can divide spelling strategies under seven corresponding headings.

Multiple Intelligences and Strategies for Spelling

1. **Verbal Linguistic**	Listening to sounds/ rhythm of words	Responding to word play, puns, jokes	Looking for order in words/syntax	Understanding meaning of words; semantics
2. **Logical Mathematical**	Observing word patterns	Analysing relationships (e.g., analogies)	Solving riddles, puzzles, codes	Categorizing/ classifying; venn diagrams
3. **Visual/ Spatial**	Noticing word shapes, configuration	Observing sequence of letters	Visual puzzles/ cloze	Charts, trees, visual groupings
4. **Musical/ Rhythmic**	Recognizing and producing rhyme	Recognizing rhythm; clapping and tapping syllables	Appreciating stress (e.g., *présent/presént*)	Enjoying alliteration, assonance, sounds of words
5. **Bodily Kinesthetic**	Keyboarding; practising letter sequence	Writing words on backs, in air, in sand	Manipulating; putting letters in order	Painting/ modelling
6. **Interpersonal**	Sharing spelling tips/strategies	Talking about learning spelling	Peer editing	Making class charts and books
7. **Intrapersonal**	Reflecting on spelling strategies; spelling self-image	Keeping a personal word list/spelling diaries	Understanding spelling strengths and weaknesses	Charting spelling growth; setting personal goals

Figure 10.28

It is important not to categorize students into any one type of intelligence. A variety of activities, from musical to intrapersonal, can be used to help students explore words and increase their oral and written vocabularies. Gardner's greatest contribution with the idea of multiple intelligences is to remind educators that there are many ways to learn, and that teachers need to be creative in helping students choose strategies that fit them and their learning styles.

SUMMARY

This chapter has presented the following main ideas:

1. **Children need to be strategic learners when it comes to spelling.**
   The best spelling strategy fits the learner and the word to be learned.

2. **Students need a wide range of spelling strategies. These can be divided into six main areas:**
   - Auditory Strategies
   - Visual Strategies
   - Tactile/Kinesthetic Strategies
   - Meaning Strategies
   - Memory Tricks and Mnemonics
   - Using the Dictionary

3. **Although there is a developmental sequence from auditory to meaning strategies as students' vocabulary increases, many students use a range of strategies throughout their learning.**

4. **Students need to reflect on and talk about how they select and use strategies.** This discussion should be part of the learning process whether it is instruction or assessment.

5. **Each category of strategies has a variety of activities to choose from to support learning.** These should be appropriate to the age and developmental stage of the learners.

6. **Howard Gardner's theory of multiple intelligences lends support to the idea that there are many ways to learn words, and that the learning style should fit the student.**

REFLECTIVE THINKING

1. "The best spelling strategy suits the learner and the word to be learned." Reflect on your own learning style. What strategies would you employ to spell a difficult word such as *cappuccino*?

2. Conduct a "spelling strategy interview" in your classroom. It could be with a student, a small group, or the whole class. What new information did you acquire about the strategies your students employ to spell unknown words?

3. What interesting facts about the history and structure of English have you learned in this chapter? How might you share this information with your students?

4. What strategies have you found useful for teaching the spelling of homophones, such as *there/ their/ they're* and *it's/ its*? Did this chapter present any further ideas you would like to try?

5. How would you answer a student who asks, "How do I check the spelling of a word in the dictionary if I don't know how to spell it?" Which dictionary skills do you address in your literacy program?

The following chart provides links with other chapters in the book:

To learn more about...	see these chapters
Strategies for ESL students	Chapter 11, page 155
Strategies for struggling spellers	Chapter 12, page 170
Strategies for skilled spellers	Chapter 13, page 182

CHAPTER 11

Second-Language Learners

ESL Terms

▶ **ESL**—English as a Second Language: commonly used for ESL programs and ESL teachers

▶ **ESOL**—English for Speakers of Other Languages: commonly used to designate students

▶ **ELD**—English Literacy Development: used in some jurisdictions for students from areas where alternate varieties of English are spoken (also referred to as ESD— English as a Second Dialect)

SPELLING FOR ESOL STUDENTS

In workshops with teachers, the issue of spelling for English as a Second Language students often arises. Yet, a search through the literature reveals little advice for ESL teachers in terms of spelling beyond "have students use a spell check" (Teachers of English to Speakers of Other Languages [TESOL], 1997). We know, however, that teachers want and need to be aware of the special problems ESOL students have with English spelling. In this chapter, we examine those problems and offer some solutions. The chapter concludes with a language profile that contrasts English and Mandarin Chinese and highlights areas of specific concern. Ironically, many of these concerns, such as confusion over plural forms, verb tenses, and homophones, are the kinds of errors that spell checks don't catch.

One school librarian relates an incident that demonstrates how spelling difficulties can be compounded by electronic media. An ESOL student in her elementary school researched a project on the environment. She presented the librarian with a project on the Envirolet, an environmentally friendly toilet. A misspelling of *environment* had led the student to a very narrow topic and some interesting research!

In the same east-end Toronto school, more than 15 languages are represented. While this is perhaps an extreme example, many students come to classrooms in Canada and the United States speaking one or more languages other than English or a dialect of English (TESOL, 1997). Some students come to school having little or no formal education in their own countries. The number of languages varies with the region and the year, but many urban schools have students from a dozen or more language groups under the same roof. In this situation, "every teacher is a second-language teacher, whether assigned to that function or not" (Handscombe, 1989, p. 12).

In using labels like ESL or ESOL, it is important that there is no implication that these students are language deficient. Many of them already speak one, two, three, or more languages (Handscombe, 1989; Urzua, 1989; TESOL, 1997). In a multinational, multicultural world, this is definitely an advantage. We want these students to know that we value their cultural and linguistic resources. They help bring the whole world into the classroom.

Although ESOL students may be sent for part of the day to special ESL classes, integrating them into the mainstream classroom as quickly as possible produces the best results both in learning English and in becoming part of the community (Urzua, 1989; Handscombe, 1989; TESOL, 1997). Interactions between ESOL students and mainstream students create benefits for both groups. In a climate where many schools are cutting back ESL services, the classroom teacher is the key.

MYTHS ABOUT TEACHING ESL

Learning English is not an easy task. In her introduction to the 1997 TESOL document on ESL standards for elementary students, Deborah Short lists three long-standing myths about second-language teaching (TESOL, p. 4):

▶ **Myth 1:** ESOL students learn English quickly and easily just by being exposed to and surrounded by native English speakers.

Fact: Learning a second language is hard work. Even the youngest students do not simply "pick up" the language. It can take six to nine years for ESOL students to reach the same level of proficiency as native speakers.

▶ **Myth 2:** When ESOL learners can converse easily in English, they are proficient in the language.

Fact: Children require both spoken and written English to learn academic content and to demonstrate that learning. They need to be able to follow instructions, both oral and written, and to communicate in the appropriate voice and patterns.

▶ **Myth 3:** In the past, immigrant children learned English rapidly and assimilated into mainstream life.

Fact: Many immigrant children in the last century did not learn English quickly or well. Many dropped out of school to work in jobs that did not require the level of English proficiency students will need in today's labour market.

These myths are important when it comes to word study: vocabulary development, word usage, spelling, grammar, and punctuation. ESOL students do not learn these skills by immersion in the culture; it takes time and good teaching. Word-study skills are vital for the sort of written communication that will help students succeed academically and in their future lives. They need academic competence, which includes literacy skills, learning strategies, and formal language, to complete assignments and meet assessment goals (Carrasquillo and Rodriguez, 1995). These skills must be taught.

In this wider context, social fluency—playground knowledge of English—is not enough. For academic presentations and writing, students must consider purpose, audience, and setting, and choose an appropriate language register, a choice that native speakers often make unconsciously. As an example, ESOL students must be able to identify and choose a more formal register when writing reports or taking a standardized test (Beckett and Haley, 2000).

> Most ESL/ELD students are able to use English to communicate in social situations and day-to-day classroom interactions within one to two years. However, students may require from *five to seven years* to develop the ability to understand the academic language used in textbooks and to use English to express the increasingly complex and abstract concepts encountered in the higher grades. (Ministry of Education, Ontario, ESL Document 2001, p. 11)

"…students may require from five to seven years to develop the ability to understand the academic language used in textbooks…" (ESL Document, 2001, p. 11).

WORD-STUDY SUPPORT FOR ESOL STUDENTS

To assist ESOL students in developing word-study skills, the following resources can provide valuable support, with study resources particularly important in the senior grades:

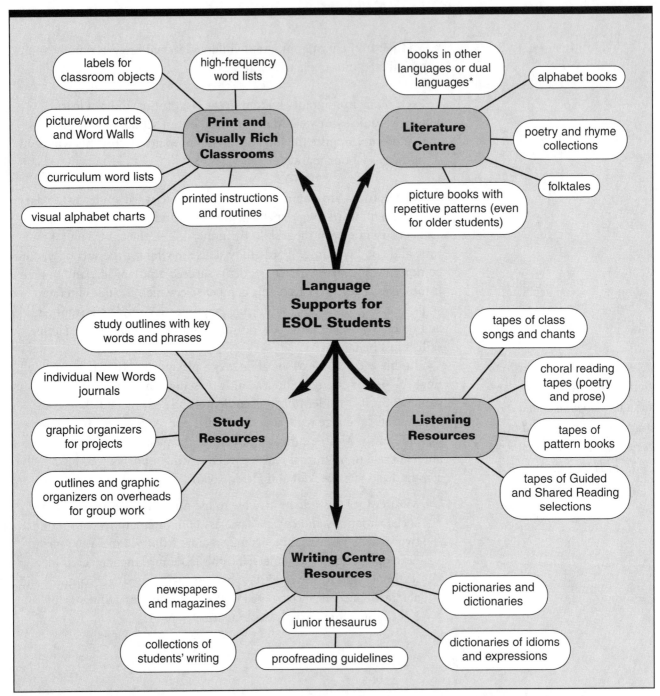

Figure 11.1 *One children's librarian in a multicultural school tells us that dual-language picture books, such as Eric Carle's *The Very Hungry Caterpillar*, which is published in English and Spanish, are valuable resources for ESOL students of all ages and their parents. They are available from specialty bookstores.

TUNING IN TO CHILDREN'S LANGUAGE

In her book, *The Languages of Learning*, Karen Gallas relates the story of Grade 2 student Imani who struggled with the question, "Where does the butterfly come from?" Imani, Gallas realized, did not know the word for *caterpillar*. Although Gallas used the word *caterpillar* often in her science lesson, she had never slowed down and pronounced it clearly. "The words I used just blended together and were indistinguishable from one another" (Gallas, 1994, p. 47). Imani also had gaps in her everyday language, particularly where abstract words such as *list, reptiles, grouping,* and *neighbourhood* were concerned. She had had limited schooling in her home country in Africa.

By learning more about Imani's dialect (Imani was listed as an English speaker) and making notes about it, Gallas narrowed the communication gap. The language differences she noted in her teaching journal are the sort that complicate all aspects of word study, from oral communication to spelling.

Teaching Journal

1. Imani's dialect has no negatives. Negative is denoted by stress.
   I *can* do it. (I can't do it.)
   I can *do* it. (I can do it.)

2. Imani's dialect has no final consonants.
   gih—girl
   buh—book

3. Imani's dialect has no plurals.
   gih—girl
   gih—girls

(Gallas, p.45)

Figure 11.2 Gallas's notes on Imani's language

Although Imani needed to learn to use final consonants and plural and negative forms to function academically, her dialect of English is a legitimate language that now finds expression in contemporary African literature. For example, when one teacher was teaching English in East Africa, she came across this phrase in a Grade 7 student's composition: "It was *arounding ten* on a rainy morning, when I first drew breath on this dear earth." Stunned by the beauty of the phrase, she didn't tell the student that *arounding* is not an English word. In that context, for an African child in an African setting, it was a perfectly good word, capturing the lilting cadence of the child's speech much more accurately than a synonym such as *nearly* or *around*.

In a Canadian setting, she would still praise the "rightness" of the word, but she might also point out the alternatives and have a group discussion about how each synonym is used. For example, *nearly ten* usually means "before the hour of ten," while *about* or *around ten* means "either before or after the hour of ten."

INTERACTIVE LEARNING: TEACHING STRATEGIES FOR ESL

A classroom teacher like Karen Gallas is often the bridge between newcomers and the classroom community. Interaction with the teacher leads to interactions with other students in a comfortable, friendly atmosphere where the new student feels safe to use her or his new skills, and receives positive feedback for communicating in English (Beckett and Haley, 2000; Lindfors, 1989). Some teaching strategies that encourage interaction in English are suggested below:

TEACHER-MODELLING THROUGH DIALOGUE JOURNALS

Dialogue journals—where students write and teachers respond—are an excellent introduction to English for learners of any age. You, as the teacher, respond to the content of the students' response, without marking errors. Instead, you provide a model of correct sentence structure, vocabulary, spelling, and punctuation. Adults use a similar strategy when they interact with children learning to speak, expanding one-word comments such as "Dog!" to whole sentences such as "Yes, darling, that's a big dog, isn't it?" Or they supply the correct past tense to an older child who says "I sleeped for a long time" by saying something like "You slept for hours!"

In responding to students' written responses or observations, teachers establish communication and offer students the chance to work out sound–symbol relationships and other patterns in a safe, authentic interchange. Peregoy and Boyle (1997, p. 170) offer this sample as a response to a child writing on the topic "What I Like to Do":

> Dec. 15: I like to play whaat butterfly de vey like to do is play a round bks Butterfy is like to eat flsr.
>
> (*I like to play with butterfly day they like to do is play around bikes. Butterfly is like to eat flowers.*)
>
> Teacher responded: I have never played with a butterfly before. It sounds like fun.

Dialogue journals also offer an excellent opportunity to observe students' progress and to plan for instruction. As a teacher looking at the student sample on the previous page, for example, you might observe that the student

- may not hear or know how to spell the *th* sound in *they* and *with*
- leaves out vowels in words such as *bikes* (*bks*) and *flowers* (*flwrs*)
- spells many sight words such as *like*, *play*, and *eat* correctly
- may not understand the plural: "Butterflies like to eat" becomes "Butterfly *is* like to eat." The student may be hearing "butterflies" as "butterfly is."

TEACHER-DIRECTED GROUP WORK

As a next step, teachers can integrate individual ESOL students into small groups that are working with pattern books, big books, songs, and chants. The repetitive language and rhythm of these selections can help students grasp the sounds and intonation patterns of the language. Here we have interaction between the ESOL student and other students in the group, supported by the teacher. ESOL students can mouth the words and sing or chant the parts they know. With encouragement from both the teacher and the group, they will join in more fully as they feel more competent.

Once the songs, stories, or poems are familiar to the students, they can be presented on large sheets of chart paper and used as a scaffold for learning syntax, semantics, morphology, phonology, and pragmatics. (See Figure 11.3 on page 162.)

Cumulative stories, such as *The Gingerbread Boy* or *Chicken Little*, have the repeating patterns so attractive to young children and useful for teaching ESOL students of any age. There are also cumulative songs, such as "She'll be Coming 'Round the Mountain," and poems such as "This Is the House That Jack Built." (This poem is particularly useful because of the repetition of the short *a*, a sound that many ESOL students struggle with.)

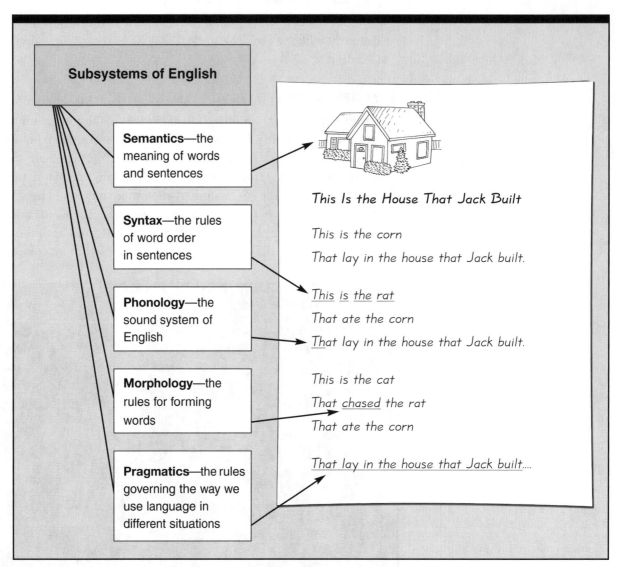

Figure 11.3 Subsystems of English

Once students are familiar with the poem or song, you can model printing it on chart paper, sweeping your hands from left to right as the students recite. Or, you can use a frame to isolate particular words and highlight sounds with coloured markers.

In addition to traditional stories, rhymes, poems, and songs, contemporary poetry that has strong speech rhythms can also be used:

Starshine

I'd like a cup of starshine please
mixed with milk and honey
And when it comes to soup
can I please
have some that's sunny?

By Romesh Gunesekera

WORD STUDY ACROSS THE LANGUAGE DIVIDE

It is a mark of respect for the students in your class who come from a variety of ethnic, cultural, and language groups, to find out as much as possible about their cultures and languages. Of course, it would be ideal if we could speak their languages, but usually this is not possible, apart from pronouncing their names correctly and learning a few words. At best, most people can struggle along in one, or possibly two, other languages. However, even this experience can help us empathize with the challenges a newcomer faces in encountering a new language.

We must be careful, in comparing languages, that we do not confuse difficulties with learning English with normal developmental stages. For example, a Grade 1 or Grade 2 student experiencing problems with multisyllabic words may be having trouble hearing unstressed vowels, a problem native speakers also experience at this stage. However, some difficulties ESOL learners face are certainly due to differences between English and their first languages.

Let's look at one language spoken by many newcomers: Mandarin Chinese. We can examine some of the areas where word-study problems may arise and look at some of the ways to offer extra support to Chinese learners of English.

Language Snapshot: Chinese

About one-fifth of the world's population speaks one of the Chinese dialects. The Mandarin dialect is the basis of the written language. Students who speak and/or write Mandarin Chinese come to us from many countries besides China, among them Malaysia and Vietnam. Not all students who speak Chinese as a first language will have problems with English spelling, grammar, and punctuation. However, Chinese and English belong to two different language families (Sino-Tibetan and Indo-European) and have major structural differences. Contrasts between the Chinese and English languages create areas of difficulty for many students.

Language Features

- Chinese uses compact ideograms to express whole ideas instead of letters to represent sounds, as in our alphabetic language. English appears "stretched out" and individual words may be hard to identify.

- Spelling problems arise because of pronunciation differences:
  - Chinese has fewer unstressed syllables and gives even these more stress than English. *Studying* may be written as *studing, unfortunately* as *unforually.*

- The phonology of Chinese and English is very different. To give a few examples:

  - Some English sounds have no equivalents. There is no *v, th, n,* or *z* in most dialects. Students can confuse words such as *night* and *light, thin* and *tin. Around* may be spelled as *aroud.*

  - Final consonants are rare and consonant clusters don't exist. Students may add a syllable, as in *sipoon* for *spoon,* or leave out a final consonant.

  - There are also many differences in vowel sounds. Chinese speakers generally hear no difference between the vowels in *eat* and *it.* There is no equivalent to short *o* as in *dog.*

- Differences in grammar are vast. For example:

  - In Chinese, there is no change in word order for questions.

  - Auxiliary verbs *be* and *do* are not used for questions or negatives.

  - Chinese expresses the idea of time very differently from English.

  - Chinese is not an inflected language (e.g., no endings such as *-s, -ing,* or *-ed*).

  - Differences in gender are not marked (e.g., by *he* and *she*).

  - There are no articles in Chinese.

  - Plurals are not expressed as in English (by adding *-s* or *-es*).

  - Some collective nouns in English, such as *weather* and *luggage,* are countable in Chinese.

Figure 11.4

DESIGNING ESL LEARNING ACTIVITIES

Besides benefiting from the interactive techniques mentioned earlier ESOL Chinese speakers need extra exposure to English print. It is important to choose a variety of learning modalities for ESL exercises: those emphasizing visual and tactile learning, as well as verbal learning. Many of the following activities are important for all students. Second-language learners can participate with the whole group, but may need more small-group practice.

---

1. Listen for the Sounds

Here is a poem that could be used with a group of older students to reinforce the long vowel sounds:

> *Butterflies*
> *By Chu Miao Tuan*
>
> *The blossoms fall **like snowflakes***
> *On the cool, **deep**, dark-**green** moss.*
> ***They lie** in **white-heap**ed **fragrant** drifts*
> *Before the courtyard **gates**.*
>
> *The butter**flies**, not **knowing***
> *That the **days** of spring are done,*
> *Still purs**ue** the **fly**ing petals*
> *Across the garden wall.*
>
> > *China, 18th century*
> > *Translated by Henry H. Hart*

- Model printing the poem on chart paper. Read it aloud as a group. Underline or highlight the words with long vowels. Then, contrast the words with long vowel sounds (*green*, *snow*) to the words with short sounds (*petals*, *moss*).

- Have one group develop a choral reading of the poem.

- Have small groups collect and record words with each long vowel sound. Print the words on cards and use them for open word sorts.

- Have the group write a new poem on the topic of *butterflies*. Or, have students draw or visually represent their impression of the poem.

2. Partner Jeopardy

In this activity, students work with a partner.* Have one partner write an answer on a card, such as "I got my socks at the mall." The challenge of his or her partner is to write the question, "Where did you get your socks?" Question words such as *how many*, *where*, *when*, and *what* can be supplied on cards.

I have two brothers.	**How many** brothers do you have?

> * **Note:** The Ontario Ministry of Education ESL document (2001) recommends choosing a co-operative, academically strong student partner (from the same language background, if possible) to work with a newcomer.

3. "See and Hear" Word Sort

Have students work with a partner or in a small group. Supply two hoops or ovals for sorting, and the following words on cards:

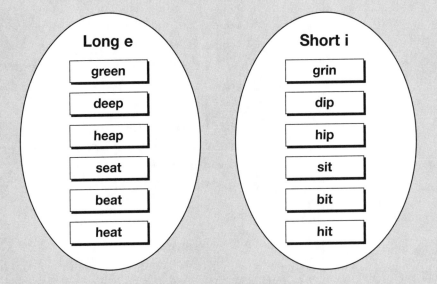

- To help students hear the difference between the long *e* and short *i* sounds, have them sort the word cards into two hoops or circles, and then say the words aloud. Words like *green/grin* are called "minimal pairs" because they are alike except for one sound. Students can then sort the words in the first oval by the two patterns for spelling the long *e*: *ea*, *ee*.

- Encourage students to work with a partner to write and share sentences using pairs of words:

  I **sit** in my **seat**.
  I **dip** my hand in the **deep** water.
  That **green** monster makes me **grin**.

KEEPING THE FAMILY INVOLVED

Students coming to Canada from other linguistic and cultural backgrounds need the support of their families to succeed in school (see Chapter 14, "Home Connections"). Families may be nervous and unsure about the school program, so the earlier and more consistently you can involve them, the better (Handscombe, 1989; Beckett, 1994). Teachers can

- Interview family members to find out as much as possible about students' educational background. Often, especially in the case of refugees, official school records may be difficult to obtain.

- Consider the students' social and emotional background. To assist in their adjustment to a new learning environment, involve their parents/guardians and other contacts from their community, perhaps counsellors and other family members, to gain as complete a picture as possible.

- Whenever possible, invite family members to help students share their culture with the whole group.

- Keep families informed about the word-study program in the school: how assessment is done, what is expected of their child, and how they can assist. Try to keep letters to be sent home simple and clear, or if necessary, find an interpreter to explain your program to parents/guardians.

Looking at Word Lists With ESOL Eyes

Examine the word list for potential pitfalls for ESOL students, such as
- ▶ silent letters
- ▶ consonant clusters
- ▶ unusual spellings of sounds, e.g., *ghost*, *rhyme*
- ▶ plurals and contractions
- ▶ homophones
- ▶ unstressed syllables

SUMMARY

This chapter has presented the following main ideas:

1. **Many students come to Canadian classrooms from other cultures.** They speak other languages, or English with a different dialect.

2. **English as a second language should not be a label that implies that students are language deficient.** It's important to recognize and value languages that students already know.

3. **Integrating students into the mainstream class as quickly as possible produces the best learning.**

4. **Myths about ESL suggest that students can learn English easily and quickly.** In fact, it takes from five to seven years for ESOL students to become fluent in English.

5. **Social fluency is insufficient for ESOL students.** They need a range of literacy and study skills to be able to function academically and in their future lives.

6. **Word-study supports for ESOL students include a classroom rich in literature, with many visual, listening, and study resources.**

7. **The teacher is the bridge between the newcomer and the classroom community.** Interactions with the teacher lead to interactions with other students.

8. **Co-operative learning is an effective strategy for ESL.** More advanced students (especially those speaking the same language) can act as interpreters and coaches. Encouraging ESOL students to respond as part of a group can help build newcomer confidence.

9. **It's a sign of respect for the languages of newcomers, as well as a useful planning tool, for teachers to learn the features of these languages,** especially those features that may cause special problems for acquiring word-study skills.

10. **The ESOL student's family is a key resource for evaluating his or her prior learning experience, and supporting his or her growth in English.**

REFLECTIVE THINKING

1. How many languages are represented by the students in your school? What resources are available to assist second-language learners?

2. The authors state, "Interactions between ESOL students and mainstream students create benefits for both groups." In your experience, what is the nature of these benefits? Are there also challenges?

3. Deborah Short lists three long-standing myths about second-language teaching (pp. 156–157). What are the implications of these myths or facts for word study with ESOL students?

4. As indicated in this chapter, families of ESOL students may be nervous and unsure about the school program. What specific steps could you and your school take to involve families in your spelling and writing program?

5. Does your school library contain literature and non-fiction materials that reflect a variety of cultures and language backgrounds? How might you acquire more such materials?

The following chart provides links with other chapters in the book:

To learn more about...	see these chapters
Spelling assessment	Chapter 3, page 32
Struggling spellers	Chapter 12, page 170
Home activities for parents/guardians and students	Chapter 14, page 196

Supporting Struggling Spellers

••

WHY DOES SPELLING MATTER?

One major reason why spelling matters is that being a struggling speller can have a devastating impact on self-esteem. Several years ago, we interviewed a ten-year-old student whose teachers were concerned about his poor spelling skills. He was tall, athletic, and loved to skateboard. As we talked, he described how embarrassed he felt whenever he was in a group and had to write. He believed his classmates thought he was stupid because he made spelling errors even in simple words. He said, "You know that television show called *Thrill of a Lifetime*? The one where they make your wishes come true? If I had one wish, I'd ask to wake up tomorrow morning and be a good speller." Not a world champion skateboarder, but "a good speller."

As teachers, how do we address this student's concern? Some teachers might assure him that spelling doesn't matter and that many very bright people are poor spellers. Yet spelling clearly does matter to this student, and he has already learned that correct spelling matters to other people— his peers, his parents, and his teachers.

Other teachers might advise him to use a spell check on the computer. Yet many errors are not picked up by this method— homophones, incorrect endings, word substitutions (*stitch* for *switch*), and words not in the computer's dictionary. Furthermore, if every other word in a composition is highlighted as an error, this student's discouragement will not go away.

Some teachers might simply tell him to be patient. It takes a long time to become a skilled speller, and he is likely just a slow starter. Eventually, he will catch up. While it is certainly true that spelling proficiency develops over many years, children who are significantly delayed in their spelling growth should not be left to flounder, nor should they be told that some people just can't spell.

"WE HAD A SPELLING BEE TODAY. I GOT STUNG ON THE VERY FIRST WORD."

All children (and adults) can become better spellers if they are given support that is geared to their needs and learning styles.

There are teachers who understand that all children (and adults) can become better spellers if they are given support that is geared to their needs and learning style. In this chapter, we outline five principles to help in planning instruction for struggling spellers.

Five Principles to Guide Instruction for Struggling Spellers
❶ Determine students' needs.
❷ Plan instruction.
❸ Conduct ongoing assessment throughout the school year.
❹ Use focused strategies.
❺ Determine what strategies will be most useful to students.

DETERMINING STUDENTS' NEEDS

Most struggling spellers show a delayed pattern of spelling development. In other words, their spelling attempts are not bizarre; they are simply not as advanced as the spelling attempts of their peers. These students have become "stuck" at some point in their spelling growth and need support to move forward.

Observing students' everyday writing, as well as the results of dictating lists of words, will reveal a great deal about their knowledge of the spelling system and the logic they use in spelling. Conversations with students about why they spell a word as they do are also a valuable source of insight for planning instruction. Ask them to identify where they were having difficulty and what choices they had to select from. At the same time, listen to students' patterns of speech. Are certain words mispronounced, indicating perhaps a hearing deficit or the use of a dialect?

It is helpful to focus on what students can do as spellers rather than on how far they are from producing perfect conventional spelling.

It is helpful to focus on what students *can* do as spellers rather than on how far they are from producing perfect conventional spelling. Most incorrect spellings are at least 75 percent accurate. Narrowing the focus to the one or two letters that are not correct puts less strain on memory and encourages students to keep trying.

You should also be aware of the normal process of spelling development. (See Chapter 1, "Learning to Spell.") Awareness of the stages of spelling development will provide you with some benchmarks for determining the needs of your students.

PLANNING INSTRUCTION

There are many ways to adapt spelling instruction to meet the needs of struggling spellers.

1. Use a combination of the following instructional techniques:
    -   Reduce the number of words students are expected to learn in a given time.
    -   Use these words frequently throughout the day.
    -   Break down the list into manageable chunks (e.g., three words a day for five days as opposed to 15 words at the beginning of the week).
    -   Use discretion in the number of errors noted when helping to proofread written work. Use the Cloze Strategy to indicate which letters are correct and which are not; for example, su_pri_e.

2. If you're using a published spelling program, select one that can be adapted to the needs of individual students. The activities you assign should be based on students' performance on a pre-test of the unit's words, as well as on information gleaned from how students apply conventions in their writing.

3. Use a variety of approaches to maintain interest and motivation, and to appeal to each student's preferred learning style. Try spelling games such as Boggle, Spill and Spell, Scrabble, and Word Mastermind, as well as computer software. Balance individual word study with peer tutoring, co-operative learning, and whole-class discussions.

4. Involve all students in a rich writing program that provides opportunities for sharing and publishing. In this way, there is a reason for editing and proofreading.

5. Teach proofreading skills and provide ample resources in the form of dictionaries, word lists, Word Walls, thesauruses, peer proofreaders, and classroom volunteers. Emphasize that the ultimate responsibility for correct spelling rests with the writer. Chapter 8, "Writing and Presenting," provides more information on proofreading.

6. Use a variety of graphic organizers to help students sort words into manageable categories and patterns.

CONDUCTING ONGOING ASSESSMENT THROUGHOUT THE SCHOOL YEAR

The best strategy is to combine both formal and informal methods of assessment to determine a student's spelling profile, to provide student feedback, and to inform teacher instruction. You can

- Track improved performance by comparing pre- and post-test results, examining the students' writing folders, and noting spelling in everyday writing.
- Provide concrete reinforcement through improvement graphs, stickers, or self-selected rewards appropriate for the students and their age.
- Encourage students to set goals and monitor their own progress through charts, learning logs, and conferences with the teacher.
- Ask students to reflect on which learning strategies work best for them. Chapter 3, "Spelling Assessment," offers more information on using ongoing assessment.

USING FOCUSED STRATEGIES

Many struggling spellers feel a sense of hopelessness when faced with the task of spelling new words. Research has shown that struggling spellers use only a narrow range of strategies for spelling and do not know how to select an appropriate strategy for specific words (Scott, 1991). Some children, for example, will try to sound out every word. This strategy is helpful for words such as *baby*, but not effective for words with silent letters (*ca_l_m*, *lis_t_en*) or schwa vowels (*depend_a_nt*, *independ_e_nt*).

Struggling spellers often do not realize that there are spelling patterns and rules that can be used to spell many words. Still other struggling spellers have learning disabilities or attention deficit disorders that make it very difficult for them to focus their attention. Some of these children have developed such strength in one modality, such as visual processing, that they have difficulty with the basic skill of sounding out words.

The following activities offer some focused strategies for spelling different types of words. Struggling spellers will often show significant improvement if they are instructed in the use of these approaches. However, spelling instruction for these students (and all others, for that matter) should be carried out in short, focused sessions of 10 to 15 minutes per day, not exceeding 60 to 75 minutes per week. **Furthermore, these activities should not take the place of rich language experiences in reading, writing, and oral language.**

"I neaver want to do this test agan!"

A Grade 6 student's comment at the end of a lengthy list of dictated words

Schwa Vowel

A *schwa vowel* /ə/ is a vowel in an unstressed syllable. Schwa vowels are often not clearly pronounced in everyday speech, as in *bask_e_t*

WHAT WORDS SHOULD BE STUDIED?

Struggling spellers should study words that will be useful to them immediately in their everyday work. You can place an emphasis on words that are part of their current reading and listening vocabularies, and on those that come from their writing. Be cautious, however, in limiting the spelling words to be studied to errors made by a student during writing, since many struggling spellers have learned to use simple vocabulary rather than taking the risk of making spelling errors. For example, a student may want to use the word *delicious* to describe a favourite dessert but substitutes *good* or *tasty* instead.

Lists of frequently misspelled words are good sources for word study (see Appendix C on page 206), especially for those words that do not fit normal spelling patterns. Specific spelling strategies can then be explored for recalling these words.

It is also important for struggling spellers to study word patterns rather than just a random list of high-utility words. The word *round*, for example, can be linked with other words in which the sound /ow/ is spelled *ou*, as in *out*, *loud*, and *house*. It also can be linked with the *-ound* word family, including *found*, *pound*, *hound*, and *mound*.

A well-planned published spelling program can provide effective support to struggling spellers in the systematic study of words. It is important to choose a text that is at the instructional level for the student (neither too easy nor frustrating), and that looks at both spelling patterns and spelling strategies.

INTRODUCING STRATEGIES

"Observations of good spellers has shown that they visualize with their eyes open and tend to look up briefly as they see the image" (Tarasoff, 1990, p. 38).

Before introducing any of the following strategies, you could explain to students the purpose of having a range of spelling strategies. For example, visual strategies help create a clear picture of the word in the brain. You can compare the brain to a camera and explain that many spelling errors result from a "photo" of the word being slightly out-of-focus. Visual strategies help to bring the word into focus so that the picture is clear and accurate.

Similarly, word families and analogy strategies create a "filing cabinet" in the brain so that words can be retrieved more easily. Words can be stored in folders of like words instead of being in a jumble on top of a messy desk.

Each spelling strategy should be modelled. You can demonstrate the thinking process out loud to explain each step in the use of the strategy.

Students then can practise the strategy and monitor their progress. Supports can be provided in the form of checklists of strategies, cue cards, classroom posters, learning logs, and so on. The strategies should be used in a variety of contexts, not just during formal spelling time. You will find opportunities for using them during the learning of words for other subject areas, studying for dictations, editing conferences, and impromptu times when you and the class brainstorm how to spell a tricky word.

DETERMINING WHAT STRATEGIES WILL BE MOST USEFUL

The following information presents strategies that may be particularly suitable for struggling spellers. Many of these approaches work best in a one-on-one setting and provide additional reinforcement beyond everyday classroom spelling activities. Consider sharing these strategies with the parents/guardians of struggling spellers so they can help their children at home. These strategies can also be modelled with "writing buddies" for use during the writing process.

1. Visual Strategies

Colour: Jeffrey Freed, author of *Right-Brained Children in a Left-Brained World*, suggests that many children who are right-brained have difficulty with auditory approaches but have strengths in the visual area. Freed advocates the liberal use of colour in teaching spelling, and notes that "Our left-brained schools teach spelling in black and white, usually using white chalk on blackboard" (p. 97). His experience has shown that children will pay more attention to letters on a screen if they are in colour. While his advice is geared to children with attention deficit disorders, it can also apply to a broad range of struggling spellers.

The use of colour can also show how words are built. Words can be broken into syllables, with each syllable presented in a different colour. Longer words can also be colour-coded according to base words, prefixes, and suffixes. For younger children, word families can be highlighted by using different colours for onset and rime.

Visualization: Both Freed and Mary Tarasoff (1990) suggest strategies for helping children see "a picture of the word in their minds." Freed recommends holding a paper on which the word is written at least a third of a metre away from the student. Direct the student to look at the word carefully until he or she can see it in his or her mind. Allow the student to take as much time as needed to "get a picture or snapshot" of the word. Then turn the paper face down and have the student spell the word *out loud*. If the spelling is correct, move on to another word.

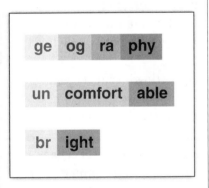

Freed also suggests asking specific questions about the targeted words after the student has gone through the visualization process; for example, "Which word has two *r*'s in the middle?" "How many *c*'s are in the word *success*?" Such questions can later become a game in which partners give clues about words on the list, and the other person must guess which word is targeted.

Tarasoff provides a variation on this visualization strategy. Using the analogy of a television screen or computer monitor, students are asked to imagine the screen, "watch" what is on it (to establish a clear picture), and then clear it off. A word is presented on the chalkboard or paper, and students are asked to "see" it on the screen and to notice the colour of the letters and the background.

Both Freed and Tarasoff recommend students "read the letters" forward and backward, relying only on their visual memory. This activity is intended to help students hold the image longer. The phrase "read the letters" rather than "spell the word" stops students from automatically using their habitual spelling strategies.

Invented Spelling and Visual Learners: The benefits of encouraging young children to use invented spelling in their writing drafts has been well supported in research (Cramer, 2001). Children in the early grades who use invented spelling show superior spelling skills both on dictated tests and in written composition.

Freed expresses concerns, however, in supporting invented spelling beyond the initial stages of composition for children who are strongly visual in their learning style. These children, if allowed to view an unconventional spelling too often (for example, *becuz* for *because*), may have difficulty re-learning the correct spelling. He advises teachers and families to encourage these children to ask how to spell unfamiliar words before writing them. Adults should also gently point out spelling errors as they assist these children.

Freed's advice, of course, could have the effect of minimizing risk-taking in spelling, with children learning to use only simple vocabulary that they already know how to spell. An alternative is to teach children a core of high-frequency words that will form the basis of their spelling vocabulary, and to expect these words to be used correctly in everyday writing. These "No Excuses Words" can be displayed on Word Walls. Invented spelling could still be encouraged for unfamiliar words, with proofreading skills being taught for effective editing.

2. Tactile Strategies

Hands-On Strategies: Many word-study techniques that are normally associated with the early grades can be very effective with older students as well. Hands-on strategies are particularly helpful for students who have strengths in the bodily-kinesthetic area.

Hands-On Activities

The following techniques highlight bodily movement and the sense of touch:

- Cut out letters from felt or sandpaper. Have students practise spelling and feeling the words.

- Students can use "wipe off" crayons on a plastic placemat to write the words.

- Students can illustrate spelling words so that the illustrations say something about the meaning of the word.

- Cut up letters and ask students to rearrange them to form the spelling words. Use letter tiles from Scrabble, Boggle, or Spill and Spell, or letters from other word-making activities in the same way.

- Have students trace words in the air, on the carpet, on their desks, or on a partner's back.

- Students can practise forming words with alphabet magnets, alphabet stampers, alphabet cards, or rubber alphabet letters.

- Have students roll out a piece of clay, and then take a sharp pencil and print a word in the clay.

- Have students trace the spelling word with their index finger on a chalkboard or in sand. Ask students to say the word aloud and say each letter as they trace.

- Students can type the words on a keyboard a number of times, or use an old typewriter.

- Have students print the word on a page, then draw a box around the configuration of each letter. Ask students to study the shape of the word, as well as its individual letters.

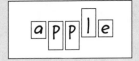

Looking for Patterns

Many spellers have a vague idea that there are spelling rules to be learned, but they have no deep understanding of these patterns. These students are left to struggle with the linguistic jargon, without seeing any real impact on their own spelling.

Much of the difficulty students experience with spelling rules rests with the way these patterns are presented. For example, when presenting the "*I before E*" rule, a teacher probably said, "*I before E*, except after *C*, and when the word says the sound *a* as in *neighbour* and *weigh*." The teacher then expected students to understand the concept, remember it, and apply it consistently in their writing. But what if their strengths are not in listening and auditory processing? What if they simply can't recall the rule, or apply it automatically to new words? Consider the cognitive overload on the brain!

The following strategies should help students grasp spelling patterns in ways other than through oral presentation:

Analogy Strategy: The strategy of applying patterns from words we know to new words is an approach shared by skilled spellers. Analogy is a particularly useful strategy with word families. By compiling lists of rhyming words, students can see that when two words rhyme, the last part of each word is often spelled the same. Struggling spellers benefit from knowing that they can quickly boost their spelling vocabulary with only a few letter changes.

Word Card Sorts: Students can be helped to grasp the "*I before E*" rule through the use of cards on which a variety of words are written. Some words should contain *ie* and others *ei*. Students can sort the words into piles, and then examine what rules can apply for when *i* comes before *e* and when *e* comes before *i*.

Graphic Organizers: Some students will be able to see patterns more clearly with the assistance of graphic organizers. These supports appeal to students who have strengths in visual/spatial awareness and logical processes. Graphic organizers can also be used as manipulatives, as in the case of hoops for Venn diagrams. As such, they appeal to the tactile senses.

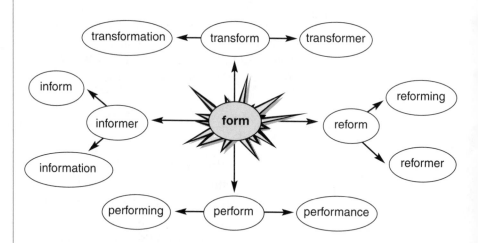

Figure 12.1 Word Explosion: building on the base word *form*

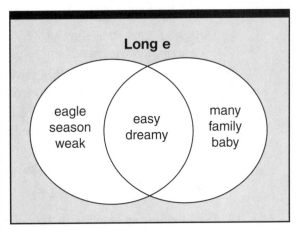

Figure 12.2 Venn diagram: long *e* spelled *ea* and *y*

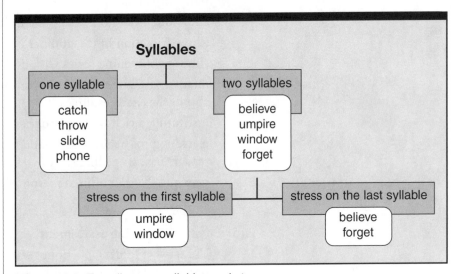

Figure 12.3 Tree diagram: syllables and stress

SUMMARY

This chapter has presented the following main ideas:

1. **Poor spelling can damage students' self-esteem.** Teachers need to be proactive in assisting struggling spellers to improve their spelling abilities.

2. **Spelling improvement can be enhanced through sound instructional practices that are geared to students' needs and learning style.**

3. **When determining students' needs, consider the following:**
   - Be aware that struggling spellers are usually delayed in their spelling development and need help to move to the next stage.
   - Teachers can observe spelling strengths and needs through everyday writing, dictated lists, proofreading conferences, and listening to speech patterns.
   - It is better to focus on what students *can do* and the strategies they use rather than on just noting errors.
   - It is important that teachers know the normal process of spelling development.

4. **When planning spelling instruction, use various forms of adaptation, including**
   - reducing the number of words studied
   - chunking lists into manageable units
   - using discretion in the number of errors noted
   - choosing a spelling series with built-in flexibility
   - maintaining interest and motivation with a variety of instructional approaches and resources
   - instituting a rich writing program as essential for all students
   - teaching proofreading skills and providing ample resources for students at all spelling stages
   - stressing that the ultimate responsibility for proofreading rests with the writer

5. **Engage in ongoing assessment.**
   - Use writing folders, portfolios, everyday writing, pre- and post-test results, and conferences with each student.
   - Provide concrete reinforcement for evidence of improvement and commitment.
   - Encourage goal-setting and self-monitoring.

6. **Struggling spellers often have a narrow range of spelling strategies and do not know how to select an appropriate strategy for specific words.** Such students need instruction in focusing on words in efficient and varied ways.

7. **Words selected for study should be within the listening and reading vocabularies of the students and be seen as useful in their everyday writing.** Sources of words may include the following:
   - students' own writing
   - lists of frequently used and frequently misspelled words
   - appropriate content-area vocabulary
   - words representing various spelling patterns
   - appropriate published spelling programs

8. **Spelling strategies should be introduced and modelled by the teacher, and practised in a variety of contexts by the student.** A broad range of strategies should be addressed. For a full discussion of spelling strategies, see Chapter 10, "Spelling Strategies and Word Study."

9. **There are a variety of ideas that are particularly useful for struggling spellers.** These include
   • Visual Strategies—colour and visualization
   • Tactile Strategies—hands-on strategies
   • Pattern Recognition Strategies—Analogies, Word Sorts, and Graphic Organizers

Reflective Thinking

1. The authors suggest that poor spelling may damage a child's self-esteem. Why might this be so? What can teachers and parents/guardians do to prevent this from happening?

2. A variety of suggestions are given for adapting spelling instruction for struggling spellers. Which of these ideas have you already used in your classroom? Which approaches would you like to try?

3. Jeffrey Freed advocates changing the way we traditionally deliver spelling instruction for struggling spellers. What strategies does he recommend?

4. Research on the stages of spelling development supports the use of invented spelling in the early grades. Freed, however, cautions that this approach may be harmful for some struggling spellers. Why? In your experience, are his concerns valid?

5. Why might graphic organizers be effective tools for helping struggling spellers? How can you utilize this strategy in your current spelling program?

The following chart provides links with other chapters in the book:

To learn more about...	see these chapters
Stages of spelling development	Chapter 1, page 4
Ongoing assessment	Chapter 3, page 35
Proofreading	Chapter 8, page 110
Spelling strategies and word study	Chapter 10, page 129

13

Challenging Skilled Spellers

· ·

When teachers think of modifying their spelling program, it is natural to consider the needs of struggling spellers. It is also important, however, to remember the students who are well advanced in their spelling development. Skilled spellers need opportunities to further their command of written language in ways that are creative and that support their inherent love of, or facility with, words.

If skilled spellers are already ahead of their peers, teachers may question whether paying further attention to their spelling is a productive use of class time. Our answer is a resounding "Yes." We do not mean that skilled spellers should simply be given more of the same spelling activities conducted with the rest of the class. Nor do we suggest that skilled spellers become all-purpose proofreaders for their classmates. We believe that learning to spell is a process that should continue for all students. In this chapter, we present four principles that will support the further growth of skilled spellers, and we suggest a number of specific word-related activities that will enrich your spelling program.

1. Skilled spellers still need to acquire an understanding of spelling concepts and vocabulary. Skilled spellers often spell simple contractions correctly or can add *-ed* and *-ing* to single syllable words, but they may not understand the patterns underlying these spellings. It may be that the student has a very good visual memory and simply "knows" these spellings are correct. The same student may not be able to apply these patterns to other words or to more sophisticated examples of the rule. Knowledge of basic vocabulary such as *vowels*, *consonants*, *syllables*, *base words*, *prefixes*, and *suffixes* should be available to all students.

Figures 1.6 (Chapter 1, page 9) and 2.4 (Chapter 2, pages 22–23), in combination with students' writing, will help you to assess specific needs and set suitable goals for each student.

2. If you are using a published spelling program, select one that provides activities to suit a wide range of student interests, learning styles, and ability levels. If it is clear from the pre-test that some students can already spell most of the words for the unit, modify the required activities to fit their needs. For example, be sure these students understand the common pattern or rule for the list and the meanings of the words, and then select activities that allow them to apply the pattern to other words, including words in their own writing and in other areas of the curriculum. Just as with struggling spellers, activities need to be selected carefully.

3. Support skilled spellers' love of, or facility with, words by examining and playing with words on a number of levels: spelling, word origins, the structure of words, and multiple meanings, including idioms, figures of speech, and shades of meaning.

4. Skilled spellers may serve as models and mentors for classmates, but should go beyond being mere proofreaders. Help these students to be skilled editors within the Writer's Workshop setting, and to use tact and helpful comments in working with their peers. Model the process for students.

The remainder of this chapter contains specific ideas for enriching your spelling program. Although skilled spellers are the primary focus for these activities, they can be used with all students. Adapt them for use with a variety of students of different ages and ability levels.

SPELLING STRATEGIES AND PATTERNS

All students need to become aware of major spelling patterns in written English. They also need to develop a wide range of spelling strategies for recalling words that do not fit common spelling patterns. Such words may include those borrowed from other languages, homophones, exceptions to spelling rules, and high-frequency words like *said*. Skilled spellers, who tend to use more complex vocabulary in their writing, will also encounter more schwa vowels (vowels in unstressed syllables). Schwa vowels are usually not enunciated clearly in speech, and often require visual strategies for spelling rather than auditory strategies, such as sounding out the word. The ability to apply spelling patterns when appropriate and to select effective spelling strategies for non-patterned words are the marks of a skilled speller.

Mnemonics

- As a class, create a collection of mnemonics, or memory cues, for difficult words. Survey students for their favourite mnemonics and start a database, chart, bulletin board, or booklet that can be added to throughout the year.

dessert: I always have seconds for dessert.

Tricky Words

- With students, brainstorm spelling strategies for recalling tricky words. Keep a list of these tricky words and a chart of ideas for spelling each word correctly.

Word	Tricky Feature	How to Remember
Wednesday	nes	say Wed nes day
muscle	silent c	think muscular
congratulations	t in the middle	think congrats!
sheriff	one r and two fs	• 1 comes before 2 • shape

Figure 13.1

Illustrate Words

- You can use concrete poetry to illustrate the meaning of words.

_{in}flation   nervous

Spelling Patterns

- Invite students to sort words by patterns. Have them generate their own word cards based on spelling patterns, common base words, and so on, and prepare decks of cards for classmates to sort. Here is an example of how this activity works:

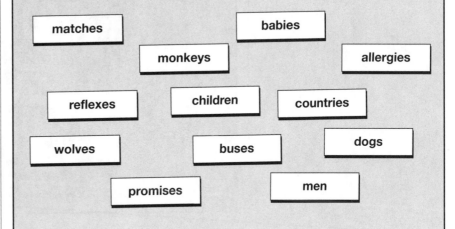

Add *s*	Add *es*	Change *y* to *i*, Add *es*	Other
dogs	matches	babies	men
promises	buses	countries	children
monkeys	reflexes	allergies	wolves

Figure 13.2

- Ask students to start a classroom collection of misspelled words viewed from signs, advertisements, and newspapers.

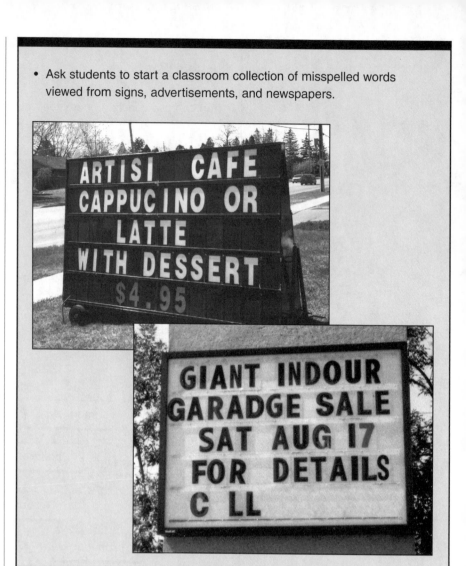

EXAMINE WORDS ON DIFFERENT LEVELS

WORDPLAY

Skilled spellers often love to manipulate words and play a variety of word games. The following activities will help these students to sharpen their spelling and vocabulary skills and enhance their natural enthusiasm for words:

Wordplay Activities

- Ask students to write a story using as many pairs of homophones as possible. Demonstrate for students how a story might begin:

  "Last night the knight rode down the road on his horse... ."

- Invite students to create wordplay books for their classmates to enjoy. Students can try some of these ideas:

  - crossword puzzles and word searches using theme words or words related to a subject area

  - rebus puzzles

R U + ing 2 M +   ?

  - lists of palindromes (e.g., *Mom, eye, pup, noon, kayak*)

  - riddles whose answers are palindromes (e.g., "A part of your face that sounds like you!" "Eye!")

  - tongue twisters for classmates to say aloud (e.g., "Much mashed mushrooms, much mashed mushrooms, much mashed mushrooms")

- Ask students to design and illustrate alphabet books on topics of interest, such as sports, music, technology, or favourite books. Older students could share these books with children in younger grades.

A is for Alligator Pie.

- Students can start a chart of abbreviations or acronyms, such as the following:

a.k.a.	*also known as*
www	*World Wide Web*
radar	*radio detecting and ranging*

- Students can design personalized licence plates using clever puns, such as the following:

2 CUTE   **SK8R**   **AV8R**

Word Meaning

Encourage skilled spellers to go beyond the literal meanings of the words they use in their writing. The activities below examine multiple meanings of words, word origins, and the meaning relationships among words. Ultimately, however, skilled spellers need to be challenged to review their use of spelling conventions in the context of their writing.

Dictionary Activities

- Encourage students to use a dictionary to discover interesting facts about words. Students can look for how many meanings a word has, what its origins are, idioms associated with the word, and other forms of the word (e.g., *nation, international*).

- Teach students to use the dictionary and thesaurus in their word-processing program. You can challenge them to identify the readability level of their words using these computer tools.

- Have students check the school library to discover how many kinds of dictionaries are available. As a class, discuss the purpose of each resource they find, such as the following:

  - monolingual dictionary
  - bilingual dictionary
  - single-function dictionaries
  - *Gage Canadian Junior Dictionary*
  - French–English dictionary
  - rhyming dictionaries, picture dictionaries, dictionary of foreign terms, dictionary of new words, dictionary of synonyms and antonyms, spelling dictionaries, crossword puzzle dictionaries

- With the students, compare print dictionaries with at least one electronic dictionary. Discuss the advantages and disadvantages of each, as well as their similarities and differences.

The following activities are suitable for the intermediate grades:

Dictionary Activities (continued)

- If the library has a copy of a rhyming dictionary, invite students to use it to create *hink pinks* for their classmates to solve. A *hink pink* is a riddle whose answer is a pair of one-syllable rhyming words (e.g., "What do you call a boiling kettle?" "A hot pot"). A *hinky pinky* riddle has two-syllable rhyming words as an answer (e.g., "What do you call a thin horse?" "A bony pony").

- Invite students to play the game "Do These Go Together?" with a classmate. Students can choose two words that are likely to be unfamiliar to the other person. The words should either go together or be very different in meaning. For example, *vivacious enthusiast* would go together, but *optimistic malcontent* would not. (Simpler examples can be used for younger students, such as g*enerous supporter* and *spacious cubicle*.)

- Have students find a thesaurus in the classroom or the library. They can make a chart of as many descriptive words as possible to replace "tired" words such as *said*, *walked*, *ate*, *sad*, or *happy*. Then, have them look at pieces of writing in their writing folders and try to use some of these words to make their work more expressive.

- Ask students to write definitions of some abstract concepts through the use of examples (e.g., "Gentleness is my grandfather holding my baby brother."). Students can define some of these words by creating sample sentences:

friendship	freedom
anger	fair play
loneliness	trust
success	fear

- Ask students to create a menu made up entirely of words borrowed from other languages, and to provide a translation of the menu (e.g., *broccoli au gratin*—broccoli with cheese). A dictionary of word origins (such as *The Concise Oxford Dictionary of English Etymology*), or books such as *An Avalanche of Anoraks: For People Who Speak Foreign Languages Every Day...Whether They Know It Or Not* will be very helpful for this activity.

- Invite students to investigate the origins of their town or city name, or the name of the street on which they live. Students may want to contact the local historical society or consult books such as *Naming Canada: Stories About Canadian Place Names* by Alan Rayburn.

- Ask students if they have ever wished there was a word for something but knew the word did not exist. Have them make up their own. They can begin with a dictionary called *Words We Want*. To help them begin, have students look at *Wanted Words* and *Wanted Words 2* by Jane Farrell et al.

SUMMARY

This chapter has presented the following main ideas:

1. **Skilled spellers still need to understand and articulate spelling concepts and terminology.** Even though students may spell words correctly, teachers should not assume skilled spellers understand the patterns underlying the way these words are spelled.

2. **All students need to develop a repertoire of spelling strategies.** Skilled spellers, who tend to use longer words in their writing, may encounter more words with schwa vowels. Since schwa vowels, for example *helmet,* cannot be sounded out clearly, visual strategies and memory tricks need to be used for spelling such words.

3. **Teachers should support skilled spellers' love of, or facility with, words by providing activities for students to examine and to play with words on a number of levels:** spelling, word origins, the structure of words, multiple meanings, idioms, and figures of speech.

REFLECTIVE THINKING

1. Describe a skilled speller in your classroom or one you have taught previously. What specific challenges do such students present for teachers?

2. Why is it important for skilled spellers to be able to articulate spelling patterns, terms, and strategies even if they are able to spell most grade-appropriate words?

3. What accommodations do you currently make in your spelling program for skilled spellers? Are you satisfied with these provisions? What concerns, if any, do you have?

4. What important spelling objectives would you try to accomplish while conducting an editing conference with a skilled speller?

5. Interview one or more of the skilled spellers in your class. What do they tell you about themselves as spellers? What needs do they express related to spelling?

The following chart provides links with other chapters in the book:

To learn more about...	see these chapters
Developmental stages of learning to spell	Chapter 1, page 4
Spelling concepts by grade	Chapter 2, pages 22–23
Spelling strategies	Chapter 10, page 129

Home Connections

THE HOME AND CLASSROOM CONNECTION

A child's first introduction to the power of words occurs at home. Family members model literacy each time they write a grocery list, leave a note for someone on the kitchen counter, or write a birthday card. Through these forms of communication, they demonstrate the importance of print and its wonderful variety, from lists to labels. It's no wonder that children soon take to writing notes on their own, as this child did at the age of six:

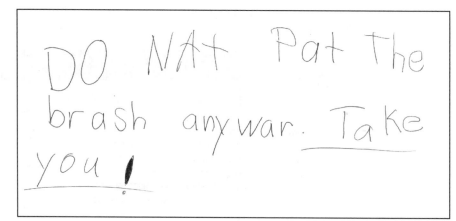

Figure 14.1 The note translates as follows: "Do not put the brush anywhere. Thank you!"

The involvement of the family with a child's literacy development begins well before he or she starts school, and cuts across ethnic and socio-economic lines (Peregoy and Boyle, 1993). In their longitudinal study of children's spelling from kindergarten to Grade 6, Hughes and Searle found that every child mentioned his or her parents when asked how they learned to spell (1997). Hughes and Searle also found family involvement was universally positive: "We haven't come across a single case where parents made things worse" (p. 168).

Many parents worry about their children's progress in writing and spelling. One of the most frequently asked questions of teachers is: "How can I help my child do better in spelling?" Underlying this question may be a perception that spelling is not taught well at school. Although there is no mark for spelling per se on many report cards, most parents want to keep track of their children's spelling progress.

From the teacher's point of view, home support is a vital component of students' learning. Teachers recognize that families are a source of information about students. Teachers need to know how much students read and write at home and how they react to homework. Of concern to teachers is how to sustain and nourish the communication between home and school. In this chapter, we will offer suggestions for successful interaction between parents/guardians and the classroom.

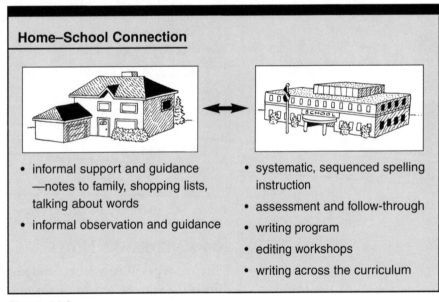

Home–School Connection

- informal support and guidance —notes to family, shopping lists, talking about words
- informal observation and guidance

- systematic, sequenced spelling instruction
- assessment and follow-through
- writing program
- editing workshops
- writing across the curriculum

Figure 14.2

COMMUNICATING WITH FAMILIES

An Introductory Letter is an excellent way to establish a home connection. It can express the school's commitment to fostering writing and spelling, let parents/guardians know the teacher's expectations and procedures, suggest how families can help, and promise continued communication. What follows is a sample Introductory Letter to families of primary students:

Dear Family,

This year, (name of child) will be learning to spell as part of the process of learning to write. Like you, we know how important writing skills are, and we are committed to helping each child grow as a writer. To assist your child in developing writing skills, our spelling program will:

(Describe the expectations and procedures of your program.)

You can help at home in many ways. You can surround your child with books and magazines, and read them aloud. You can make your child aware of the words in the world outside school—the print on the cereal box, the newspaper flyer, the sign in the doughnut shop window. You can help with homework. Most importantly, you can show your child that you think writing and spelling are important as you write letters, shopping lists, directions, and thank-you notes.

As the school year goes on, we will be sending home regular newsletters offering suggestions as to how you can help with the words we are studying in the classroom. Your help and encouragement are two of the most important factors in your child's success. Let's stay in touch!

Yours sincerely,

(teacher)

Figure 14.3 Sample Introductory Letter

NEWSLETTERS AND NOTES

Different types of newsletters and notes sent to parents and guardians during the year are other valuable resources for maintaining a home connection. These letters and notes do not need to be long, and they can take many different forms. For example, they can be entries on a homework calendar, a brief note in a dialogue journal, or a general note to the whole class. Alternatively, families can be supplied with an evaluation sheet (see Figure 14.4), on which students can record the words they need to study. One teacher sends home a spelling study book with study steps glued inside the front cover to serve as a reference for students and family members.

Student Record Sheet

Name: _____

Date: _____

List Words	Words I Need to Study

Figure 14.4 Evaluation sheet

Other newsletters can be brief and helpful, letting family members know the focus of the week's or month's program, or enlisting the family's help with reinforcement activities. Here is a sample newsletter for the families of junior level students:

Dear Family,

We are working on alphabetical order in our class. You can help at home.

Give your child a list of three or four food items, articles of clothing, names, or games that begin with the same letter, and help to put the words in alphabetical order by looking at the second letter.

Thanks,

Figure 14.5 For use with junior level students

LETTERS TO PARENTS OF SECOND-LANGUAGE STUDENTS

In many classrooms, there will be students whose families don't speak English. Families new to your community may be concerned about their children's progress, particularly in spelling, and need a communication bridge to be reassured (Beckett, 1994; Ministry of Education, Ontario, ESL Document, 2001, p. 15). If possible, have letters that are to be sent home to families where English is not spoken translated into a language they speak or read. To do this, schools may need to request assistance from social organizations that provide services for immigrants and refugees. It is necessary, especially for these parents, to keep messages simple and as free of educational jargon as possible.

TAKE-HOME ACTIVITIES

Jim Giles, an Ontario teacher, has developed a "Book and Backpack" program for take-home writing activities. In each backpack are writing and drawing materials, such as pencils, markers, crayons, and paper. A book or magazine from the classroom library is also included. Students read the book with a family member and then respond to it in some way, such as drawing their favourite part of the story, writing a letter to classmates about the book, or writing a story based on the book's pattern (Giles, 2002). Families are also encouraged to write comments and questions in a journal, which then becomes a forum for discussion between home and school.

Activity sheets that focus on specific topics can also be sent home as a way to review the current spelling words. For example, Figure 14.6 is an activity that gives students practice with sorting nouns, verbs, and adjectives.

Simple activity sheets can be made by creating word searches with list words, or words that fit a spelling pattern. To create a word search, fill in the words on a squared grid in all directions, and then fill in letters of the alphabet randomly. (Hint: Don't forget to check for unintentional embarrassing words. Students are certain to find them!)

PROOFREADING

Parents and other family members can be encouraged to help their children revise and proofread. If unpolished drafts are sent home, it is important to let family members know that this is a work in progress, not a finished copy. An editing stamp that makes this clear is a useful device for letting families know the stage of a writing sample. For example:

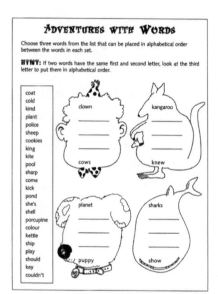

Figure 14.6 Activity sheet

Rough Draft

This draft has been checked for:

___ Punctuation

___ Spelling

___ Grammar

Figure 14.7 Editing stamp

Engaging family members in proofreading may help remind them what a rigorous process writing is!

In other newsletters or notes, parents and guardians can be encouraged to play word games with their children. For example, they can play a game where they look for compound words in the home (*bedroom*, *toothbrush*), in supermarket ads, or in the environment. Points can be awarded for every compound found and recorded in a list.

Older students' families may enjoy playing a game that will help students remember confusing word pairs, such as *desert* and *dessert*.

Dear Family,

This week we are studying pairs of words that are easily confused, such as *quite* and *quiet*. A variety of memory strategies are needed to learn the spelling of these words. One way to tell these words apart is to create nonsense sentences with personal memory clues. For example:

Bob built qu**ite** a k**ite**!

Dad went on a qu**iet** d**iet** of chocolate chips.

Using the names of people you and your child know, work with your child to make up nonsense sentences for these tricky words:

desert—dessert   **dairy—diary**

angle—angel   **loose—lose**

close—clothes   **accept—except**

Have your child record the sentences in a "Memory Trick" list that can be added to at a later date.

Figure 14.8

SPELLING ACTIVITY NIGHT

An excellent way to foster home–school connections is to invite parents and guardians to a Spelling Activity Night early in the school year. At this time, the program is outlined, and parents'/guardians' questions are answered. It is a good opportunity for teachers to outline expectations for students and their families, and to present spelling in the context of reading and writing. If weekly word lists are used, teachers can explain the selection criteria for words on the list. (See Chapter 2, "What Does the Research Mean for the Classroom?")

You and the other organizers can present a selection of activities and games that demonstrate a range of strategies that family members can foster at home. An invitation to parents and guardians should explain the agenda for the evening, as in the sample letter on page 198:

Criteria for Word Lists

▶ developmental appropriateness

▶ high-utility words that all students need to know how to spell

▶ words that fit common spelling patterns, some from other curriculum areas

▶ words chosen by students

Dear Parents and Guardians,

On Wednesday, October 7, we are holding a Spelling Activity Night at James Street Public School.

We would like to extend an invitation to you and the children of the primary division to this event. It will be held in the school's gymnasium from 7:00 to 8:30 p.m.

The purpose of the evening is to explain our spelling program, answer questions, demonstrate some spelling strategies you can reinforce at home, and HAVE SOME FUN doing spelling activities with your children.

We hope you can attend this interesting and informative evening. Please indicate below if you are able to come. We look forward to seeing you on the 7th!

Yours truly,

> >
❑ Yes, I will be able to attend the Spelling Activity Night on October 7th.
❑ No, I will not be able to attend.

Name: _____

Figure 14.9 Invitation to a Spelling Activity Night

At Spelling Activity Nights, students and their families work together on activities such as word sorts (see Figure 14.10). Hands-on practice with sorting words or doing cloze activities can cut through educational jargon and help families see how such strategies work. You can have word cards and sorting hoops on hand, as well as chart paper for other activities.

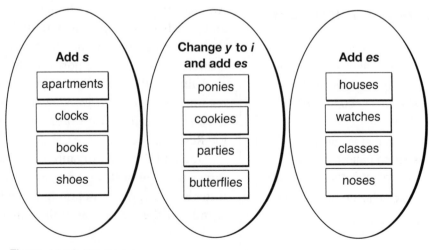

Figure 14.10 Word sort

Teachers can demonstrate and discuss activities that are easy to do at home. Families can also play commercial spelling games such as Spill and Spell, or do co-operative crossword puzzles and word searches. Word wheels (see Figure 14.11) or alphabet cards that students can take home are spelling aids that families can use for reinforcement. These aids are especially important for second-language families.

At the end of the evening, an evaluation sheet can be supplied for participants to comment on the proceedings (Baskwill, 1989).

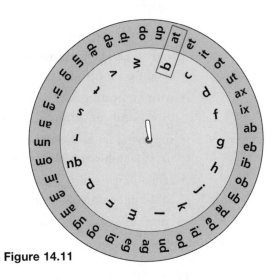

Figure 14.11

THE PARENT/GUARDIAN INTERVIEW

Jane Baskwill takes slides of students "in action" to display on a big screen at parent/guardian interviews. Pictures of students writing can help families get a sense of the classroom at work. Writing portfolios, results of student spelling surveys, and other assessment information provide a sense of how their child is progressing. (See Chapter 3, "Spelling Assessment.")

Another way of demonstrating student progress is to dictate to a student a piece of his or her own writing from earlier in the year. This provides a window into spelling growth over an extended time.

Graphs showing personal spelling profiles, or progress on pre- and post-tests of spelling words are other concrete illustrations of progress. The interview is also a good opportunity to obtain feedback on how the student is doing at home and what factors may be influencing progress.

Families and teachers working together can build confidence in students that they, in turn, can communicate successfully in print by writing well, spelling correctly, and creating a finished piece of work. Whether it's a poster, story, or learning-log entry, students can communicate information, thoughts, feelings, and ideas. When they can write well, they will have the confidence to carry this skill into their work and personal lives.

SUMMARY

This chapter has presented the following main ideas:

1. **Children's early literacy development takes place in the home.**

2. **Communication between home and school is vital to students' progress.**

3. **Parents'/guardians' involvement with their children's spelling progress can be fostered in the following ways:**
   - sending an introductory letter home early in the school year
   - communicating with families through regular newsletters, notes, and other kinds of communication
   - supplying "at home activities" and opportunities for family members to help children with spelling practice, writing, and proofreading
   - scheduling Spelling Activity Nights that highlight spelling activities that can be done at home
   - communicating children's spelling progress at parent/guardian interviews

REFLECTIVE THINKING

1. List the ways in which you communicate with the parents/guardians of your students about the nature of your language program.

2. How do you answer parents who ask, "Why do you not mark every spelling error in my child's work?"

3. What questions would you like to ask parents/guardians when you encounter a new classroom of students?

4. What arrangements are made in your school for communicating with families who do not speak English?

5. How can you use student writing as a way of discussing a child's progress in spelling with parents?

The following chart provides links with other chapters in the book:

To learn more about...	see these chapters
Selection of word lists	Chapter 2, page 25
Spelling Assessment	Chapter 3, page 32

APPENDIXES

APPENDIX A: Reproducible Pages

APPENDIX B: Resources to Support Language Development

APPENDIX C: Frequently Used Words

APPENDIX D: Common Spelling Patterns

STATUS-OF-THE-CLASS SHEET

Spelling	Word Study		Capitals/Periods/Commas			Paragraphing		Other:
Holistic	Holistic		Plot	Setting		Writing Organization	Draft	Edit
Punctuation	Writing		beginning, middle, ending	Presentation			Rev.	
4 3 2 1	4 3 2 1		4 3 2 1			4 3 2 1		4 3 2 1
4 3 2 1	4 3 2 1		4 3 2 1			4 3 2 1		4 3 2 1
4 3 2 1	4 3 2 1		4 3 2 1			4 3 2 1		4 3 2 1

Outcome/Expectation

Student Groupings and Focus

© 2004 Gage Learning

SPELLING CHECKLIST

Student _____

	Sometimes	Always	Never
1. I try to spell words the way they sound.			
2. I try to use spelling rules to spell words.			
3. I try to remember the shape of words or where the tricky parts are.			
4. If I cannot spell a word, I think about the meaning.			
5. I break words into syllables to spell them.			
6. I listen for smaller words inside the bigger word.			
7. I spell a new word by thinking of other words that rhyme with it.			
8. I use a dictionary, Word Wall, or other type of word list to help me spell.			
9. I can tell if a word I have written "does not look right."			
10. I proofread for spelling errors when I write a first draft.			
11. I proofread for spelling errors when I edit something I have written.			
12. I misspell the same words over and over again.			
13. I think that correct spelling in a polished piece of writing is important.			
14. I find spelling easy.			

SPELLING PROFILE

Student _____

	Sources	Knowledge	Strategies	Instructional Goals
Date:				
Date:				
Date:				
Date:				
Date:				
Date:				
Date:				
Date:				
Date:				
Date:				
Date:				
Date:				

Resources to Support Language Development

KINDERGARTEN TO GRADE 3

Bennett, J. (Ed.). (1991). *A cup of starshine: Poems and pictures for young children.* London: Walker Books.

Bonder, D. (2002). *Accidental alphabet.* Vancouver, BC: Whitecap Books.

Booth, D. (Ed.). (1993). *Dr. Knickerbocker and other rhymes.* Toronto: Kids Can Press.

Dunn, S. (1993). *Primary rhymerry.* Markham, ON: Pembroke Publishers.

Fitch, S. (1992). *There were monkeys in my kitchen.* Toronto: Doubleday Canada.

Harrison, T. (1989). *A northern alphabet.* Toronto: Tundra Books.

Kovalski, M. (1987). *The wheels on the bus.* Toronto: Kids Can Press.

Lear, E. (1997). *A was once an apple pie.* Cambridge, MA: Candlewick Press.

Lee, D. (1983). *Jelly belly.* New York: Macmillan.

Lee, D. (2001). *Alligator pie.* Toronto: Key Porter Kids.

Lesynski, L. (1999). *Dirty dog boogie.* Toronto: Annick Press.

Lesynski, L. (2003). *Cabbagehead.* Toronto: Annick Press.

Martin, B. J. (1983). *Brown bear, brown bear, what do you see?* New York: Henry Holt.

Martin, B. J. (2000). *Chicka, chicka, boom boom.* New York: Alladin Paperbacks.

McPhail, D. (1993). *Pigs aplenty, pigs galore!* New York: Dutton Children's Books.

Parry, C. (1991). *Zoomerang a boomerang: Poems to make your belly laugh.* Toronto: Kids Can Press.

Prelutsky, J., & Nobel, A. (1983). *The Random House book of poetry for children.* New York: Random House.

Prelutsky, J. (1996). *A pizza the size of the sun: Poems.* New York: Greenwillow Books.

Thornhill, J. (1988). *The wildlife abc: A nature alphabet.* Toronto: Greey de Pencier Books.

GRADES 4 TO 8

Agee, J. (1991). *Go hang a salami! I'm a lasagna hog! and other palindromes.* New York: Farrar, Straus, and Giroux.

Eckler, R. (1996). *Making the alphabet dance: Recreational wordplay.* New York: St. Martin's Press.

Farrow, J. (2000). *Wanted Words: From amalgamots to undercarments—Language gaps found and fixed.* Toronto: Stoddart.

Heller, R. (1989). *Many luscious lollipops: A book about adjectives.* New York: Grosset and Dunlap.

Lear, E. (1994). *There was an old man...A collection of limericks.* Toronto: Kids Can Press.

Lederer, R. (1990). *The play of words: Fun and games for language lovers.* New York: Pocket Books.

Maestro, G., & Terban, M. (1982). *Eight ate: A feast of homonym riddles.* New York: Clarion.

Terban, M. (1985). *Too hot to hoot: Funny palindrome riddles.* New York: Clarion.

Terban, M. (1988). *The dove dove: Funny homograph riddles.* New York: Clarion.

Terban, M. (1991). *Hey, hay! A wagonful of funny homonym riddles.* New York: Clarion.

White, R. J. (1994). *An avalanche of anoraks: For people who speak foreign languages every day whether they know it or not.* New York: Random House.

Frequently Used Words

200 WORDS USED MOST FREQUENTLY IN WRITING

a	do	himself	much	she	up
about	does	his	must	should	us
after	don't	home	my	since	use
again	down	house	never	small	used
against	during	how	new	so	very
all	each	however	no	some	want
almost	even	I	not	something	was
also	every	if	now	state	water
always	fact	in	number	still	way
an	far	into	of	such	we
and	few	is	off	take	well
another	find	it	old	than	went
any	first	its	on	that	were
are	for	just	once	the	what
as	found	know	one	their	when
away	four	last	only	them	where
back	from	left	or	then	which
be	get	less	other	there	while
because	give	life	our	these	who
been	go	like	out	they	why
before	going	little	over	thing	will
being	good	long	own	think	with
between	got	look	part	this	without
big	government	made	people	those	work
both	great	make	place	though	world
but	had	man	play	thought	would
by	hand	many	put	three	year
came	has	may	right	through	years
can	have	me	said	time	you
come	he	men	same	to	your
could	her	might	saw	too	
course	here	more	say	two	
day	high	most	school	under	
did	him	Mr.	see	until	

200 USEFUL HOMOPHONE SETS

KINDERGARTEN TO GRADE 3

ad, add
ant, aunt
ate, eight
be, bee
bare, bear
beach, beech
beat, beet
blew, blue
bough, bow
brake, break
buy, by, bye
caught, cot
cell, sell
cent, scent, sent
cheap, cheep
chews, choose
close, clothes
creak, creek
chute, shoot
coarse, course
days, daze
dear, deer
dew, do, due

fair, fare
feat, feet
fir, fur
flew, flu
flour, flower
for, four
gait, gate
gnu, knew, new
grate, great
groan, grown
hall, haul
hare, hair
he'll, heal, heel
hear, here
heard, herd
him, hymn
hoarse, horse

hole, whole
hour, our
in, inn
its, it's
knead, need
knight, night
knot, not
know, no
lead, led
made, maid
mail, male
main, mane
meat, meet
oar, or, ore
one, won
pail, pale
pain, pane
pair, pare, pear
passed, past
peace, piece
peak, peek
plain, plane
prince, prints
rain, reign, rein
rap, wrap
read, red
read, reed
real, reel
right, write
road, rode, rowed
root, route
rose, rows

sail, sale
scene, seen
sea, see
seam, seem
side, sighed
size, sighs
so, sew, sow
some, sum
son, sun
soar, sore

stair, stare
stake, steak
steal, steel
straight, strait
sundae, Sunday
tee, tea
tacks, tax
tail, tale
taught, tot
team, teem
their, there, they're
threw, through
tide, tied
to, too, two
toe, tow
vale, veil
vain, vein
weak, week
wade, weighed
waist, waste
wait, weight
war, wore
way, weigh
who's, whose
whole, hole
wood, would
you're, your

GRADES 4 TO 8

air, heir
aid, aide
aisle, I'll, isle
allowed, aloud
altar, alter
arc, ark
ascent, assent
band, banned
berry, bury
berth, birth
billed, build
board, bored
bread, bred
brews, bruise

carrot, karat
ceiling, sealing
cereal, serial
chili, Chile, chilly
chord, cord
crews, cruise
check, cheque
complement, compliment
correspondence, correspondents
council, counsel
currant, current
descent, dissent
died, dyed
doe, dough
dual, duel
ducked, duct

facts, fax
find, fined
flair, flare
flier, flyer
foreword, forward
genes, jeans
gorilla, guerilla
guessed, guest
higher, hire
idol, idle, idyll
laid, layed
leased, least
links, lynx
manner, manor
marry, merry
medal, meddle
mil, mill
mind, mined
miner, minor
missed, mist
muscle, mussel
naval, navel
packed, pact
patience, patients

pause, paws
pedal, peddle
pistil, pistol
pleas, please
prays, praise, preys
presence, presents
pried, pride
principal, principle
profit, prophet
raise, rays, raze
rapper, wrapper
residence, residents
right, rite, wright, write
ring, wring
rough, ruff
rung, wrung

seas, sees, seize
seller, cellar
sight, cite, site
slay, sleigh
soared, sword
stalk, stock
stationary, stationery
step, steppe
serf, surf
sweet, suite
symbol, cymbal
teas, tease, tees
tacked, tact
taught, taut, tot
tense, tents
throne, thrown
thyme, time
urn, earn
vary, very
walk, wok
weave, we've
whoa, woe
wretch, retch

Common Spelling Patterns

KINDERGARTEN TO GRADE 3

Consonant Blends—Initial Two Letters

with *r*	with *l*	with initial *s* and other letters
br brush	**bl** blue	**sc** scatter
cr crack	**cl** climb	**sk** skid
dr drag	**fl** fly	**sm** small
fr frog	**gl** glue	**sn** snow
gr grass	**pl** please	**sp** spark
pr present	**sl** slow	**st** star
tr treat		**sw** sweet

Consonant Blends—Initial Three Letters

ending in *r*	ending in *qu*	ending in *l*	ending in *ch*
scr screech	**squ** squish	**spl** splash	**sch** school
shr shrill			
spr spread			
thr threw			

Consonant Digraphs

Initial		Final	
ch	chum	**ch**	rich
sh	ship	**ng**	ring
th	thin	**nk**	think
wh	what	**sh**	wish
		th	with
		tch	catch

Consonant Clusters—Final

ct	fact	**nce**	once
dge	edge	**nge**	lunge
ft	soft	**nk**	rink
nd	send	**nse**	dense
lt	felt	**pt**	lept
mp	bump	**sk**	desk
nch	lunch	**sp**	lisp

Short Vowels

ab	grab, tab, slab
ack*	black, back, tack
act	fact, pact,
ad	bad, lad, mad, sad
aft	raft, craft, shaft
ag*	bag, wag, tag
am	yam, ham, gram
amp	lamp, clamp, tramp
an*	ran, man, pan, tan
ance	dance, lance
and	hand, grand, band
ang	bang, sang, rang
ank*	tank, bank, thank
ant	ant, pant, slant
ap*	gap, trap, snap
ash*	rash, crash, trash
at*	hat, bat, sat, that
atch	catch, batch, snatch
ead	head, bread, read
eck	neck, peck, deck
ed	bed, led, fed
ell*	bell, well, sell, tell
end	spend, bend, mend
ent	tent, went, bent
est*	best, test, west
et	let, bet, wet, met
ick*	thick, brick, stick
id	kid, bid, lid
ig	pig, wig, big
ill*	will, pill, still, bill
in*	pin, bin, grin, spin
ing*	king, ring, sing, thing
ink*	drink, sink, think
ip*	dip, sip, lip, tip
it*	fit, bit, sit, lit

ob	job, mob, rob
ock*	knock, sock, block
og	frog, log, bog,
op*	hop, stop, mop, shop
ot	got, lot, hot, spot
ub	tub, rub, stub, cub
uck*	duck, luck, stuck
ug*	tug, rug, mug
um	gum, hum, glum
ump*	jump, thump, bump
unk*	sunk, bunk, drunk
ush	brush, slush, gush

Long Vowels

ace	face, grace, space
ade	fade, made, grade
age	sage, wage, page
aid	maid, laid, braid
ail*	pail, nail, tail, jail
ain*	brain, grain, train
ake*	take, bake, make
ale*	sale, pale, tale, whale
ame*	name, same, tame
ane	lane, mane, cane
ape	cape, drape, shape
aste	paste, taste, waste
ate*	plate, state, date
ave	cave, wave, shave
ay*	play, day, say, may
each	beach, teach, reach
ead	bead, lead, read
eak	beak, leak, peak
eam	team, stream, beam
eat*	seat, treat, meat
eed	need, feed, seed
eep	sleep, deep, steep

ice*	nice, mice, twice
ight*	right, night, bright
ike	bike, like, spike
ime	time, dime, lime
ine*	fine, mine, spine
oke*	joke, broke, poke
old	sold, bold, told
one	bone, cone, phone
ope	hope, mope, lope
ow	snow, low, grow

Other Vowel Sounds

air	hair, fair, stair
all	ball, tall, hall, fall
are	care, bare, stare
ew	few, new, grew
ook	book, look, took
oom	room, zoom, boom
oop	swoop, troop, loop
ore	more, store, core
ound	sound, round, bound
out	shout, out, stout
ow	cow, how, now

*Most commonly used phonograms. Wylie and Durrell (1970) quoted in G. Pinnell & I. Fountas, (1998). *Word matters: Teaching phonics and spelling in the reading/writing classroom* (Appendix 15). Portsmouth, NH: Heinemann.

IE and EI Words

ie			*ei* After *c*	Long *a* Spelled *ei*	Common Exceptions to the Rule
achieve	fiery	priest	ceiling	beige	conscience
apiece	friendship	relief	conceit	eighth	foreign
belief	grieve	review	conceive	freight	forfeit
believe	handkerchief	shield	deceive	neighbour	height
brief	hygiene	siege	perceive	reign	leisure
chief	mischief	thief	receipt	veil	neither
diesel	niece	yield	receive	vein	seize
field	piece			weigh	species
fierce	pierce			weight	weird

Common Prefixes

Negation		Number		Again		Direction	
in	inconsiderate	**uni**	unicorn	**re**	return	**trans—across, over, down, beyond**	transport, transnational, transfusion
il	illegal	**bi**	bicycle				
ir	irregular	**tri**	tricycle			**sub—under, beneath**	suburban, subway, subcommittee
im	impossible	**semi**	semifinal				
un	uncommon					**inter—between, among**	international, intermediate, interracial
non	non-profit						
dis	disappear						

Common Suffixes

ness—nouns
  happiness, sadness

less—adjectives meaning "without"
  helpless, hopeless

ly—adverbs
  lovely, slowly

ment—nouns
  entertainment, government

tion—nouns
  action, suggestion

sion—nouns
  omission, possession

ful—adjectives meaning "full of"
  hopeful, helpful, joyful

er—added to verbs to make nouns meaning "one who does the action"
  swimmer, thinker, writer

or—similar to *er* nouns
  actor, editor, visitor

able—adjectives
  acceptable, enjoyable, evaluable

ible—adjectives, similar to **-able**, but not as common
  edible, terrible, impossible

ian—nouns, meaning "someone who does something"
  electrician, magician, politician

Bibliography

Early reading strategy: The report of the expert panel on early reading in Ontario. (2003). Toronto, ON: Ministry of Education.

Adams, M. J. (1990). *Beginning to read: Thinking and learning about print.* Cambridge, MA: MIT Press.

Allal, L. (1997). Learning to spell in the classroom. In C. A. Perfetti, L. Rieban, & M. Fayol (Eds.), *Learning to spell: Research, theory, and practice across languages* (pp. 129–150). Mahwah, NJ: Lawrence Erlbaum Associates.

Atwell, N. (1998). *In the middle: New understanding about reading, writing, and learning.* Portsmouth, NH: Heinemann.

Au, K., Carroll, J., & Schen, J. (1997). *Balanced literacy instruction: A teacher's resource book.* Norwood, MA: Christopher-Gordon Publishers.

Barber, C. (1997). *The English language: A historical introduction.* Cambridge, UK: The Cambridge University Press.

Barrett, N. (1995). *Word origins: Chambers fun with English.* London: Chambers.

Baskwill, J. (1989). *Parents and teachers: Partners in learning.* Toronto: Scholastic.

Bear, D., Invernizzi, M., Johnston, F., & Templeton, S. (2000). *Words their way: Word study for phonics, vocabulary, and spelling* (2nd ed.). Englewood Cliffs, NJ: Prentice Hall.

Bear, D., & Templeton, S. (1998). *Explorations in developmental spelling: Foundations for learning and teaching phonics, spelling, and vocabulary* (Vol. 52).

Beckett, C., & Haley, P. (2000). Using standards to integrate academic language into ESL fluency. *Clearing House, 74*(2), 102.

Beers, J. W., & Henderson, E. H. (1977). A study of developing orthographic concepts among first grade children. *Research in the Teaching of English, 11*(2), 133–148.

Bennett, J. (Ed.). (1991). *A cup of starshine: Poems and pictures for young children.* London: Walker Books.

Berent, M. (1995). *Weird words.* New York: Berkley Books.

Bosman, A., & Van Orden, G. (1997). Why spelling is more difficult than reading. In C. A. Perfetti, L. Rieben, & M. Fayol (Eds.), *Learning to spell: Research, theory, and practice across languages* (pp. 173–194). Mahwah, NJ: Lawrence Erlbaum Associates.

Bowers, V. (1999). *Wow Canada! Exploring this land from coast to coast.* Toronto: Owl.

Broukal, M. (1994). *Idioms for everyday use.* Lincolnwood, IL: National Textbook Company.

Bryson, B. (1990). *Mother tongue: English and how it got that way.* New York: Avon Books.

Burgstahler, S., & Utterback, S. (2000). *New kids on the net: Internet activities in elementary language arts.* Boston: Allyn and Bacon.

Calkins, L. M. (1983). *Lessons from a child: On the teaching and learning of writing.* Portsmouth, NH: Heinemann.

Calkins, L. M. (1994). *The art of teaching writing.* Portsmouth, NH: Heinemann.

Carrasquillo, A., & Rodriquez, V. (1995). *Language minority students in the mainstream classroom.* Briston, PA: Multilingual Matters.

Chang, J. (1995). Chinese speakers. In M. Swan & B. Smith (Eds.), *Learner English: A teacher's guide to interference and other problems.* Cambridge, UK: Cambridge University Press.

Cleary, B. (1999). *Ramona's World.* New York: Morrow Junior Books.

Cramer, R. (1998). *The spelling connection: Integrating reading, writing, and spelling instruction.* New York: The Guilford Press.

Cramer, R. (2001). *Creative power: The nature and nurture of children's writing.* New York: Longman.

Cramer, R. L., & Cipielewski, J. (1995). A study of spelling errors in 18,599 written compositions of children in grades 1–8. In *Spelling research and information: An overview of current research and practices.* Glenview, IL: Scott Foresman Co.

Crystal, D. (1995). *The Cambridge encyclopedia of the English language.* Cambridge, UK: The Cambridge University Press.

Cunningham, P., & Cunningham, J. (1992). Making words: Enhancing the invented spelling-decoding connection. *The Reading Teacher, 46*(2), 106–115.

Cunningham, P., & Hall, D. (1994). *Making big words: Multilevel, hands-on spelling and phonics activities.* Torrance, CA: Good Apple.

Cunningham, P., & Hall, D. (1998). *Month-by-month phonics for upper grades.* Greensboro, NC: Carson-Dellosa.

Cunningham, P., Hall, D., & Sigmon, C. (1999). *The teacher's guide to the Four Blocks*: *A multimethod, multilevel framework for grades 1–3*. Greensboro, NC: Carson-Dellosa.

Dixon-Krauss, L. (1996). *Vygotsky in the classroom*: *Mediated literacy instruction and assessment*. White Plains, NY: Longman.

Dunn, S. (1993). *Primary rhymerry*. Toronto: Pembroke Publishers.

Ehri, L. C. (1997). Learning to read and spell are one and the same, almost. In C. A. Perfetti, L. Rieban, & M. Fayol (Eds.), *Learning to spell: Research, theory, and practice across languages* (pp. 237–269). Mahwah, NJ: Lawrence Erlbaum Associates.

English as a second language and English literacy development: *A resource guide, 2001*. (2001). Toronto, ON: Ministry of Education.

ESL standards for pre-K–12 students. (1997). Alexandria, VA: Teachers of English to Speakers of Other Languages (TESOL).

Farrow, J. (2000). *Wanted Words: From amalgamots to undercarments—Language gaps found and fixed*. Toronto: Stoddart.

Fountas, I., & Pinnell, G. (Eds.). (1999). *Voices on word matters: Learning about phonics and spelling in the literacy classroom*. Portsmouth, NH: Heinemann.

Fountas, I., & Pinnell, G. (2001). *Guiding readers and writers grades 3–6: Teaching comprehension, genre, and content literacy*. Portsmouth, NH: Heinemann.

Freed, J. (1997). *Right-brained children in a left-brained world*. New York: Simon & Shuster.

Fresch, M. J. (2000). What we learned from Josh: Sorting out word sorting. *Language Arts*, 77(3), 232–240.

Fulk, B., & Starmont-Spurgin, M. (1995). Fourteen spelling strategies for students with learning disabilities. *Intervention in School & Clinic*, 31(1), 16–21.

Gallas, K. (1994). *The languages of learning: How children talk, write, dance, draw and sing their understanding of the world*. New York: Teachers College Press, Columbia University.

Gardner, H. (1983). *Frames of mind: The theory of multiple intelligences*. New York: Basic Books.

Gentry, R. (1993). *Teaching kids to spell*. Portsmouth, NH: Heinemann.

Giles, J. (2002). Book backpack: Home and school partnerships that keep going and going…. *ETFO Voice* (Spring), 9–13.

Glazier, T. (1993). *The least you should know about vocabulary building: Word roots*. New York: Holt, Rinehart and Winston.

Graves, D. (1983). *Writing: Teachers and children at work*. Portsmouth, NH: Heinemann.

Graves, D., & Stuart, V. (1985). *Write from the start: Tapping your child's natural writing ability*. New York: E. P. Dutton.

Handscombe, J. (1989). A quality program for learners of English as a second language. In P. Rigg & V. Allen (Eds.), *When they don't all speak English*. Urbana, IL: National Council of Teachers of English.

Head, J. C. (1986). *Monday morning: A first lick at the lolly*. London: Macmillan.

Henderson, E. (1981). *Learning to read and spell: The child's knowledge of words*. DeKalb: Northern Illinois University Press.

Henderson, E. (1990). *Teaching spelling* (2nd ed.). Boston: Houghton Mifflin.

Hoad, T. (Ed.). (1986). *The concise Oxford dictionary of English etymology*. Oxford: Clarendon Press.

Hughes, M., & Searle, D. (1997). *The violent e and other tricky sounds: Learning to spell from kindergarten through grade 6*. York, MA: Stenhouse.

Jenkins, C. (1999). Assessing spelling knowledge: The child as a reader and writer. In I. Fountas & G. Pinnell (Eds.), *Voices on word matters* (pp. 67–88). Portsmouth, NH: Heinemann.

Johnson, D. (2001). *Vocabulary in the elementary and middle school*. Boston: Allyn and Bacon.

Johnston, F. (1999). The timing and teaching of word families. *The Reading Teacher*, 53(1), 64–75.

Johnston, F. (2001). Spelling exceptions: Problems or possibilities? *The Reading Teacher*, 54(4), 372–378.

Lederer, R. (1987). *Anguished English*. New York: Dell Publishing.

Lederer, R. (1990). *The play of words: Fun and games for language lovers*. New York: Pocket Books.

Lederer, R. (1991). *The miracle of language*. New York: Simon and Schuster.

Lederer, R. (1993). *More anguished English*. New York: Dell Publishing.

Lederer, R. (1994). *Adventures of a verbivore*. New York: Pocket Books.

Lederer, R. (1998). *Crazy English: The ultimate joy ride through our language*. New York: Pocket Books.

Lee, D. (1974). *Alligator pie*. Toronto: Macmillan of Canada.

Lesynski, L. (1996). *Boy soup or when giant caught cold*. Toronto: Annick Press.

Lindfors, J. (1989). The classroom: A good environment for language learning. In P. Rigg & V. Allen (Eds.), *When they don't all speak English*. Urbana, IL: National Council of Teachers of English.

Maestro, G., & Terban, M. (1985). *Too hot to hoot: Funny palindrome riddles*. New York: Houghton Mifflin.

Marsh, C. (2001). *The big Canada reproducible activity book*. Toronto: Gallopade International.

Martin, B. J. (2000). *Chicka, chicka, boom boom*. New York: Alladin Paperbacks.

McFarlane, J. A., & Clements, W. (1996). *The Globe and Mail style book*. Toronto: Penguin.

Miles, R. (Ed.). (2000). *Canada*. London: Dorling Kindersley.

Moore, C. (2002). *The big book of Canada*. Toronto: Tundra Books.

Nunes, T., Bryant, B., & Bindman, M. (1997). Spelling and grammar - the necsed move. In C. Perfetti, L. Rieben, & M. Fayol (Eds.), *Learning to spell: Research, theory, and practice across languages* (pp. 151–170). Mahwah, NJ: Lawrence Erlbaum Associates.

Payne, J. (1995). *Collins Cobuild English guides: no. 8: Spelling*. London: Harper Collins.

Peregoy, S., & Boyle, O. (1997). *Reading, writing, and learning in ESL: A resource book for K–12 teachers*. New York: Longman.

Perfetti, C. (1997). The psycholinguistics of spelling and reading. In C. Perfetti, L. Rieben, & M. Fayol (Eds.), *Learning to spell: Research, theory, and practice across languages* (pp. 21–38). Mahwah, NJ: Erlbaum Associates.

Pinnell, G., & Fountas, I. (1998). *Word matters: Teaching phonics and spelling in the reading/writing classroom*. Portsmouth, NH: Heinemann.

Rayburn, A. (2001). *Naming Canada: Stories about Canadian place names*. Toronto: University of Toronto Press.

Read, C. (1971). Preschool children's knowledge of English phonology. *Harvard Educational Review, 41*, 1–34.

Rees, N. (1994). *Dictionary of word and phrase origins*. London: Cassell.

Rhodes, L., & Dudley-Marling, C. (1988). *Readers and writers with a difference: A holistic approach to teaching learning disabled and remedial students*. Portsmouth, NH: Heinemann.

Rosenbloom, J. (1999). *The little giant book of tongue twisters*. New York: Sterling Publishing.

Scott, R. (1991). *The student editor's guide to words*. Toronto: Gage Learning.

Scott, R. (1991). *Spelling and reading strategies of seventh grade good readers/good spellers, good readers/poor spellers, and poor readers/poor spellers*. Toronto: OISE/FEUT.

Scott, R., & Siamon, S. (1994). *Sharing the secrets: Teach your child to spell*. Toronto: Macmillan Canada.

Shlagel, R., & Shlagel, J. (1992). The integral character of spelling: Teaching strategies for multiple purposes. *Language Arts 69*(6), 418–424.

Siamon, S. (1991). Five years in transition: Profile of an invented speller. In D. Booth (Ed.), *Spelling links: Reflections on spelling and its place in the curriculum*. Markham, ON: Pembroke Publishers.

Sigmon, C. M. (2001). *Modifying the four blocks for upper grades: Matching strategies to students' needs*. Greensboro, NC: Carson-Dellosa.

Solski, R. (1998). *Exploring my school & local community*. Napanee: S & S Learning Materials.

Solski, R. (2000). *Canadian provinces and territories: grades 4–6*. Napanee: S & S Learning Materials.

Tarasoff, M. (1990). *Spelling: Strategies you can teach*. Victoria, BC: Pixelart Graphics.

Templeton, S., & Morris, D. (1999). Questions teachers ask about spelling. *Reading Research Quarterly, January/February/March*, 102–112.

Terban, M. (1991). *Hey, hay!: A wagonful of funny homonym riddles*. New York: Houghton Mifflin.

Treiman, R., & Cassar, M. (1997). Spelling acquisition in English. In C. Perfetti, L. Rieben, & M. Fayol (Eds.), *Learning to spell: Research, theory, and practice across languages* (pp. 61–80). Mahwah, NJ: Erlbaum Associates.

Turbill, J. (2000). Developing a spelling conscience. *Language Arts, 77*(3), 209–217.

Urzua, C. (1989). I grow for a living. In P. Rigg & V. Allen (Eds.), *When they don't all speak English*. Urbana, IL: National Council of Teachers of English.

Varnhagen, C., McCallum, M., & Burstow, M. (1997). Is children's spelling naturally stage-like. *Reading and Writing: An Interdisciplinary Journal, 9*, 451–481.

Vygotsky, L. (Ed.). (1962). *Thought and language*. Cambridge, MA: MIT Press.

White, R. (1994). *An avalanche of anoraks: For people who speak foreign languages every day...whether they know it or not*. New York: Random House.

Wilde, S. (1992). *You kan red this!: Spelling and punctuation for whole language classrooms, K–6*. Portsmouth, NH: Heinemann.

Willows, D. (2002). The balanced literacy diet. *The School Administrator*.

Glossary

●●

acronym: a word formed from the first letters or syllables of other words (e.g., *NATO*)

affixes: a syllable or syllables added to the stem or base of a word to modify the meaning (e.g., *un-*; *-ly*)

alliteration: the repetition of the same first sound in a group of words (e.g., *silky satin*)

analogy strategy: the use of known spelling patterns to spell unknown words (e.g., *house* to spell *mouse*)

assonance: a kind of rhyme in which the vowel sounds are alike but the consonants are different (e.g., *brave/vain*)

base word: a word to which prefixes or suffixes are added (e.g., *comfort* in *uncomfortable*)

blend: a written letter combination in which the sounds are blended (e.g. *blast*; *crush*)

Cloze Strategy: in spelling, selectively leaving a space for letters that have been misspelled or that provide spelling challenges (e.g., *su_ prise*)

compound word: a word made up of two or more smaller words. There is a logical connection between the two separate words and the new word (e.g., *basketball*).

consonant cluster: a group of two or three consonants that are often clustered together in words (e.g., *stuck*; *splash*)

decoding: in reading, the ability to sound out words and letters

derivational constancy: consistency in the spelling of words that are derived from the same base or root (e.g., *sign/signal*)

dialect: a form of speech characteristic of a fairly definite region or class. It may involve variations in pronunciation, grammar, or vocabulary from the standard form of the language.

digraph: two letters used together to spell a single sound (e.g., *each*; *thing*). In phonics instruction, digraphs usually refer to consonants (*chin*, *phone*, *thumb*, *whistle*, *laugh*, *ring*, *watch*), but there are also vowel digraphs (*hook*, *bread*, *enough*, *sauce*).

diphthong: two vowel sounds pronounced in one syllable (e.g., *house*; *noise*)

ELD: English Literacy Development; used in some jurisdictions for students from areas where alternate varieties of English are spoken (also referred to as ESD—English as a Second Dialect)

eponym: a word named after a person (e.g., *sandwich* for the fourth Earl of Sandwich)

ESL: English as a Second Language; commonly used for ESL programs and ESL teachers

ESOL: English for Speakers of Other Languages; commonly used to designate students

etymology: having to do with the origin and history of words

euphemism: the use of a mild or indirect expression instead of one that is harsh or unpleasantly direct (e.g., "to pass away" instead of "to die")

grapheme: the smallest unit of written language that represents a sound in spelling (e.g., *c*, *k*, *ph*, *igh*)

graphic organizer: the use of a visual (graph, picture, or chart) to generate or organize information

homograph: words having the same spelling but different meanings (e.g., *wind* as in "air" and *wind* as in "turn")

homophone: words having the same pronunciation but different meanings, origins, and sometimes spellings (e.g., *horse/hoarse*)

ideogram: a symbol used in a writing system to stand for a whole word or concept

invented spelling: spelling an unknown word as it sounds, or as the student thinks it should be spelled

linguistics: the study of language, both human speech and the structure of languages

minimal pairs: words that are alike except for one sound (e.g., *green/grin*)

mnemonics: a strategy to aid memory (e.g., *strawberry shortcake* for *dessert*)

morpheme: the smallest meaningful element of a language (e.g., *un-*; *take*; *-ed*). Free morphemes can stand on their own as words (e.g., *bus*); bound morphemes cannot stand on their own but need to be used with words (e.g., *bus<u>es</u>*).

morphology: the branch of linguistics that deals with the forms of words

morphosyntactic awareness: awareness of how words fit into grammatical patterns

onomatopoeia: the use of words whose sound suggests a particular meaning (e.g., *buzz*, *splash*)

onset: the initial consonant sound in a single syllable or word (e.g., /s/ in *sip*; /sl/ in *slip*)

orthography: the writing system of a language, particularly the correct sequence of letters, characters, or symbols. In most instances, orthography refers to the spelling system of the language.

palindrome: a word or phrase spelled the same way both backward and forward (e.g., *dad*, *mom*, *eye*)

phoneme: the smallest unit of speech that distinguishes one word from another (e.g., the *h* of *hack* and *t* of *tack* are phonemes in English)

phonemic awareness: awareness of the sounds that make up words

phonogram: a symbol representing a single speech sound, syllable, or word. It is sometimes used to describe the vowel and following consonant(s) in a one-syllable word (e.g., *-ast*, *-ip*, *-og*).

phonological awareness: awareness of the constituent sounds of words in learning to read and spell

phonology: the sounds and systems of sounds used in a given language at a particular time

polysyllabic: a word containing more than one syllable

portmanteau: a word made by combining parts of two other words (e.g., *smog*, from *smoke* and *fog*)

positional constraints: the restrictions placed on letters that can spell specific sounds based on their position in the word (e.g., *gh* can spell the sound /f/ in the middle or at the end of words but not at the beginning)

pragmatics: the realization that context affects meaning. For example, the statement "Good luck!" can mean different things depending on the situation and the tone of voice.

prefix: a syllable or syllables added to the beginning of a word to change its meaning (e.g., *<u>un</u>likely*)

rhyme: words or word segments that sound alike in the last part (e.g., *light/kite*)

rime: the vowel and any of the following consonants within a syllable (e.g., *ag* in *flag*, *ight* in *night*)

r-influenced vowel: when an *r* influences the pronunciation of a preceding vowel (e.g., *c<u>a</u>r* vs. *c<u>a</u>t*; *c<u>or</u>n* vs. *c<u>o</u>n*; *b<u>ur</u>n* vs. *b<u>u</u>n*; *h<u>er</u>* vs. *h<u>e</u>n*; *f<u>ir</u>st* vs. *f<u>i</u>st*)

root: a word or word element from which others are derived. (e.g., *<u>graph</u>ic*)

scaffolding: instructional support to assist learners in acquiring new concepts

schwa vowel: an unstressed vowel sound (e.g., *<u>a</u>bout*, *circ<u>u</u>s*, *lem<u>o</u>n*)

semantics: the meanings of words and sentences

suffix: a syllable or syllables added to the end of a word to form another word of a different meaning or function (e.g., *good<u>ness</u>*)

syllable juncture: the transition from one syllable to the next. It often involves spelling changes, such as the doubling of consonants or dropping the final *e* (e.g., *hop/hopping*, *hope/hoping*).

syntax: in grammar, the way in which words are arranged to form sentences, clauses, or phrases

word solving: taking words apart while reading for meaning, and spelling words while writing to communicate

word sort: the process of classifying words (usually presented on word cards) into appropriate categories. An "open sort" is one in which the categories are left open for the students to decide. In a "closed sort," the categories have already been determined.

Word Wall: an alphabetic list of words displayed in the classroom. Teachers use Word Walls to help students recognize and use high-frequency words when they are reading and spelling.

Index

Acknowledgments

• •

Every reasonable effort has been made to trace the ownership of copyrighted material. Information that would enable the publisher to correct any reference or credit in future editions would be appreciated.

2 Family Circus © Cowles Syndicate Inc. 1996. Reprinted by permission King Features Syndicate. 6 © Tribune Media Services, Inc. All Rights Reserved. Reprinted with permission. 10 PEANUTS reprinted by permission of United Feature Syndicate, Inc. 15 PEANUTS reprinted by permission of United Feature Syndicate, Inc. 21 © Tribune Media Services, Inc. All Rights Reserved. Reprinted with permission. 24 © Lynn Johnston Productions, Inc./Distributed by United Feature Syndicate, Inc. 40 THE BUCKETS reprinted with permission of United Feature Syndicate, Inc. 50 PEANUTS reprinted by permission of United Feature Syndicate, Inc. 70 "Billy Batter" from *Alligator Pie* by Dennis Lee. Macmillan of Canada, 1974, p. 18. "My Cat Can Stalk" by Sonja Dunn from *Primary Rhymerry*. Pembroke Publishers 1993. 71 "The Elephant" from *Daily Poetry* by Carol Simpson. GoodYear Books, 1995, p. 101. 73 "Monday Morning" used by permission of John C. Head. 74 "Have You Ever Seen a Sheet on a River Bed?" from *Daily Poetry* by Carol Simpson. GoodYear Books, 1995, p. 101. 79 © The New Yorker Collection 2001 Jack Ziegler from catoonbank.com. All Rights Reserved. 85 Bizarro 6-19, 1989. Reprinted by permission King Features Syndicate. 92 "The Gnome, the Gnat, and the Gnu" from *Falling Up* by Shel Silverstein. Reprinted by permission Edite Kroll, Literary Agency Inc. 99 DILBERT reprinted by permission of United Feature Syndicate, Inc. 112 ADAM@2002 HOME © UNIVERSAL PRESS SYNDICATE. Reprinted with permission. All rights reserved. 163 "Starshine" from *A Cup of Starshine: Poems and Pictures for Young Children*, Walker Books 1991. Reprinted by permission of the author. 165 "Butterflies" by Chu Miao Tuan. Reprinted by permission Stanford University Press. 170 Art Bouthillier © 2003.

Visual Credits

Front cover (left) Bonnie Kamin/PhotoEdit Inc.; (top right) © ROB & SAS/CORBIS/MagmaPhoto.com; (bottom) Richard Hutchings/PhotoEdit. 1 PhotoDisc/Getty Images. 20 Courtesy of Ruth McQuirter Scott. 65 © ROB & SAS/CORBIS/MagmaPhoto.com. 81 (top, centre, bottom) Courtesy of Sharon Siamon. 128 The Image Bank/Getty Images. 155 Bonnie Kamin/PhotoEdit. 161 Elena Rooraid/PhotoEdit Inc. 186 (top, bottom) Courtesy of Ruth McQuirter Scott.